"BLOOMING IS EXTRAORDINARY. . . . EMOTIONALLY HONEST AND OBVIOUSLY A WORK OF LOVE."
—*The Cleveland Plain Dealer*

"An important book on coming of age in the breadbasket of America . . . A delicious, witty, insightful autobiography. It will make you rethink your girlhood, raise your consciousness, and brighten your day."
—Maxine Kumin

"Susan Allen Toth has recreated childhood in Ames, Iowa, with clarity and charm. . . . Her vivid descriptions of Midwest life . . . have a humorous lilt and a sensitive perception. . . . As adults, we still find comfort in shared experiences; Toth's memoir is a friendly gift."
—*Los Angeles Times*

"This is a book for anyone who survived adolescence and bloomed in the Midwest, or it's enough to make you wish you had; maybe it's just a book for anyone who ever grew up."
—*The Boston Globe*

"A sweet, funny, and true remembrance . . . The evocation of small-town life in the 1950s goes beyond nostalgia to understanding."
—Richard Lingeman
Author of *Small Town America*

"She examines her early life in all its varied forms but preserves its integrity by describing it without condescension or embellishment. She certainly understands how memories of childhood influence later life, but she treats the relation lightly and never belabors it. This is a charming and well-written book."
—*The Washington Star*

"The pages dance with stories."
—*Publishers Weekly*

By Susan Allen Toth

Blooming
Ivy Days
How to Prepare for Your High-School Reunion
Reading Rooms (editor, with John Coughlan)
A House of One's Own (with James Stageberg)
My Love Affair with England
England as You Like It
England for All Seasons

Susan Allen Toth

BLOOMING:

A
SMALL-TOWN
GIRLHOOD

with a new introduction
by the author

BALLANTINE BOOKS • NEW YORK

A Ballantine Book
Published by The Ballantine Publishing Group

Introduction copyright © 1998 by Susan Allen Toth
Copyright © 1978, 1981 by Susan Allen Toth

All rights reserved under International and Pan-American Copyright Conventions. Published in the United States by The Ballantine Publishing Group, a division of Random House, Inc., New York, and simultaneously in Canada by Random House of Canada Limited, Toronto. Originally published by Little, Brown and Company in 1981.

A slightly different version of "Science" appeared in *Great River Review*. "Girlfriends" has appeared in *McCall's Magazine*.

http://www.randomhouse.com

Library of Congress Catalog Card Number: 97-94055

ISBN: 0-345-42115-9

Cover design by Ruth Ross
Text design by Jie Yang

Manufactured in the United States of America

First Ballantine Books Mass Market Edition: June 1985
First Ballantine Books Trade Edition: February 1998
10 9 8 7 6 5 4 3 2 1

For my mother,
Hazel Erickson Allen Lipa,
who taught me the best of what I know

Author's Note

Soon after *Blooming* was published in 1981, I began writing a sequel, *Ivy Days*, and then eventually went on to other books. After a year or two, except for an occasional public reading, I had no pressing reason to return to *Blooming*. Whatever I was writing at the moment interested me more.

So when I recently picked up my first memoir after seventeen years, I was uneasy. I am not sure what I expected to find. When I wrote it, I was forty, divorced, a teacher, with a ten-year-old daughter who was at the center of my life. (Even the original jacket photograph showed the two of us together.) Now, a full-time writer, remarried, with an adult daughter (now a painter) living far away, I knew that my life—and some of my perceptions about it—had changed in many ways. I wondered if perhaps I would need to change my narrative as well.

But when I began to re-read *Blooming*, I soon stopped trying to measure distances between perspectives. Instead I was quickly caught up again in reliving my childhood and adolescence in Ames, Iowa, in the 1940s and 1950s. I'd forgotten some vignettes. Others came sharply back into focus: that high-school championship basketball game, for instance, when I was fifteen. Yes, I could still evoke all the excitement: the midnight parade, the hoarse cheering, the sense of making history.

I am not the only one who remembers. Not long ago, at my

fortieth high-school reunion, I was struck by how various speakers kept returning to their own vivid recollections of that champion-ship night, or to the famous Marshalltown game with seven over-times, or, yet more nostalgically, to the football team's annual "fireside" farewell. When we all finally stood to sing (somewhat abashedly, then with fervor) the Ames High Fight Song, our for-mer cheerleaders even came to the front of the room to clap and kick a little.

Although I sang as determinedly as any of my reunion class-mates, I realized then, and in re-reading *Blooming* shortly afterward, how much boys' athletics had dominated high-school life. Boys played, girls clapped. It is not hard to trace obvious connections to American culture today, in which (mostly male) athletes have be-come fabulously overpaid heroes, and taxpayers subsidize stadiums rather than schools. Re-reading *Blooming*, I could also note, pain-fully, how obsessed I was with clothes, appearance, and body shape. I am wryly amused at how often I describe myself as plump, when, in fact, reassuring snapshots show that I look just fine. Like many girls, I simply thought of myself as fat. Here too I could easily draw depressing conclusions about women's self-esteem.

But none of this critical commentary belongs in *Blooming*. It is a memoir, not a polemic. I wanted to record, as accurately as pos-sible, what it was like for me, a middle-class girl, to grow up in a Midwestern small town. Though occasionally troubled, those years were mostly happy—even, sometimes, magical. But as I wrote my story, I was acutely aware of what some of it implied: certain assumptions, prejudices, unthinking acceptance of pre-vailing conditions. So I chose my details very carefully. They could provide, I hoped, all the irony and commentary I needed.

My readers have been wonderful. They have sent me long let-ters describing their growing up in other—and sometimes, very different—towns, states, even countries. I have learned about their swimming pools, Carnegie libraries, slumber parties, high-school formals, boyfriends and girlfriends. Often they tell me about their later lives, too. One man, now middle-aged, used my memoir as an excuse to contact an old sweetheart from whom he had long been estranged. Though both were now happily married, they renewed a long-distance friendship. He told me part of his past had been restored, which is what I wished I could do for readers.

A few were skeptical. At book-signing events more than one queried me suspiciously: "Are you sure you didn't make any of this up?" Some—frequently younger and non-Midwestern—could not quite believe I had detasseled corn or tramped for miles to sell Camp Fire candy or danced in my socks on a gym floor. One woman said, almost accusingly, "But you *must* have invented the Mystery Farm of the Week!" (In the chapter, "Preparation for Life," I describe doing research for this weekly feature on the farm page of the Ames *Daily Tribune*.) Such questions always astonish me. Why *would* anyone make up a Mystery Farm of the Week?

Except for changing names and a few facts to hide identities, I told the truth as meticulously as I could. My truth isn't, of course, everyone else's. My old friend Larry ("Charlie" in the book), now a retired banker, maintains fiercely that I never went to see the movie, *The Barefoot Contessa,* with the particular group of friends I mentioned. He was there, he says, but I was not. No, I tell Larry just as fiercely, I *was* there. If we were put in a witness box, who would the jury believe? (A banker, I fear, rather than a writer.)

Although I told the truth as I knew it, I did not always tell everything. I left out a few scenes, or characters, because including them would have caused someone unnecessary pain. Other omissions involved more complicated reasons. Only when readers asked why I'd said so little about my father, who died when I was seven, did I realize how completely my mother had tried to lock out her terrible grief with stoic silence. We almost never mentioned my father. Years too late, I have tried to learn more about him—but that effort is not part of *Blooming*.

Some stories I just did not know. As I look back, I am sure that Ames had its share of closeted fear, shame, and secrecy. I think of the few people of whom neighbors murmured disapprovingly, "He

drinks too much," and I realize that they were talking about alco-
holics. At least two of my friends from high school—one a boy I
dated for some time—have died, tragically young, of AIDS. I did
not know then they were gay, and, just possibly, they didn't either. I did not hear about child abuse, incest, and wife-beating
(with an exception I noted, wonderingly, in my chapter on "Girlfriends"), but perhaps these were stories no one ever told.

If I had to paint some of the tones in *Blooming* darker, I would
also have to make my highlights even brighter. "It was a quiet
town and a quiet time," I wrote in 1981, and added, "Against that
background . . . a girl could listen to her heart beating." Having
raised a daughter in the 1970s and 1980s in a large city, I can say
without hesitation that, by comparison, she had the background
of a raucous rock concert.

Writing *Blooming* changed my life in many ways. Some months
after its publication, I took a phone call from a stranger. "My
name is James Stageberg," the man said. "I've just read half of
Blooming, and I'd like to take you out to lunch."

I thought for a brief moment. I was intrigued. I didn't get invited to lunch very often. But should I take a chance? "Why
don't you finish the book and then call me back?" I said politely.
He didn't miss a beat. "Let me tell you a litle about myself," he
went on. "I'm an architect, I'm divorced, and I'm from a small
town too."

We met for lunch, and now we have been married for thirteen
years. No wonder I think of *Blooming* with affection.

—February 1998

Author's Note
to the original edition

My memories of growing up in Ames are as true as I could make them, but I have changed names, and often places or contexts, in order to avoid embarrassing or injuring anyone. One factual error is deliberate: Ames High did indeed once beat Marshalltown in seven overtimes, but not in the championship game of 1955; I transferred a rhythmic chant from one memory to another. Others will remember Ames differently, and I look forward to their versions of a childhood I saw through very particular eyes.

I have always wanted to write this book, though only recently did it suddenly become possible. I have had the encouragement of many wonderful friends who were interested in this small segment of one woman's life. Several cheerfully read and commented on all or portions of this manuscript: Katharine Chrisman, Valerie Monroe, Patricia Kane, Felicity Thoet, Susan Welch, Kiki Gore, Joanne Von Blon, Harley Henry, Truman Schwartz, Peter Shriver, Lon Otto, and Timothy Slade. Kay Crawford added intelligence and patience to her skill as a typist. My editor, Mary Tondorf-Dick, and my agent, Molly Friedrich, gave me wholehearted support. A grant from the Minnesota State Arts Board, through funds appropriated by the Minnesota State Legislature and the National Endowment for the Arts, and a leave from Macalester College combined to give me time. I am grateful for all this assistance.

Contents

Nothing Happened

When she was four years old, my daughter, Jennifer, began to develop a sense of history. "What was it like in the old days, Mommy? Did you wear long dresses? Did you ever ride in a covered wagon?" As I struggled with her questions, I realized that to her the "old days" encompassed a cloudy past when I was young, as well as when her grandmother was young, and whatever dim days extended beyond Gramma's childhood. I could not distinguish among these histories nor tell her exactly when the "old days" ended and the present began.

I have some of the same difficulty trying to explain to friends who did not grow up in a small Midwestern college town in the 1950s what life was like then. Those "old days" have disappeared into an irretrievable past that seems only faintly credible to those who did not live it. Does any girl today have the chance to grow up as gradually and as quietly as we did? In our particular crucible we were not seared by fierce poverty, racial tensions, drug abuse, street crime; we were cosseted, gently warmed, transmuted by slow degrees. Nonetheless we were being changed, girls into women. The kind of woman we thought we would become was what Ames, Iowa, saw as the American ideal. She shimmered in our minds, familiar but removed as the glossy cover of the Sears, Roebuck catalogue. There she rolled snowballs with two smiling red-cheeked children, or unpacked a picnic lunch on emerald grass as an Irish setter lounged nearby, or led a cherubic toddler into *blue water. Her tall, handsome husband hovered close, perhaps with his hand protectively on her shoulder. Pretty and well dressed, she laughed happily into the KodaColor sunshine that flooded her future.*

I do not think any of us would fit into such a simple picture today. During the past twenty years, that gleaming ideal has become tarnished, scratched and blackened as deeply as the copper bottoms on the shiny saucepans we got as wedding presents. Many of us have gone through painful reassessments that have made us question the kinds of assumptions upon which we so confidently based our lives. We look to the past to try to discover how we got here from there. I look at my own childhood and adolescence in Ames and wonder: was such innocence constricting, or did it give me shelter and space to grow? What do I see in that past I can still value? What did I get for the price I paid? What was the price, anyway?

I cannot sum it up. I do not see my life as a cost-accounting sheet, this friend a profit, that time a dead loss, cause and effect neatly balanced on a ledger line. Instead, when Jennifer asks, "What was it like in the old days, Mommy?" my mind begins to spin with images. I want to describe for her the tension of the noisy, floodlit night we won the state basketball tournament; how sweat dripped down my dirty bathing suit as I detasseled corn under a July sun; the seductive softness of my red velveteen formal; the marble hush of the Ames Public Library; the feeling of choking on the cold chlorinated water of Blaine's Pool when a boy cannonballed on top of me.

What will these images tell her about love, sex, pride? Self-esteem, ambition, fear? I do not know. Examining my childhood has not brought me any easy answers. Sometimes I wish it had. Once I read aloud passages from these memoirs to some local alumnae of an Eastern women's college I had always feared but respected. They were intelligent listeners, and I know many of them had grown up in times and towns like mine. When I had finished, I waited anxiously for their response. What conclusions had they reached? Everyone was silent for a few moments, hesitant to begin the discussion. Then one intense young woman, a recent graduate, would contain herself no longer. Her lips were drawn tight with suppressed indignation, her voice trembled with feeling. "Where," she demanded, "is the admission that it was hell?" She paused for effect, giving me just time to open my mouth and close it again. "Where is your acknowledgment of the smugness, the hypocrisy, the prejudice?"

Suddenly several women spoke at once, agreeing, disagreeing, and sharing their own stories. Underneath the clamor I thought, "But it wasn't hell. Not for me. It wasn't perfect, but mostly I was happy. Yes, I saw provincial smugness, but I didn't always realize what it was. I can report its effects now, but I didn't suffer from them then. I wish I had known more about some things, absorbed less about others, but that's the way it was. Of course we weren't prepared for life. Who ever is?" I paused, trying as I often have to sum up, reach a judgment, and deliver a final verdict on my childhood. My antagonist, seeing me silent, returned to the attack. "You see?" she said triumphantly, pointing her finger at me. "You're ambivalent! Admit it, you're ambivalent!"

Of course I admit it. Even if I could change the ways in which I grew up, I would not know where to start or stop. On the way home after that alumnae meeting, I was still arguing in my head, partly with myself, partly with the finger-pointing moralizer. Whoever I became, who I am now, is the result of many tangled circumstances, and I cannot single one out for praise or blame and say, "There!"

I wished I had thought to tell her about my garden. Maybe that would have been an answer. It is a small garden, carved from the back lawn of a city lot, but gradually I have replaced more and more grass with flowers, herbs and vegetables. I don't have much space, so I plant my perennials carefully: three gray-green bunches of English lavender, some Iceland poppies, one shaggy white Shasta daisy, other small clusters of plants that must be nurtured carefully in the violent Minnesota climate. I weed, water, mulch, pinch and spray. In the fall I bury the tender ones with leaves and straw. Most of my plants endure the winter; though I mourn some losses, I will try again, perhaps with a new variety or stronger seedlings. A few survivors grow and thrive with such sturdiness and vigor that I marvel at their bloom.

I have a friend who gardens too. She is cheerfully careless, scattering seeds in odd places, buying faded flats of petunias in mid-July, and *accumulating clumps from whatever her neighbors want to get rid of. She weeds occasionally and waters during droughts, but otherwise she gardens lazily. She doesn't bother with winter covering. "I figure any plant of mine has got to be tough," she said to me last fall. I would like to be able to report that her garden is a disaster, but it's not. Her backyard has as much color as mine, with pink bleeding heart in spring, gaudy tiger lilies in midsummer, the yellow fire of mums in the fall. True, she doesn't have any English lavender, Iceland poppies or Shasta daisies, but she doesn't care. "I only plant what I know can make it without too much fuss," she explains.*

Her flowers survive and bloom, and so do mine. We both have successful gardens. I would like to have told my moralizer that we are simply cultivating different plants. When I look at the time, the town, the customs, the people who surrounded me when I was growing up, I cannot wish I had been nurtured in a different place. It was the only garden I knew.

We huddled together in the cool spring night, whispering in hoarse voices, thrumming with the excitement that vibrated through the crowd gathering in the parking lot outside the Ames train station. All the way home from Des Moines we had hugged each other, laughed, cried, and hugged each other again. When we passed through the small farming towns between Des Moines and Ames, we rolled down the windows of the Harbingers' station wagon and shouted down the quiet streets, "We beat Marshalltown in seven overtimes! We beat Marshalltown in seven overtimes!" It had a rhythmic beat, a chant we repeated to each other in unbelieving ecstasy. We beat Marshalltown in seven overtimes! For the first time in ten years, Ames High School had won the state basketball championship. Most of us sophomores felt nothing so important could ever happen to us again.

As a string of cars began threading off the highway, filling up the lot, someone turned the lights along Main Street on full. It was close to midnight, but families were pouring down the street toward the station as though it held a George Washington's

Birthday sale. We were all waiting for the team. The mayor had ordered out the two fire engines, which were waiting too, bright red and gleaming under the lights. When the bus finally came around the corner, a cheering erupted from the crowd that didn't stop until the boys had walked down the steps, grinning a little sheepishly, and climbed onto the engines. The coach rode on one, the mayor on another. Following our cheerleaders, voices gone but valiantly shrieking, who were leading the way in their whirling orange pleated skirts and black sweaters, we snake-danced down Main Street behind blowing sirens and paraded to the high-school auditorium. There we listened to speeches from the mayor, the principal, the coach, and the team captain. We would have no school tomorrow, the principal told us (we cheered again), just a pep assembly, then dismissal. Then Mr. J. J. Girton, who owned all three movie theatres in Ames, came to the mike and said that in honor of the occasion he would show a free movie at the New Ames tomorrow at two P.M. We cheered, but this time not as loudly. We knew whenever Mr. Girton showed free movies, he always picked the oldest Looney Tunes and a dull Western. The coach thanked everyone and sat down quickly; he looked tired. But when he introduced the team cap-tain, who made his teammates rise, we jumped to our feet and clapped and stomped.

I was filled with love and admiration for all of them, for stocky little Tom Fisher, who had made a critical free throw; for tall, gangly Charlie Stokowski, who had racked up thirty points; for George Davis, who usually stood most of the game in front of the bench with his mouth hanging open, but who tonight in the midst of the team looked like a hero. Next to me Patsy Jones, George's girlfriend, looked smug and proud. We knew she was planning to meet him backstage for a few moments after the as-sembly. When our new celebrities filed off the stage, our parents, who had been sitting together in the last rows, took us home. Next morning at breakfast we could read all about ourselves, with headlines and pictures, in the Des Moines *Register*. Though we

knew other stories would topple ours after a few days, it didn't
matter.

Perhaps I remember that night so vividly because it stands out
like a high hill in the flat, uneventful landscape that was both the
physical and emotional setting for our town. Our lives were not
dull, oh, no; but our adolescence bubbled and fermented in a
kind of vacuum. In Ames, in the 1950s, as far as we were concerned, nothing happened.

Ames had once had a murder. It had happened a few years before we were in junior high, to someone we didn't know, a man
who hadn't lived in Ames long. He had somehow accumulated
gambling debts, probably on his travels out West, and one night
he was found shot to death at the Round-up Motel. No one ever
found a weapon or the murderers. After a few blurred photographs in the Ames Daily *Tribune* and interviews with the cleaning woman who'd found him, the motel owner, the county sheriff
and local police, even the newspaper abandoned the story. But
for many years afterward, when we drove with strangers past the
Round-up, we would point it out in reverential tones. It might
look just like a tidy modern bungalow, stretched out into longer
wings than usual, but we knew it was a bloody place.

Other than our murder, we had little experience with violence.
Sometimes there were accidents. One of my girlfriends had a
brother who had lost an eye when another boy had aimed badly
with a bow and arrow. We stared surreptitiously at his glass eye,
which was bigger and shinier than it ought to be. Someone else's
sister, much younger, had toddled in front of a truck on the highway and been killed. Her picture, done in careful pastels by an
artist from Des Moines, hung over the sofa in her parents' living
room. When they spoke of her, I tried not to look at the picture,
which made me feel uncomfortable.

When death came to Ames, it seldom took anyone we knew.
We were all shocked when one morning we saw our high-school
teachers whispering in the halls, a few of them weeping openly,
over the history teacher's four-year-old daughter, who had been

rushed the previous night to the hospital and who had died almost immediately of heart failure. Visitation was to be that night at the Jefferson Funeral Parlor. Those of us who felt close to Mr. Sansome wanted to go to "pay our respects," a phrase someone had heard from another teacher. We discussed solemnly what to wear, what to do, what to say. When two girlfriends came to pick me up, I was nervous, with a sinking feeling in my stomach because I did not know what to expect. I had never seen a dead person before.

We didn't stay at the funeral parlor long. The room was crowded with friends of the Sansomes. Mrs. Sansome wasn't there—home, in bed, someone said sympathetically—and Mr. Sansome stood with a glazed expression on his face, shaking hands, muttering politeness, to everyone who came up to him. We shook his hand and moved on to the coffin. Mary Sansome looked just as she always did, dressed perhaps more neatly in a Sunday dress with bright pink bows tied onto her long pigtails. As we leaned closer, I thought her skin looked rubbery and waxen, like a doll I had once had. Her eyes were shut, but she looked as though she might wake up any minute, disturbed by the murmured talk around her. I looked over at Mr. Sansome, usually a gesturing, dramatic man, standing woodenly a few feet away, staring straight ahead of him. The feeling in my stomach got worse. I wanted to cry, but I couldn't. Soon my friends and I went silently home.

The few deaths we knew in those years seemed rare and accidental. Once Mrs. Miller, an elderly neighbor, came fluttering to our house in high excitement. She didn't want my sister and me to hear what she had to tell my mother, but we hovered quietly in our room with the door open a crack and listened intently. Behind Mrs. Miller lived Sam and Martha Doyle, five children, a collie, and a tiger cat. It was a large, noisy, happy family. Mr. Doyle was like any other father, kindly, offhand, seldom home. But for some reason no one understood, not even patiently inquisitive Mrs. Miller, Mr. Doyle had tried to kill himself that morning. "I heard screams," she said breathlessly to my mother, "and when I ran to the back door, there was Martha Doyle stand-ing in the driveway trying to open the garage door. I guess it must have stuck. Right behind her was Sam, with some kitchen towels wrapped around his wrists all covered with blood. Then she got the door open, they both got in the car and drove off."

We never heard what happened after the Doyles got to the hospital, but everything was quickly hushed up. Soon afterward the whole family moved away. I thought about Mr. Doyle for a long time. What could ever be so bad you would want to hurt yourself, make yourself bleed like that? Tragedy, as far as we knew it existed in adult lives, merely extended to freakish twists of fate, like the death of little Mary Sansome. Most of us were convinced that life was going to be wonderful.

As far as we knew, people in Ames didn't get divorced. But one woman did. Sallie Houlton, the divorcée, looked like any other grown-up. In her late twenties, she had an average figure, nonde-script brown hair, a pleasant but undistinguished face. Sallie lived sometimes with her arthritic aunt, Miss Houlton, on the far side of town. Mother knew them both because an aunt of mine had taught with Miss Houlton years ago in Minnesota. Sometimes Sallie disappeared for temporary employment in other cities. She was a dietitian, Mother said, and ran hospital kitchens. All I really knew about Sallie Houlton was that she had been divorced. No one would say why, but once Mrs. Miller had been talking about Sallie to Mother and I heard her say, with disapproving fer-vor, "And on top of all that, he *drank*." I was very curious to know what "all that" was. Mother, usually fairly straightforward in her replies to my questions, hedged this one; she said it was very com-plicated, hard to explain. Many years later, when for some igno-ble reason I was still curious about "all that," Mother said simply, "He was impotent." Oh, I said. Her answer was something of a letdown.

It was almost as difficult to understand what could happen to a husband and wife so terrible that they would want a divorce as it was to understand what had driven Mr. Doyle to cut his wrists.

As I grew older and moved through high school, I began to have occasional focus, as though a blurred picture had suddenly sharpened, on a few of the marriages I had taken so far for granted. My first illumination took place outside our house one hot summer night, when my mother had given one of her four-to-six sherry parties. Her friends, all married couples, came to sip a little Taylor's Cocktail Sherry or ginger ale, smoke, talk, sip some more and go home at a decent hour. But at this party, four of the guests stayed until past ten. Two were Australians, a visiting professor of agricultural economics and his pale blonde wife, who was a part-time secretary in the foreign students' office; the others were my mother's old friends, Mike and Helen Snyder, who had lived next door to her before I was born. The Snyders were probably in their forties then, the Australians in their twenties. Mike always liked to stay late at parties, and he and Helen had begun to snipe at each other about whether it was time to leave. I had heard their rapid fire before, seen Helen's mouth tighten at the corners, watched Mike defiantly pour more sherry into his glass; neither I nor anyone else ever took their bickering seriously. Mike was a sharp-tongued mathematician, and his cutting edge seemed almost professional. Tonight Mike kept his back turned to Helen as much as possible and talked vehemently to the Australian wife. Sometimes when he got particularly excited he picked up her hand and held it for a while. Finally the Australian economist got up. His wife rose obediently, and Mother, who was looking tired, rose too to walk them to their car. I tagged along, bored with the party, and, surprisingly, found that Mike Snyder was walking beside me.

"So how's your summer going?" he asked me absentmindedly, but he was watching the light-haired woman in front of him. He swayed, bumped into me, and straightened up again. At the car, after her husband got in, he reached through the front window and patted her on the shoulder. "Lucy, Lucy, Lucy," he said in a kind of singsong. The car pulled quickly away from the curb. Mike turned to my mother. With astonishment, I could see that he had tears in his eyes. "What am I going to do, Hazel?" he said in a voice in which anguish had conquered the alcohol. "I love her so damn much. What am I going to do?" Mother put her arm around Mike and began to guide him back to the house. "It's going to be all right, Mike," I heard her say comfortingly, just as she did to me when I was overcome with despair. "It's all right. You know they're leaving soon. It's going to be all right."

Maybe for a while it *was* all right. The summer passed. The Australian visitors went back to Melbourne, and the Snyders continued to come to Mother's sherry parties. I tried not to talk to them much. I had been both confused and embarrassed by what I had seen. Four or five years later, when I was in college, one of the bits of news that Mother had for me at Christmas vacation was that the Snyders were getting a divorce. It was not the shock it would once have been. I asked Mother about the Australian woman, but Mother looked surprised. That was a long time ago, she said, and had nothing to do with it anyway.

If I knew little about love, I knew nothing about sex. The closest thing Ames had to offer as sex education was the Hudson station, a rickety gas outlet beyond the city limits that sold rubbers in a coin-operated machine in its men's room, or so we girls were told. A girl's reputation could be ruined if her date stopped for gas at the Hudson station. A lot of us had to ask more knowing friends what a rubber was. That piece of information was conveyed to me in patronizing tones by a fellow sixth-grader, Joyce Schwartz, who motioned me upstairs one day to her parents' bedroom when they were out. She carefully opened her father's top drawer, lifted up a pile of neatly folded handkerchiefs, and showed me a small cardboard box. "Those are rubbers," she said wisely. She let me open the top of the box but didn't want me to take anything out. I couldn't make much of what I saw anyway.

Not long after that, another friend, Emily Harris, also mature beyond my years, took me for a walk behind her house to an old deserted greenhouse that had once belonged to the college. There couples came sometimes at night and did things, she said.

"Sometimes I find rubbers here in the grass," she added, staring intently around her feet, and I stared at my feet too, though I wasn't sure what I was looking for. I only saw bits of broken glass from long-gone windows, bottle caps, and used Kleenex. Suddenly Emily shouted, "There's one!" She looked around quickly for a stick, and then fished in the grass until she managed to hoist aloft a squishy shapeless piece of latex. It was the fleshlike color that seemed obscene to me. "Don't touch it," Emily warned. "You can get awful diseases from these things." I thought you could also get awfully cold out here at night. What could drive anyone to such an uncomfortable spot to do something with that icky piece of rubber?

Besides having had a murder and a divorce, Ames had a prostitute. Her name was Nancy, and all the boys in high school joked about her. She lived near the college, but I never saw her until one dark rainy night when I was a senior in high school, almost ready to graduate. It was late in May, the kind of balmy weather that opened up the promise of a long drowsy summer ahead. My friend Charlie, who had dropped over on a dull evening just to talk awhile, agreed to walk with me in the rain all the way to Campustown, the tiny shopping district about a mile distant.

When we were dressed for outdoors, we looked like brothers in our wrinkled trenchcoats, the Penney's double-breasted poplin style that was practically unisex even in those days. I borrowed Charlie's shapeless old hat and jammed it down over my short hair. You couldn't see much of me except my nose, though I would lift my face up from time to time to catch the fresh feel of the rain. It was a lovely walk, as we sloshed through puddles, stared at the bright glowing lights in all the darkened houses, reveled in the quiet of the deserted streets. It seemed to me as if we were all alone in the world, wet and happy, with only the faint whooshing of tree branches and the occasional splash of passing cars to interrupt our intent conversation. When we got to Campustown, it too was deserted, the stores shuttered tight, a few small neon signs flashing in dark windows, "Cat's Paw," "Pop's Grill,"

"Cigars." Tonight we seemed to own this little main street, which echoed to our steps and low voices.

Striding along, matching Charlie's pace as best I could, I soon saw someone approaching from the other direction. I didn't bother to notice who it was until she drew abreast of us, paused for a moment, and said quickly but distinctly, "Want to fuck?" I looked up in disbelief. I caught a glimpse of a lined face, bright yellow stringy hair, garish lips, and then it was gone. Charlie, though startled, was beginning to laugh. "Did she say what I thought she said?" I asked anxiously. "Yup," he said, now laughing openly. "That was Nancy. She probably thought you were a boy. She must've been really startled when she saw you up close." I turned and looked behind me, but Nancy was gone. Charlie, who kept chuckling for a long while, couldn't understand why I seemed upset; I wasn't sure myself. But it seemed as though the interruption had broken something fragile, as evanescent as the rainbow oil slick in the gutter at our feet.

If I was vouchsafed some faint but definite glimmerings about sex in Ames, I saw little else troubling that small society. One reason I was so blind to common attitudes toward blacks was that Ames didn't have any. Or rather, like everything else, Ames had only one. For most of the years I was growing up, there was a single family in town who were black, or, to be precise, an unassuming shade of brown. The Elliotts, quiet and hardworking, lived far from the college campus in an unfashionable section where small businesses, warehouses and rundown older houses crowded together. It wasn't exactly a slum, but it wasn't a place where anyone I knew lived either. Alexander Elliott was in my class, his younger sister two classes behind me. They too were hardworking and quiet, always neatly dressed, pleasant expressions on their faces, ready to respond politely. What went on behind those carefully composed smiles no one then ever wondered.

We thought the Elliott kids were nice enough, we exchanged casual greetings with them, but Alexander was never invited to any parties. He did not belong to any social groups. I do not re-member seeing him anywhere, except in a crowd cheering at a football game or sitting a little apart in school assembly. Once or twice I think I remember Alexander's bringing a date, also black—though "Negro" was what we called them, enunciating the word carefully—to the Junior-Senior Prom. Wherever she was from, it wasn't Ames. They danced by themselves all eve-ning. Yet none of us thought we were prejudiced about Alex, and almost every year we elected him to some class office. The year Alex became student-body president, our principal pointed to Ames High proudly as an example of the way democracy really worked.

If I was unaware that Ames was prejudiced toward blacks, I could not miss the town's feeling about Catholics. I myself was fascinated by the glamour that beckoned at the door of St. Ce-cilia's, the imposing brick church defiantly planted right on the main road through town. Every Christmas St. Cecilia's erected a life-size nativity scene on its lawn, floodlit, Mary in blue velvet, glowing halos, real straw in the wooden manger. None of the Methodists, Lutherans, Baptists or Presbyterians did anything quite so showy. I always begged Mother to slow down as we drove by so I could admire it. Sometimes I could see one of the nuns from the small convent behind the church billowing in her black robes down the street. If I was with my friend Peggy O'Reilly, who was Catholic, she would stop and greet the nun respectfully. She knew each one by name, though they all looked alike to me.

Peggy told me bits and pieces about Catholic doctrine, which was so different from the vague advice I was gathering hap-hazardly in my own Presbyterian Sunday School that I didn't know what to make of it. Catholics had exotic secrets. One of the saints—was it Bernadette?—had been given the exact date of the end of the world, Peggy said, and she on her death had be-queathed it to the Pope. Every Pope kept this secret locked in a special case, and when he was about to die, he opened it, read the date, and expired—probably, I thought, out of shock. Why didn't the Popes share this wonderful knowledge with the world, so we could all get ready for the end? I asked Peggy. Peggy couldn't say.

Even if we hadn't known from friends like Peggy that Catholics were different, our parents would have told us. One of the few rigid rules enforced on many of us was the impossibility of "getting serious" about a Catholic boy. For a Protestant to marry a Catholic in Ames produced a major social upheaval, involving parental conferences, conversions, and general disapproval on both sides. Even our liberal minister, who encouraged his Presbyterian parishioners to call him "Doctor Bob" because he didn't want to appear uppish about his advanced degree, came to our high-school fellowship group one night to lecture on Catholicism. He probably knew that one of his deacons' daughters was going very steadily with a Catholic boy. Warning us about the autocratic nature of the Catholic Church, its iron hand, its idolatry, and most of all the way it could snatch our very children from us and bring them up in the manacles of a strange faith, Doctor Bob heated with the warmth of his topic until his cheeks glowed as he clenched and unclenched his fists.

Since I never fell in love with one of the few Catholic boys in our class, I never faced such direct fire. But my friend Peggy did. Much to her parents' disapproval, she began going steadily with Alvin Barnes, a Methodist boy who had never dated at all before he discovered Peggy. He was a quiet, withdrawn boy who seldom talked about anything, let alone his feelings, but we could all tell by the way he looked at Peggy that he loved her with a single-minded devotion. Her parents tolerated the romance for a year, though we knew they often had long talks with Peggy about it. But during their senior year, when Peggy and Alvin were still holding hands in daylight, Peggy's family decided that enough was enough. They gave Peggy an ultimatum, which she repeated to us, sobbing, one night when we girls had gathered together at someone's house for popcorn and gossip. She was distraught, but she had no thought of disobeying them; she was going to tell

Alvin they must break it off. We were indignant, sympathetic, but helpless; the price Peggy's parents were willing to pay was a year away at college, and no one thought Peggy could give that up instead.

A few days later Alvin was absent from school, and the whispers were alarming. After hearing Peggy's news, he had come to her house to try to argue with her parents. They had refused to let him in, had told him to go home and not to bother their daughter again. When he called their house, they wouldn't let Peggy come to the phone. So later that night, he had returned. There in the sloping driveway he had lain down behind the rear wheels of the O'Reilly family car. All night he lay there, waiting for the still-dark morning when Mr. O'Reilly would come out, start the engine, and back the car down the driveway on his way to work.

Of course, when morning finally came, Mr. O'Reilly saw Alvin at once. Horrified, he called Alvin's parents. They came and took Alvin away, and he did not come back to school until close to the end of the semester. Then he kept aloof, refusing to talk about what had happened, and hovered silently at the edges of our games and parties. Soon we all graduated, Alvin left town, and we lost track of him entirely. But I felt as though he had somehow been sacrificed, offered up to the fierce religious hatred I had seen gleaming in Doctor Bob's eyes. For several years, until even more bitter images etched over this one, I thought of the effects of prejudice as embodied in Alvin's quiet figure, lying patiently and hopelessly in the chilly darkness behind the wheels of the O'Reilly car.

Such drama, however, was rare. It was a quiet town and a quiet time. That may be why I can still hear the whispers of notebooks slapping shut and a pencil-sharpener grinding in the high-school study hall; the scratchy strains of "Blue Tango" on an overamplified record-player at the Friday dance; the persistent throb of grasshoppers in a rustling cornfield on a summer night when my boyfriend Peter parked his old Ford on a country road. In a world where nothing seemed to happen, small sounds were amplified so clearly that they still echo in my mind. So now on a hot summer night, when I sit by myself on my city steps, trying to block out nearby traffic and concentrate instead on the slightest rustle of leaves in the warm breeze, I remember the years of my growing up in Ames. Against that background of quiet, a girl could listen to her heart beating.

During the summer the long hot weekend days seemed to stretch out like the endless asphalt ribbons of highway winding into the country. We never had quite enough to do, especially on Saturday mornings. So we often drifted in and out of Olson's Bowling Alley, just a few lanes, hand-set pins, a quarter a line. Tucked on the second floor above a Spiegel catalogue order house at the end of Main Street, it was a most unlikely location for a bowling alley. Although the nearby high school hired it for occasional gym classes, I doubt that it ever paid its way. Sometimes we arrived at Olson's Alley early, by nine o'clock, when the downtown stores were opening their doors and hosing down their sidewalks. The heat was beginning to pour in the open windows, streaking sunshine across the dirty wooden floor and the three brightly gleaming lanes. We settled haphazardly into a game. Before long our hands were sweaty; we'd wipe them on our shorts, hoping the crispness of our carefully ironed blouses wouldn't wilt too much before the boys came.

Some boys always did drift through Olson's on those long hazy mornings, as aimlessly as the dusty sunshine. They banged noisily up the stairs, yelling to each other, and clambered over the church-pew benches to hoot at our self-conscious strides as we struggled to aim our bowling balls straight. The girl whose turn it was to be pin-setter, huddled behind the racks at the end of the long alley, looked through the intricate metal network at the far-away girls laughing and flirting with the boys. Even a boy who liked you was too embarrassed to walk all the way to the back of the lanes when everyone could see where he was going.

Though it seems odd to think of a bowling alley as a quiet place, Olson's was. Though we girls giggled and gossiped, the only other sounds beyond those occasional noisy interruptions of the boys were the heavy thud of the bowling balls, the clang of the pin-setting rack, and the flap of the torn shade at the open window. The morning seemed to stretch on forever. When we'd used up our quarters and given up on seeing any more boys, we'd tuck in our blouses, comb our hair, and emerge from the oppressive sweaty room into the blinding full-noon sun. Down Main Street we'd hurry to the Rainbow Cafe, newly air-conditioned, and treat ourselves to icy root-beer floats before taking the bus home.

When I plunge back into those uneventful Saturday mornings, I am once more lapped around by waves of time, repetitious, comforting, like the gentle undulations of Blaine's Pool when the late-afternoon breezes blew over its empty blue-green water. We all felt as though summer would go on forever. I would go to Olson's, or not; I would bowl a little, or not; I would see the boy I cared about, or I wouldn't. Other Saturday mornings stretched ahead like oases in the shimmering sun.

As I grew older, I began to realize that this quiet was not going to last. Time was speeding up; at some sharply definable point I would grow up and leave Ames. At odd moments in those last years I would be surprised by sadness, a strange feeling that perhaps I had missed something, that maybe life was going to pass me by. At the same time I nestled securely in the familiar landscape of streets whose every bump and jog I knew, of people who smiled and greeted me by name wherever I went, of friends who appeared at every movie, store, or swimming pool.

Nowhere did I feel this conflicting sense of security and impending loss as sharply as I did at the train station. Ames lay on some important transcontinental routes, and trains passed through daily on their way from Chicago to Portland, San Francisco, Los Angeles. I had ridden on trains for short trips, but I had never been on one overnight and I was too young to remember clearly what the country was like west of Ames when the prairies stopped and the mountains began. From a long auto trip when I was eight, I only remembered endless spaces punctuated by the

Grand Canyon. So for me the crack passenger trains, the *City of San Francisco*, the *City of Denver*, the *City of Los Angeles*, had titles that rang in my imagination like the purest romance. Big cities, the golden West, life beckoned to me from every flashing train window.

On slow spring or summer nights I would often ask my friend Charlie to take me down to the station to watch the trains come in. The *City of San Francisco* was due to pass through at ten o'clock, the *City of Denver* at eleven. Down at the deserted station we sat on an abandoned luggage cart near the tracks, staring into the darkness, listening for the first telltale hoot of a faraway whistle. The night was so quiet we whispered, hearing above our voices the grasshoppers, a squeal of brakes three blocks away at the beer parlor, the loud click of the station clock. The trains were always late, but we were in no hurry.

Eventually we'd hear a rumble on the tracks and then see a searching eye of light bearing down on us. Quickly we'd leap to our feet and get as close to the tracks as we dared, plugging our ears as the train ground to a stop in front of us, its metallic clamor deafening, its cars looming in the night like visitors from another world. As we stood there, we could see people moving back and forth inside the lighted windows. If we were outside a Pullman car, we might catch a glimpse of someone seated next to the window staring wordlessly back at us. I wondered why everyone wasn't asleep. A frowsy-haired woman with a brown felt hat pinned to her graying curls looked like someone I might know but didn't. Two young boys, jumping on their seats and pounding silently on the glass, could have been the Evans kids down the street, but weren't. They were strangers, separated from us not only by thick glass but by chance, being whisked away from their old lives to new ones. I felt the pull of the future, of adventure waiting for them and someday for me.

After a few moments, an exchange of luggage flung by the stationmaster, who had suddenly emerged from inside the darkened hut, a few shouts, the train began to grind again. As we winced with the jarring sound of metal against metal, it picked up speed. I tried to watch the car with the frowsy-haired woman and the two jumping boys, but it was soon lost in a blur of streaming silver metal. A last long low shriek, and the train was gone, off to Denver or San Francisco.

I always felt let down when Charlie and I walked back to his car. I comforted myself with thinking that someday I too would be traveling on one of those trains, leaving Ames for college someplace far away, maybe even Denver or San Francisco. When I got on that train, I would head into a new and wonderful life. It never occurred to me that I would be taking my old self, and Ames, with me.

Swimming Pools

We were talking, my friend and I, about our children. Almost every day for nine years we have called each other to exchange anecdotes, complain, congratulate, and reassure ourselves that we aren't such bad mothers after all. That day I was complaining. I was suddenly bone-tired of worrying, fussing, arranging. I gritted my teeth as I told my friend how I suddenly, desperately, didn't want to listen to piano lessons, fix dinner, scrape dishes, run a bath, comb tangly hair, fix the wobbly night-light. I went on and on, cataloguing weariness, winding down in a disheartened gasp.

"I know, I know," said my friend soothingly, as she always does. "But think of how much easier it is now than it was three years ago. Remember when they were two? Or when they were just crawling?" We were both silent for a moment, evoking those breathless days. "I was just thinking today," my friend went on, "as I saw Katy riding down the block on her bicycle, that this spring she is finally launched. She can ride a bike, and she can swim all the way across the pool. Now I think she can make it on her own. As soon as the baby gets a little older . . ." Her voice trailed off too, and we began to talk of other things.

After we hung up, I pondered what my friend had said. Is that what it means to be launched into life, to be able to ride a bike and to swim? The bike I understood quickly, because I remember myself on my first blue fat-wheeled Schwinn, weaving crazily down the sidewalks at first, then soon riding in gangs down the empty streets, riding to school and to stores and to the park. *But swimming? Why should a girl know how to swim? Even here in Minnesota, land of ten thousand lakes, we may not get to one of them in a whole summer. None of our friends owns a boat. Jennifer's social life would hardly be damaged if she stayed out of the water.* Yet, like my friend, I hurried to sign up Jennie for Water Babies when she was an infant. I shivered through endless hours in the YWCA pool as she clung and tugged fearfully at my swimsuit. I was overwhelmed with pride when I saw her finally leave my arms and swim all by herself two feet to the side of the pool. What had she mastered? The ability to save her own life? I would not always be near her; if she were fishing, on a yacht, in a sailboat, could she now swim to shore? Was I happy because I had given her the self-sufficiency to survive one of the myriad dangers she will face in the years ahead?

Or was I pleased to see her swim because I now felt she had begun to master her own body? Because she could make her muscles move in a coordinated way, force them to do what she wanted? Was she learning to enjoy the way her body moved? Did I see in her early flappings and splashings some promise of grace? Was I foreseeing her physical pleasure in being a woman?

I didn't know then, and I still don't know. Since that conversation with my friend, I have wondered about the ways in which I myself was launched many years ago. My friend is intuitively right: though born and raised inland, I connect many of my most vivid memories about growing up with water. When I dip into the past, I often come up gasping in a swimming pool.

I always ask for a window seat so I can see the swimming pools. As we descend over the suburbs, I stare like a child with nose pressed to glass at the brilliant blue eyes that stare back at me from the ground. They blink in the sun with affluent pride. What would it be like, I wonder, to live in a neighborhood where every yard had its pool? When I was growing up, our town had ten thousand people and only three swimming pools for us all, so that on hot days we were packed like Vienna sausages into the water. The pools I see below me look empty and lonely, unable to convey the intense excitement and fear I remember. My own swimming pools were three enchanted places, each casting a different spell, and we girls growing up in Ames passed through certain rites there.

All this was besides the swimming lessons. Girls didn't have many other lessons to worry them. Nobody owned horses, except a few farmers, and we didn't mix much with their kids anyway. A few girls took dancing from a dark-haired lady downtown, and once a year they gave a recital in the high-school gym. Draped in flags or dressed like soldiers, they tap-danced vigorously as their teacher played the piano. A few star pupils, all much older then we, were ballerinas who spun through a spotlight carefully wielded by the teacher's son. Their layers of net, painstakingly sewed together like giant nylon pot-scrubbers, whirled as they danced so you could see lots of pink, perspiring legs. It somehow seemed not quite socially acceptable. But instinctively we agreed that we ought to learn how to swim, and so every spring we signed up for Saturday morning lessons at the college pool.

Why we were so determined to swim would have mystified any outsider. The nearest lake of any size was a two-hour drive, far away in the corner of the state, and few of us knew anyone with a cabin there. We simply wanted to hold up our heads at Blaine's Pool, the town's only public swimming place, and to do that we had to know how.

Entering the college gym was like edging into a strange and vaguely threatening world. Partly, of course, we were in awe of any place that belonged to college students, those noisy, reckless grown-ups whose fraternity parties and pep rallies often lit up the lives of those of us who lived near the campus. As we entered the dark brick building, and descended the cold tiled staircase, a smell of old sweat, dampness, chlorine and mildewing towels seemed to creep up the stairs and beckon down the halls where we were not allowed to go. Here in some hidden labyrinth the Iowa State athletes "worked out." From one of these doors, opening off a hall we couldn't see, they emerged to the open field next door into a chorus of cheers. Walking outside the stadium walls on Saturday afternoon, I could often hear the cheering rise and fall like a giant inarticulate voice. "OOOOOH," the voice cried, "AAAAAH." Then it would be silent, as though the giant had fallen back into his cave. These shouts of incomprehensible pleasure or disappointment seemed to hover in the air as I now found my way to an empty locker and started to slip into my swimming suit.

Even changing into a swimsuit was part of the physical education of swimming lessons. I wasn't all that shy; after all, I had a sister. But still it was unsettling to get undressed in a line of other freckled, tanned or pale bodies that looked so critically different from mine. Even though my best friend was famous for her golden hair, I was still surprised to see that the little fur of hair between her legs was blonde too, not brown like mine. I had thought everybody's was probably brown.

As I unfastened my cotton-knit band that masqueraded as a bra, I looked surreptitiously around at the other girls. Some of them had actual breasts. I looked away again quickly. I only wore my "bra" because recently one of the cruder boys in our seventh grade had told me he could see my titties through my sweater. I wasn't sure what he meant, until he pointed. Then I held back tears, and embarrassment, until I could get back home for lunch and demand that my mother take me out right away, that noon, to Younkers to buy a bra. I wondered why she hadn't seen that I needed one. As I pulled my swimsuit up to fasten it, I looked down at myself and felt once again that somehow all the bumps fell in the wrong places.

All this examination of bodies, furtive as it was, made me feel as though there were something faintly medical about the college pool. We had to splash through a footbath of gray, smelly disinfectant before we trooped down the inner stairs to the pool. This footbath, we were informed, was to guard against all kinds of fungi, like athlete's foot; I wasn't sure what that was but knew that it must be very personal, infectious, and unpleasant. I associated it

in my mind with rumors I had heard about something called
syphilis. Even today, when someone mentions v.d., I sometimes
think of footbaths.

Once we were assembled, shivering, along the pool edges,
sniffing the chlorine and watching the black marking bands on
the pool floor waver through the gently moving currents, I was in
a daze. Stripped of my dignity, cowed, I held my knees tightly and
listened to Big Mike O'Donnell tell us what we would do today.
Big Mike was the college swimming coach. We all thought he
was very handsome and a fitting imperial figure to strut up and
down the pool sides, surveying us struggling swimmers. He had a
muscular, hairy chest, usually covered by a sort of terry shirt left
unbuttoned, and he wore trim black racing trunks that contrasted
with our variously flowered swimcaps, bright cotton suits, little
skirts and ruffles. He was obviously efficient, powerful and knowing, a man to be feared as well as admired. As I slipped with a
gasp into the cold water, I would look up with eyes blurred by
chlorine and see Big Mike sternly patrolling above me, poking a
long pole into the water. If you misbehaved, he would rap you on
the head. But if you were in trouble, or seemed about to drown,
he would extend the pole to you so you could grab it and get
pulled out.

I suppose there were women's swimming teams somewhere in
those ways, but I could never imagine them practicing in the college pool. Big Mike was the men's coach, and I always thought of
his precincts as a man's pool. Later in the day boys we knew
would come to take their swimming lessons. We knew, because
one of them had told one of us, that they swam naked. Without
any suits at all. I never thought much about male bodies: I had no
brothers, I had not yet been exposed to art, and I simply could
not picture all those boys in the pool. I would shudder a bit and
feel very cold. I was glad I wore a suit.

Sometimes after lessons we could stay and watch the advanced
class, older high-school girls who practiced diving and fancy
strokes. Once I was very late in getting dressed, and on an im-

pulse I climbed up the back upper stairs to the tiny gallery over-looking the pool. There I could see six girls, dressed in identical one-piece striped suits, all with dolphin insignia, performing a sort of water ballet. They were Big Mike's synchronized swim-mers, special protégées, and he even occasionally smiled at them as they dipped and dove, turned and flipped, kicked in unison like submerged cancan dancers. I stared, entranced, until Big Mike glanced up and saw me. He frowned, waved his hand, called some-thing, and I backed away. But I carried home with me the vision of those lovely, beautiful bodies, all grace and precision, moving in the water as though they were sleek fish.

When summer finally came and I was ready to go with my friends down to Blaine's Pool, how I longed to be able to swim like a fish. My lessons always seemed to leave me half-finished, almost passing advanced beginners, or just a few backstroke lengths short of moving on from intermediate. It wasn't so much that I wanted to *swim* like Big Mike's special girls, I just wanted to *look* like them in the water. As I tried on swimsuits at Younkers, sucking in my stomach, I looked in the mirror and saw nothing there but plump discouragement in a bright shirred Hawaiian print. All the elastic in the world wouldn't transform me into a dolphin.

But I bought the suit, hoped I would magically turn sleeker, and agreed to make the first trip to Blaine's. School was out, and a few weeks might have passed between the last classes and the first really hot day. None of us girls had seen any of the boys, except during chance encounters at the ice-cream store, or down-town, or perhaps at a Sunday matinee. Many of them had sum-mer jobs, earning real money, and they were glad to emerge on the weekends to show off their new muscles and their purchasing power. They all knew that Blaine's was the place to do it.

Even the setting of Blaine's Pool made it a place apart. Outside the city limits, it was dug out of the ground in a small hollow sur-rounded by a scraggly woods and a dirty, meandering river. Blaine's had a remote air about it, a kind of isolation. As one of our mothers drove, very carefully, down a steep hill that curved sharply, we heard the noise of splashing and confused shouts, screams, and the lifeguard's whistle before we could see the pool itself. We bounced up and down on the back seat, giggling and chattering in high-pitched voices, until the mother, made nervous by the hot rods that zoomed past her up the hill, snapped crossly. We subsided and clutched our rolled-up bathtowels in anticipation.

As we pulled into the parking lot, where the mother would pick us up a few hours later, we all strained to see what faces we could make out at the poolside, in the bleachers, or at the pop stand. Much of our anticipation depended on just this uncertainty. Who was here? Would Bob O'Brien and Lon Sell have already come? Or gone? Were we too late? Or too early? Was that Tommy Sandvig on the diving board? The mother was probably glad to escape from our gasps, pointings and smothered cries. No matter whose mother she was, though, she never commented on this aspect of the swimming pool ritual. By eleven or twelve, we were all expected to have boyfriends, or at least to want to have them. Blaine's Pool was a proper place to find them.

I sometimes think I learned about sex at Blaine's Pool. Oh, not the hard facts (it was years before I knew what they really were, and there are still some days when I don't feel too sure). So what jagged bits of knowledge did I take home from Blaine's, along with a bent locker key and someone's used Tangee orange lipstick, rescued from the dressing-room floor? Mostly stinging bits of intense physical sensation. Looking back to those green, dreaming summers, I always think of blistering heat and ice-cold water. Some afternoons, when I couldn't go to Blaine's, I sat in my shorts and halter in our steaming living room, damply reading, feeling the old wool upholstery of the comfy Morris chair rub against my thighs, while I sucked and chewed on ice cubes and balanced the glass, painfully cold, on my knee for as long as I could stand it. That was the kind of intensity I felt at Blaine's. Emerging from the shaded dressing room, I always blinked, temporarily blinded, in the dazzling light that reflected from the white bleachers, shining metal slides, and of course the glittering blue water. It was as though all the colors had been turned up just a bit too bright.

As the sun beat down on my head, shoulders and thighs, I had to decide how to get into the water. It was inviting, but very cold. So my friends and I edged gingerly into the shallow end, stepping daintily down the little children's steps, and then began rubbing our tummies cautiously with the cold water. We seldom got the chance to edge much farther, because by that time one of the boys saw us. Whooping and splashing, he leaped into the water, scooping up water with the palm of his hand in a practiced, skidding gesture, covering our exaggerated screams with shock waves. By the time the lifeguard blew his whistle and shook a finger at us, we were wet, initiated, ready to paddle down to the deep end and continue the Blaine's ritual. Some afternoons I was braver. Standing for only a few moments on the pool's edge, before anyone could push me in, I looked down and anticipated with a delicious shudder how the water would feel, closing over me in a total embrace. Then I jumped. For one brief moment as I went under I wondered if I would ever come up again. Then I surfaced, blowing, laughing, and waited for the others to join me.

Then, of course, we swam. We girls never did laps, and we seldom even swam in a straight line. Instead we darted back and forth, moving to parts of the pool where someone we hoped would notice us had last dived in. As we hung, treading water, chatting together in brief gasps, Tommy or Bob or Lon glided under water toward us, often in twos or threes, as though they needed support. We girls pretended not to notice them coming until they spouted to the top, with loud shouts, and pounced on us to dunk us. The lifeguards were supposed to stop any horseplay (a sign by the pool read: "No running. No bottles by the pool. NO HORSEPLAY."). But they usually looked the other way at such simple stuff as dunking. Being shoved under water was recognized as a sign that a boy had noticed you. He had at least taken the trouble to push you down. We certainly never complained, though I sometimes swallowed water and came up coughing. At other times the boys would ignore us and engage in their own elaborate games, diving for pennies or playing tag. We girls clung to the side, hanging on to the gutters, and watched.

When I grew older, I heard for the first time about something called the battle of the sexes. It brought to mind an image that would doubtless seem ludicrously inappropriate to Millett or Mailer, but that's because neither one of them ever held on for dear life to the giant tops at Blaine's Pool.

Once there must have been two tops; one rusting anchor was still fastened to the bottom, a melancholy reminder of summers long gone. But by the time I was there, only one top was left intact, and we all wrestled and struggled to be among the few its surface could hold. The top was maybe six feet in diameter, with a steering wheel at the center that you turned to make the top revolve as you stood on its slanting, slippery surface. It spun on a slightly askew axis, so that as you turned the wheel faster, and the top whirled faster, it was harder and harder to hang on. The boys always had control of the steering wheel; at least, they felt they had a right to it, so that if we girls climbed on board when the top was empty, they soon spied us from wherever they were in the pool and came splashing noisily over to assume charge. Those of us girls who were sturdy, not easily scared off, or perhaps a bit foolhardy, stayed on the top. As the boys turned the wheel, we clung to whatever part of its metal rim we could grab. Faster and faster it spun, and before long girls would begin to fall off, like bits of spray dashed away from a fierce centrifugal force. Even a boy or two might lose hold, pretending, if possible, that he had just decided to dive from the edge, or that he wanted to jump on one of the girls who had just fallen off, cannonballing on top of her.

Whoever stayed on the top longest won. When competition got down to the last two swimmers, anything was acceptable, from prying someone's fingers off the wheel to tripping and pushing. The boys had fewer inhibitions about those tactics, and consequently one of them always won. I wish I could say I was often one of the last girls to leave the top, but I wasn't. I got dizzy quickly, and, stomach churning, ended up gulping mouthfuls of chlorine as I tumbled ignominiously into the water.

Climbing out, waterlogged, I felt heavy and washed out, so tired I forgot to hold in my stomach as I walked away. Stretching out on a wooden bleacher, I closed my eyes and listened to the shouting and splashing, which seemed dimmer and far away, even though the pool was just a few feet off. With dulled vision, I occasionally squinted at the swimmers hurrying along the pool deck to see who was still in action. But I was warm, drying, and strangely invisible. I can still feel how comforting the sun seemed then, how blissfully tired and somehow virtuous I felt, worn out by all my social exertions. As I shifted position, very carefully, I could feel the rough grain of the wood. The paint was worn off in many spots, and once when I moved too fast, I got a splinter in my hand. There I lay in the sun and baked, letting time pass over me.

When I finally got up, I could look down and see damp cool stains on the wood where I had been. Tired, but still anxious to extract the last bit of possible pleasure from the afternoon, I jumped in quickly. Soon we had to trudge to the dressing room; it was almost time for the mother to return.

Not everything connected with Blaine's Pool is illuminated in my memory with the blinding glare of sun and water. Though it was by day filled with open games, battles on the top, flirtations in the water, Blaine's Pool was reputed to be quite another sort of place at night. Its hidden location, surrounded by trees, naturally made it a favorite spot for "parking," or so the stories went. None of us girls had ever parked anywhere yet, so we didn't know. But sometimes, floating on my back in a quiet moment, I would look up at the overhanging trees and wonder. Occasionally a lifeguard left his post for a few minutes and walked over to the rattly stands placed just outside the pool enclosure for observers. Once I saw the guard talking to a pretty girl with red lipstick who stood, casually brushing back her hair, on the lowest step. After a bit he returned to his chair, and she left. I thought they were probably arranging to meet later that night, somewhere in the trees.

This suggestive air of illicit sex that hung over the pool, or so I thought, crystallized for me one late afternoon when we were still halfheartedly messing about in the almost empty pool. Most of the boys had gone home. Among the stragglers were an older girl with long black hair and lots of curves that owed nothing to elastic, and her boyfriend, who we knew was a football player on the high-school team. They were swimming lazily in the deep end, diving under water, tagging and laughing. As I bounced on the bottom of the shallow end, wondering if I could rub out the seat of the new swimsuit I now hated, Peggy O'Reilly came striding through the water toward me as fast as she could. "Susan!" she said breathlessly. "Guess what! I just saw Cindy and Steve! Do you know what they were *doing?*" No, I said, I didn't know. "Well," she announced with a sense of real importance, "they were *kissing under water.*" We were both silent. With one instinct, we turned to look at the deep end. Holding hands, Cindy and Steve were climbing out of the water. They walked toward the dressing rooms, and we watched them until they passed out of sight.

Soon we too left the pool. Dressing hurriedly in a tiny cubicle, I kept a close watch on the floor. A few of the booths had gaps in the floorboards, and several weeks earlier they had caught some boys underneath the girls' dressing room, peering up. If you dressed in the open, walled section, where the sun could dry your hair, you had to look above the wall toward the trees. Sometimes a few boys shinnied up the trunks in order to be able to get a good view. It is only now as I remember these small terrors, our automatic precautions, that I realize with surprise we never dreamed of invading the boys' dressing room in return.

After we were all ready, we turned in our locker baskets and rolled our damp suits in our towels. Then we loitered around the pop stand, hung on the fence, or made patterns in the dust with our sneakers, talking about everyone we'd seen that day and what he had done and what we had said in return. The mother was later than she'd promised. I walked around the pool enclosure to the bleachers near the trees. The ground was littered with torn popcorn boxes, green Coke bottles, and candy wrappings. The grass there and under the trees was sparse and brown. It was hard to imagine anyone wanting to linger there, even at night. When I finally heard a horn honk, impatiently, I was glad to hurry over to the parking lot and squeeze comfortably into the back seat with my friends.

A few years after I began going regularly to Blaine's Pool, my mother joined the Country Club for one season. I may have learned something about sex at Blaine's, but I learned about social nuance at the Country Club. I'm still not sure how Mother got us in, though I think it must have been a sympathy vote. She was a widow, we were almost poor—the way an English instructor at a state college was poor in those days, three thousand a year in dollars and in freshman themes—and as a family, we had a noticeably deserving character. As I remember, they gave Mother a "single" rate, and for that both my sister and I were able to use the club's pool. I think I also remember that Mother had to promise them that none of us played golf, so we wouldn't take advantage of our bargain by crowding the greens. We were, however, all allowed to swim.

Compared to Blaine's, the Country Club pool was small. One diving board, no spinning top. But its size only seemed to me to be a measure of its exclusiveness. Whoever had laid out plans for the Country Club was an entrepreneur with an eye for the one beautiful, rolling and wooded piece of land outside Ames. He must have known immediately that such an acreage had to be saved; he had a true aristocrat's instinct and converted it into a private preserve. Instead of the scraggly woods around Blaine's, the club had a real forest, shady oaks and maples that had escaped wholesale conversion into farmland. These trees clustered around a clear, grassy-edged creek, where white golf balls shone unexpectedly in the water. Dipping and swooping toward the creek, the hills were high enough so that at the bottom you couldn't even see the clubhouse. They were the only real hills for miles, and in the winter we children sneaked onto the golf course for forbidden toboggan parties. Those were the only times I ever saw the Country Club until the summer we joined.

Now that I have seen other private clubs, much larger and glossier, I realize that the Ames Country Club wasn't much: a nine-hole golf course, a ranch-style clubhouse built like a log cabin, a small pool, two picnic tables, and an outdoor water fountain. But its size merely insisted on its intimacy, that of a self-confident and rather comfortable small family. That whole summer I never really felt we belonged there. Mother, who was always anxious to please my sister and me, must have decided to join for our sake. But she didn't realize that we couldn't see any of our friends there. They were all down at Blaine's.

Instead we saw mothers. Nobody's mother ever went to Blaine's, except maybe at empty hours, like Sunday morning or very late afternoon. But every day at the Country Club, two or three women would pull up in their Oldsmobiles and stroll down to the pool together. They wore bright scarves around tightly curled hair and very dark sunglasses. Propped discreetly on the grass next to the pool, they sunned and tanned. Many of them lived in the only part of town that had a signpost, a fancy development called Colonial Village, with expensive New England saltboxes on curving streets. They were mothers who didn't have to work, though they belonged to organizations, with mysterious names and initials, P.E.O., A.A.U.W., O.R.T., Jayceettes. All afternoon these mothers basked and browned, watching the pool through dark glasses, staying carefully just out of range of splashes. At the end of the day their husbands puffed over the hill, pulling golf carts, wiping sweat from red faces. The women rose, slipped their baked feet into sandals, and went home.

Sometimes if my sister and I stayed late enough, close to supper-time, we could see the same mothers and fathers return to the club for a dinner-dance. Now the women had on gaily printed dresses with full skirts and bared shoulders, and the men's red faces looked even more burned above white shirts. Earrings sparkled, and polished black shoes gleamed in the dusk. We wheeled our bicycles away very slowly so we could see and hear as much of the party as possible before leaving. The pool closed early on those nights. Someone said it would open later so the adults could swim in the dark under floodlights. From the bar, a musty pine-paneled room just inside the clubhouse, where we never could go, we could hear laughter, glasses clinking, loud voices and music. Years later, when I read *The Great Gatsby* for the first time, I realized that I had always imagined parties like Gatsby's taking place at the Country Club: drinking, dancing, flashing color, romance.

The tinge of glamour that still invests the Country Club in my memory was probably also due to the presence there of some of the Central boys. Ames had two junior high schools, Welch for the college half of town, Central for the downtown half. Until they merged into one high school, the two sides never had much chance to meet each other, except perhaps at church youth groups, or the annual rival games. We Welch kids had always heard that the Central kids were "fast," familiar not only with parking but also with drinking beer. We learned to recognize a few Central boys from their appearance on basketball or football teams; they seemed taller, older, and much more attractive than the boys we knew at Welch. Jay Gordon, for instance, always wore pale pastel shirts, pink or yellow or green, while the Welch boys invariably dressed in red checks from Penney's.

Jay's parents belonged to the Country Club, and so did Jack Bolton's. Jack was tall, already six feet, with an appealing shamble, and my heart leaped when he dribbled down the court in the midwinter Welch-Central game. Now in the summer he played golf with his father, and once in a while, with a shy smile, he would appear at the pool for a quick swim. A few girls from Central of course belonged too, and if they were together, Jay or Jack would stop to talk and joke with them. Sometimes they all teased and pushed their way to the water together, jumping in with loud splashes and laughter, just as we all did in a larger, noisier gang at Blaine's. Only here at the Country Club I wasn't one of them; I sat on my beach towel alone and felt awkward. In fact, I didn't enjoy swimming very much on the days when both the Central boys and girls were at the club. I was left out, a very different feeling from just being alone. One of the Central girls belonged to my church youth group, and sometimes she said hello, casually, as she passed by. That greeting was worse than anonymity, because it meant that she, and the others, knew I was there. I was acutely conscious that my little potbelly, easily lost in the crowd at Blaine's, seemed to stick out, downright protuberantly, at the Country Club.

If I became too depressed, I jumped up from my towel and headed toward a deserted part of the pool. Swimming under water, I pretended I was invisible. Or I did a vigorous sidestroke, as though I were practicing laps. Just being in motion made me feel better, and the cool water closing over my head calmed my feelings so I could emerge with some dignity, towel myself off, and go home. After a while, I simply stopped going to the Country Club. My sister found other things to do too. The next summer Mother didn't renew our membership.

Whatever impressions I soaked in with the chlorine or sun at those three swimming pools of my childhood must have stained me somewhere ineradicably. For ever since then, at bad times I have headed, like a lemming, to the water. When in pain, I can be found in a pool. Perhaps the noise of yelling children reminds me of happy afternoons at Blaine's, or perhaps I am obscurely pleased that I no longer need to be part of that boisterous group and that I can just swim, by myself, with my own thoughts. I don't know. Last summer, when a man I had much loved and I suddenly parted, I fled the house every afternoon at five for the new municipal pool in the city where I now live. This pool is much bigger than Blaine's, quite an impressive place, and at that hour the guards cordon off lengths for laps. I felt the tightness in my chest and stomach begin to ease the minute I stepped out of my car and saw that huge pool, almost empty, waiting for me. A few swimmers, whom I didn't know, already churned up and down the black lines: company without the responsibility of conversation. They might comment on the weather, or the temperature of the water, but they wouldn't know or care about what I was feeling. As I undressed in the shower room, I could pat my snug, now familiar body, to reassure myself that it was still there, and I knew that swimming helped, as Big Mike always said, to "keep in shape."

Once in the pool, doing my laps, I felt a kind of anesthetic set in. Cold water slithered over me, a numb caress, promising relief. It seemed to wash off some of the unhappiness that clung to me all over like mosquito repellent. Even the chlorine helped: as I mechanically stroked, back and forth, I hoped it would disinfect my brain. Clinging to the pool edge between laps, breathing hard, I could look up at the empty sky and see blue peace mirroring back to the pool. Everything seemed far away, except the water, the cold tile I grasped, the blue of sky and water. No one knew who I was, and I didn't have to remember. When I climbed out, tired, after an hour, I had the same feeling I used to have after an afternoon at Blaine's: exhausted, satisfied, with the hope of perhaps yet another hot afternoon before the summer ended. I was glad to be tired. I could tell I was still alive. Tomorrow I could go back to the swimming pool.

Boyfriends

"Come on, Sarah," hisses my daughter excitedly. *The two six-year-olds tear up the stairs, giggling loudly. Jennifer sees me standing there and stops to explain. "There are some boys out there, Mommy," she says with emphasis. "Sarah and I are going to get them." Sarah nods, they giggle again, and disappear into Jennie's bedroom. They don't say how they plan to "get" those boys, but they'll probably run into the front yard, hide behind the big maple tree, stare at the boys, giggle even more loudly, and then run back into the house. Even at six, Jennie's feelings about boys are complex.*

So far I've been able to answer most of Jennie's questions about sex. I've had help: carefully illustrated books, mainly about chickens and eggs; a tour through a life-sized prenatal exhibit at a science museum that showed everything except how babies got started; feminist essays reminding me to use words like vagina *instead of* bottom, uterus *as the wonderful thing to tell her she's got instead of a* penis.

Speaking of penises, I am reminded of one question of Jennie's I didn't answer. She was only four then, beginning that rapid flow of interrogation that still startles me. I was cleaning the house, dusting in a concentrated fury, when suddenly she appeared beside me to ask in a thoughtful voice, "Mommy, are penises nice?" I stopped dusting. Whatever I said was bound to be repeated somewhere: "My Mommy says," Jennifer announces proudly. Did I want to be quoted enthusiastically? Yes, penises can be lovely? Did I want to be judiciously comparative?

Some are nicer than others? As I paused, thoughts racing, my daughter as usual whizzed by me to the finish line. "You know, Mommy, I think they're yucky," she said firmly, and left the room.

A little dazed, I continued to dust. I tried to think back to my first awareness of that basic fact, that boys do have penises, but I could not. When did I first realize that boys were different? How did I feel about them then? I remembered a cluster of boys snickering at our fifth-grade class picture when one girl's little white triangle of underpants showed. The time I got blisters from the teeter-totter. The piece of lead in my right middle finger. A silver cross on a chain. A jigsaw puzzle of irrelevancies that somehow fit together.

I can't remember when I didn't want a boyfriend. Walking timidly for the first time into my sunny kindergarten room, I noticed immediately two play areas, one with a complete toy kitchen, pots and pans, tiny brooms and mops; the other with a miniature carpenter's shop, filled with wooden blocks, hammers, glue. Although I delightedly fussed in the elaborate cardboard kitchen, I kept sneaking curious glances at the boys who were hammering real nails in their adjoining shop. I wanted one of them to notice I was there.

In those early years boys seemed very strange. I had no brothers, and the only boys I knew were those on the playground at Louise Crawford Elementary School. They were loud, rough, and dangerous. During recess we girls had to stay out of their way, usually on the swings while the boys whirled over the hanging bars nearby. A square skyscraper of a jungle gym dominated the playground; from its top, clinging tightly to the bars, you could look out over the whole sandy yard. But the boys scrambled on it faster than we girls ever could, hampered as we were by our skirts and the care we had to take not to let our underpants show from below. If I saw the jungle gym vacant, I would sometimes try to get to the top, skirt tucked safely under, before one or two of the boys could invade and drive me down.

My first boyfriend didn't last long. When I was in first grade,

Johnny Prince, who was a year older, would sometimes wander over to me during recess and ask if I wanted to teeter-totter. He had freckles, a nice grin, and an exciting double bounce. When my end of the teeter-totter went up, Johnny could give the board two flips so that I sailed a few inches into the air, landing with a satisfying *thwat* back on the board. It felt a little like flying. But after a week, my mother noticed some blisters on my bottom and wondered where they were from. When I made the mistake of telling her, she called Johnny's mother. The next day Johnny passed me at recess with a look of disgust. "Tattletale!" he jeered, and then ignored me. I felt bereft.

One reason I had been so happy to have Johnny Prince bounce me was that he was one of the more desirable boys in second grade. Already I knew that some boys were worth wanting and others weren't. I would never have gotten on a teeter-totter with Jack Holmgren, who lived alone with his father in a dark and dirty house down the street. He wore scruffy clothes, picked his nose, and said "ain't." When I look at my first class picture, taken in third grade, I am amazed that even now I can remember precisely who the acceptable boys were and which particular one of them I wanted for my boyfriend. In third grade it was Lou Jones, who was solid, big, neither smart nor dumb, and president of our class. By fifth grade I began to look longingly at the set of boys who could sass the teacher and get away with it, who hung around together after school, who shot baskets and made rude jokes as we girls trailed past on our way home. But by then I also knew I wasn't likely to land one of them; I was a bit too brainy and somewhat plump. Acceptable, but not wildly desirable.

So it is not surprising that in sixth grade my first great passion was for a boy on the fringes rather than in the center of popularity. Doug Boynton was within my range, though he kept just out of reach like a moving target. I still associate Doug with speed and motion because of his bicycle. He owned the first bike with gears I'd ever seen, a thin-wheeled Raleigh as foreign to our dented, fatwheeled Schwinns as Doug was when he moved to Forest Avenue. If our windows were open, I could hear the whirr and click-click-click of those gears whenever Doug was cruising down the street. I would dash to the back door to see if he might pull into our driveway and pause, one foot still on the pedal, to talk to me for a few moments before taking off again. Sometimes he stayed a while, but he never got off his bike. When my mother asked him if he would like to come in, he shook his head and backpedaled a little. I was embarrassed that she didn't understand; of course he couldn't come in, he was only just passing, he hadn't come to see me at all, he was on his way somewhere else.

What did I find so attractive about Doug Boynton? I peer into the past now trying to see some hidden qualities in that sixth-grader that might explain why I was drawn later to other difficult relationships. Doug wasn't handsome at all. Tall, scrawny, with unruly hair, he seemed mainly composed of elbows and side-stepping feet. But he had a fast, crooked grin that signaled a slightly wild sense of humor. Now I can't remember a single funny thing Doug said or did, although everyone treated him as a comedian. I do remember once when our sixth-grade classroom was filled with an overpowering smell from someone's explosive fart how Doug confessed, laughed, and rushed around opening windows and making jokes. He was one of the few boys who could have gotten away with such bravado.

Although Doug was partial to me in some ways, he never openly claimed me as his girlfriend. This made me very unhappy. My mother didn't like to see me unhappy, and she took an early dislike to Doug. She suspected something hidden and cruel in his nature, and maybe she was right. Somewhere in those few years I remember standing half-undressed in my bedroom, hearing a funny scratching noise, and looking upward at the back wall windows. There I saw two peering faces that disappeared the minute I screamed, but not before I had recognized them as Doug and one of his friends. When my mother rushed out, they were gone, and I had to beg her not to call their mothers and complain. But I felt frightened and exposed and didn't like to stay alone in our house for a long time afterward.

In the sixth-grade classroom, however, Doug and I carried on an odd courtship. He sat in the front desk of our row, and I sat in the back. Whenever I walked up to the teacher's table or the pencil sharpener, I had to pass Doug's desk, and he was always waiting for me. As I slid by, as fast as I could, he would try to stab me with his pencil. I knew these pokes were really expressions of attention, and I played along willingly, jabbing back. He was faster and more coordinated, and he scored more often. Twice his pencil left bits of lead under my skin, one in my left elbow, another in my middle finger. A doctor reassured my mother that I wouldn't get lead poisoning from them, pencils were mainly graphite anyway, but she told me to stop playing that stupid game. I did. Twenty-five years later those bits of lead are still there. I stare at them sometimes, tiny blue-black dots blurred under layers of skin, and gloomily wonder if they are testimonials to a masochistic streak in my nature. Though I have long since lost track of Doug Boynton, his affections left a permanent mark.

I don't pretend that I was always uncomplainingly on the receiving end of Doug's small cruelties. I tried to give Doug as good as I got, though the odds were uneven, because I loved him. Once he broke his leg and had to wear a huge cast, lugging it awkwardly up and down the school stairs. Soon after he returned to class from the hospital, he stood in the hall one noon teasing me mercilessly until I couldn't stand it any longer. I drew my foot back, meaning to kick him in his good leg, but I lost control of myself. Instead I kicked him in his cast. It must have hurt terribly, because Doug began to cry. I was terrified at what I'd done, and I burst into tears too. Everyone came running. This time Doug's mother called my mother, and after that we had a truce for quite a while.

I never had a chance to find out if Doug could be a real boyfriend, because he moved. Just before seventh grade, Doug's family went to Alaska for a year. Though they returned for our eighth-grade year, they then left permanently for Alabama. This was my first experience of having someone I loved literally move out of my life, a helpless feeling that most of us eventually learn to live with but that is particularly bewildering when you're young. Why could grown-ups move wherever they wished and drag us kids along? I was angry at the unfairness of it all. I was sure when I was a grown-up I would be able to keep my friends around me forever. No one would ever force them to leave.

During that first year Doug was gone, he wrote regular letters to our seventh-grade class. Since I was class secretary, I had to read them aloud during homeroom period, blushing at Doug's scattered references to me. I liked the feeling that everyone knew Doug had singled me out; even a long-distance boyfriend who really wasn't a boyfriend conferred status. Once he sent me a tiny pair of Alaskan wooden dolls, whose heads nodded loosely on small pins, and I kept them in my bedroom as totems. I had their heads turned so they were facing each other, woodenly kissing, and I cherished a superstition I invented that as long as they touched faces everything would be all right.

Although Doug was no longer a physical presence in my life, I never forgot him, I kept my kissing dolls on my shelf, and I had romantic dreams about him for years. We continued to correspond sporadically, though life in Alabama sounded so strange that I had a hard time imagining what Doug might now be like. In one letter he talked about "chasing jig-a-boos," a remark that puzzled me and horrified my mother. When he graduated from high school, he sent me a snapshot of himself, leaning languidly against a fireplace, dressed in a white tuxedo, and holding a cigarette in one hand. Such sophistication awed me. If we ever met again, I doubted that I'd be able to talk to him.

My mother hadn't forgotten Doug, either. When she learned that he was going to attend Dartmouth while I was at Smith, she thought he would be far too close. So when she had to sign what was then infelicitously called "blanket permission" for off-campus overnights, she wrote that I could go anywhere I wanted, any time, but I was never to go to the Dartmouth Winter Carnival. One fall night my first semester in college, I did see Doug Boynton again. Huddled in a crowd of girls at a noisy mixer, I felt someone tap my elbow. A young man stood in front of me. Something about his crooked grin looked familiar. "Don't you know who I am, Susan?" he said. "Doug BOYNTON!" I shrieked. For a while all I could say was his name.

Remembering my dreams, my wooden dolls, my years of hopeful letters, I would like to report that we then danced into the sunset together. But one evening was enough to disperse five years of Hollywood haze from Doug Boynton. He wasn't quite as funny as I remembered. Nor was he as sophisticated as his high-school graduation picture had suggested. No longer the breezy boy from Forest Avenue, he seemed uncertain, awkward, a little scared about keeping up at Dartmouth. I now wanted to be dazzled beyond what sparkle he could supply. When he called me after the mixer to try to arrange a date, I turned him down. He stopped writing, I stopped thinking about him, and one day I gave my Alaskan dolls to a little girl who probably lost them.

Just because I dreamed about Doug Boynton for years, I didn't stop hoping for a suitable boyfriend closer at hand. Seventh grade was the first year most mothers allowed girls to go out on real dates, but to do that you had to have someone to go out on a date with. Not all the seventh-grade boys were as ready as we were. You had to take what you could get. In my case that meant Kurt Peterson, a silent, short, unnoticeable boy who went to my Sunday school. One day he asked me if I wanted to go to a movie. I did. I was nervous, because I knew the First Date had great significance. But nothing happened. Kurt lived close enough to walk to my house and to the movie theatre a mile away. He found it very difficult to talk, and though I babbled on as best I could, he only responded in monosyllables. It was a long mile to the movie and an even longer mile back. For about a block on the way home Kurt held my hand; his palm felt cold and damp.

When I reported all these details to my best friend the next morning, she thought for a moment and then announced: "Sounds to me like he's a real dead fish." I was struck with the soundness of her judgment.

By eighth grade most of us could recognize real Romance when we saw it. A year ahead of us we watched the uncrowned kings and queens of ninth grade pairing off. One couple came every Wednesday to junior-high Presbyterian Fellowship, so I could see them close up. Larry Matthiessen was dark and handsome, with a misset broken nose that gave him a tough, world-wise air. He went with Sara Ward, a girl of delicate prettiness who reminded me of an ad I'd seen in *American Girl* of a blue-eyed blonde in a flowered raincoat with matching umbrella who was surrounded by boys wanting to carry her books. Larry's father ran a grocery store; hers did something vague but so impressive that he could afford to build the first house in town that cost twenty thousand dollars. I had heard Mrs. Miller down the block tell my mother that every brick in that house had been specially ordered from Des Moines. We all knew that the Wards wished Sara would find somebody more suitable to go steady with, which made their romance seem somehow threatened and even more exciting to watch. We had heard of Romeo and Juliet. After Presbyterian Fellowship was over at nine o'clock, everyone walked home. Most of us walked with girlfriends or in groups, boys hanging behind the girls. But Larry and Sara walked alone, holding hands, sometimes with their arms around each other. From the half-block my girlfriends and I kept behind them, we could see their heads close together and hear their laughter, Larry's deep and short, Sara's light and long. As we bobbed along in the darkness, we hoped for brief glimpses of their faces under the occasional streetlights. They looked very happy.

Although a year later Sara moved away, and Larry, to my immense disappointment, did not mourn forever but started dating someone else, not all the couples who formed during those eighth- and ninth-grade years were so ephemeral. By the time we were thirteen, Romance had begun to attack us seriously. I knew several couples who started to go steady, continued together throughout high school and got married. Though I knew that I would not get married for years and years, still I could sense that love was not always indefinite, that it could lead somewhere. Our parents, of course, warned us about where it *might* lead, but since few of us had done more than hold hands, furtively, on church-sponsored hayrides, nobody was very much worried. We were all shocked, parents and children alike, when a whispered rumor reached us from the downtown high school that Elena Novak, runner-up to the Snow Queen and still only a sophomore, had gotten pregnant. She was pretty, popular, vivacious, the only daughter in a proud family with four older sons. How could it have happened? We all felt as though she had died. Perhaps in a way she did; she quit school, got married, and hid at home for several years. One summer I caught sight of her in the high school, where she was taking special courses to try to finish her diploma. The halls were empty, darkened, echoing to my foot-steps. From my distance Elena seemed a little like a ghost, a plumpish matronly one in a shapeless dress, as she turned the cor-ner and disappeared.

As boys began to circle more closely around us girls in ninth and tenth grades, I found dishearteningly that I wasn't very inter-ested in the ones who hovered near me. My mother usually liked them. But I almost always wanted a boy I couldn't have. I in-vested these hopeless romances with so much tragically unful-filled potential that an artificial aura hung about them for years. Not long ago, an old Ames friend told me that Jay Gordon was now a jowly disc jockey somewhere in Arizona. I don't believe it.

My crush on Jay Gordon should seem funny after all this time, but it doesn't. It taught me something about self-deception and betrayal, and those elementary lessons are especially painful be-cause you don't know then that you will be able to survive them. When I first saw Jay at a Welch-Central junior-high basketball game, he was wearing a pale pink button-down shirt. Too short to be on the team, he was leaping confidently up and down the bleachers, talking to the Central girls and laughing, cracking gum, hands carelessly in his pockets. Something about his laugh struck me; it was easy, delighted, inviting.

I don't remember how or where Jay first noticed me, but he did. I found this out from my friend Marcie Hampden, who called me one night full of excitement. I thought to myself I was lucky to have Marcie for a friend. Cute, giggly, with a naturally flirtatious air, she had been a ninth-grade cheerleader and a steady girlfriend of our homeroom president until a new girl in town had suddenly eased her out. Now in the summer between junior high and high school, she could have had several boyfriends with a wink and a toss of her head. Marcie basked in popularity from both sexes. Somehow she had managed to make friends with the important girls from Central, the downtown junior high, and so she had an entrée we all envied into the new, scary, high-school world ahead. Everyone agreed she wasn't the least bit stuck-up, though, which was evident in the fact that she liked me.

Jay Gordon liked me too, she told me. He thought I looked like fun. He was too shy to call me himself, she explained, but since he knew her a little from her Central friends, he had called her as a kind of substitute. I was transported. He was thinking of asking me to go to a movie with him sometime this summer, she said. I clutched the phone as though I could squeeze this wonderful news into my hand. To go to a movie with Jay Gordon!

For several weeks I was deliriously happy. Of course I didn't see Jay often, only coming out of Moore's Dairy occasionally or leaving the swimming pool, and then he didn't talk to me for long. I tried to think of clever things to say to him, but after these brief encounters I felt stupid and awkward. Almost every night, though, Marcie called me to tell me that she had been on the phone with Jay. They always talked about me, she promised, though she became less and less specific about what exactly they had said. I was a little uneasy, but I didn't want to seem anxious. I knew these things took time. Meanwhile I dreamed about going to the movies with Jay, dating a boy from Central, maybe somehow getting close to that pink or blue or green Oxford-cloth button-down shirt. Underneath it he looked strong and solid. I wondered how he felt.

Although maybe I sensed it coming, I don't remember exactly when Marcie told me that Jay's affections had shifted. That wouldn't have been exactly how she put it, either. She probably explained that Jay had asked her out to a movie, and she had been surprised out of her mind, but she didn't know how to say no. Maybe he just wanted to talk about me face-to-face with her. So she went, and that was that. Before long they were going other places together, and Marcie no longer called me to report on her conversations. Intermediary friends tried to assure me that she felt terrible, that she hadn't meant to hurt me, that she couldn't help it. I tried to be nice about it, but I never forgave her. Years later, when we were all in college, I crossed the street to avoid speaking unnecessarily to Marcie Hampden.

One particular scene remains in my mind from that bitter summer, although I have no difficulty recalling my feelings of rejection and despair. I lugged all that anguish around without any idea of how to get rid of it. Once I almost threw it up. Marcie and some other friends invited me to meet them for lunch at the Rainbow, a cafe that specialized in pork tenderloin sandwiches with lots of juicy fat. I ordered my usual sandwich and chocolate milk, but when it was plunked down in front of me, I couldn't eat. I was staring, not caring who noticed, at Marcie's wrist. She was wearing Jay's silver identification bracelet, a sign, we all knew, that things were really serious. You had to be In Love to wear someone's i.d. bracelet. Nobody I knew had ever worn one before. The other girls tried not to comment on it, but they couldn't stop themselves. Marcie giggled and giggled. I stared at her bracelet and felt sick.

That loss is what I remember. It doesn't help to remind myself that a year or two later, I didn't want Jay anymore. He turned out to be nice but not too bright, a little conceited, something of a loudmouth. By the time we were seniors, we were friends, talking and joking together in the halls with an ease I would have given anything to have known a few years before. I still liked him, but he no longer mattered. That is not the Jay who haunts my memory, though, any more than I really believe in a middle-aged Jay now casting his spell over a teen-age audience in Arizona. I will always think of him with a pastel shirt, carefree grin, and a confident leap up the bleachers.

One recent night when an old friend and I were talking about men we had known, boys we had once loved, I told her all I remembered of Doug Boynton, Jay Gordon and the rest. She hooted a bit, then looked thoughtful. "They're all abstractions," she said. "No wonder." "No wonder what?" I asked defensively. "Remember Scott?" she said and smiled. I had to smile too. Once I had told my friend about a musician I adored, someone I saw as vital, sexy, enchanting, with a twinkle in his eye no woman could resist. She had seen Scott soon afterward; she was appalled. "But he's *motheaten*," she had wailed to me, describing with lethal accuracy his paunch, his greasy long hair and an oversized fur hat that made her think of rodents. "Did any of those boyfriends back then ever survive your illusions?" my friend went on to ask. "Was there a single one you came to see in time as a real person?" "In time for what?" I snapped back. But I knew what she meant. Yes, there was, I said after a while. There was Peter Stone.

Just when I was approaching sixteen, I found Peter Stone. Or did he find me? Perhaps I magicked him into existence out of sheer need. I was spooked by the boys who teased us nice girls about being sweet-sixteen-and-never-been-kissed. I felt that next to being an old maid forever, it probably was most demeaning to reach sixteen and not to have experienced the kind of ardent embrace Gordon MacRae periodically bestowed on Kathryn Grayson between choruses of "Desert Song." I was afraid I would never have a real boyfriend, never go parking, never know true love. So when Peter Stone asked his friend Ted to ask Ted's girlfriend Emily who asked me if I would ever neck with anyone, I held my breath until Emily told me she had said to Ted to tell Peter that maybe I would.

Not that Peter Stone had ever necked with anyone either. But I didn't realize that for a long time. High-school courtship usually was meticulously slow, progressing through inquiry, phone calls, planned encounters in public places, double or triple dates, single dates, hand-holding, and finally a good-night kiss. I assumed it probably stopped there, but I didn't know. I had never gotten that far. I had lots of time to learn about Peter Stone. What I knew at the beginning already attracted me: he was a year ahead of me, vice-president of Hi-Y, a shot-putter who had just managed to earn a letter sweater. An older man, *and* an athlete. Tall, heavy, and broad-shouldered, Peter had a sweet slow smile. Even at a distance there was something endearing about the way he would blink nearsightedly through his glasses and light up with pleased recognition when he saw me coming toward him down the hall.

For a long while I didn't come too close. Whenever I saw Peter he was in the midst of his gang, a group of five boys as close and as self-protective as any clique we girls had. They were an odd mixture: Jim, an introspective son of a lawyer; Brad, a sullen hot-rodder; Ted, an unambitious and gentle boy from a poor family; Andy, a chubby comedian; and Peter. I was a little afraid of all of them, and they scrutinized me carefully before opening their circle to admit me, tentatively, as I held tight to Peter's hand. The lawyer's son had a steady girl, a fast number who was only in eighth grade but looked eighteen; the hot-rodder was reputed to have "gone all the way" with his adoring girl, a coarse brunette with plucked eyebrows; gentle Ted pursued my friend Emily with hangdog tenacity; but Peter had never shown real interest in a girlfriend before.

Although I had decided to go after Peter, I was hesitant about how to plot my way into the interior of his world. It was a thicket of strange shrubs and tangled branches. Perhaps I see it that way because I remember the day Peter took me to a wild ravine to shoot his gun. Girls who went with one of "the guys" commiserated with each other that their boyfriends all preferred two other things to them: their cars and their guns. Although Peter didn't hunt and seldom went to practice at the target range, still he valued his gun. Without permits, "the guys" drove outside of town to fire their guns illegally. I had read enough in my *Seventeen* about how to attract boys to know I needed to show enthusiasm about Peter's hobbies, so I asked him if some day he would take me someplace and teach me how to shoot.

One sunny fall afternoon he did. I remember rattling over gravel roads into a rambling countryside that had surprising valleys and woods around cultivated farmland. Eventually we stopped before a barred gate that led to an abandoned bridge, once a railroad trestle, now a splintering wreck. We had to push our way through knee-high weeds to get past the gate. I was afraid of snakes. Peter took my hand; it was the first time he had ever held it, and my knees weakened a little. I was also scared of walking onto the bridge, which had broken boards and sudden gaps that let you look some fifty feet down into the golden and rust-colored brush below. But I didn't mind being a little scared as long as Peter was there to take care of me.

I don't think I had ever held a gun until Peter handed me his pistol, a heavy metal weapon that looked something like the ones movie sheriffs carried in their holsters. I was impressed by its weight and power. Peter fired it twice to show me how and then stood close to me, watching carefully, while I aimed at an empty beer can he tossed into the air. I didn't hit it. The noise of the gun going off was terrifying. I hoped nobody was walking in the woods where I had aimed. Peter said nobody was, nobody ever came here. When I put the gun down, he put his arm around me, very carefully. He had never done that before, either. We both just stood there, looking off into the distance, staring at the glowing maples and elms, dark red patches of sumac, brown heaps of leaves. The late afternoon sun beat down on us. It was hot, and after a few minutes Peter shifted uncomfortably. I moved away, laughing nervously, and we walked back to the car, watching the gaping boards at our feet.

What Peter and I did with our time together is a mystery. I try to picture us at movies or parties or somebody's house, but all I can see is the two of us in Peter's car. "Going for a drive!" I'd fling at my mother as I rushed out of the house; "rinking" was our high-school term for it, drawn from someone's contempt for the greasy "hoods" who hung out around the roller-skating rink and skidded around corners on two wheels of their souped-up cars. Peter's car barely made it around a corner on all four wheels. Though he had learned something about how to keep his huge square Ford running, he wasn't much of a mechanic. He could make jokes about the Ford, but he didn't like anyone else, including me, to say it looked like an old black hearse or remind him it could scarcely do forty miles an hour on an open stretch of highway. Highways were not where we drove, anyway, nor was speed a necessity unless you were trying to catch up with someone who hadn't seen you. "Rinking" meant cruising aimlessly around town, looking for friends in *their* cars, stopping for conversations shouted out of windows, maybe parking somewhere for a while, ending up at the A&W Root Beer Stand or the pizza parlor or the Rainbow Cafe.

Our parents were often puzzled about why we didn't spend time in each other's homes. "Why don't you invite Peter in?" my mother would ask a little wistfully, as I grabbed my billfold and cardigan and headed toward the door. Sometimes Peter would just pause in front of the house and honk; if I didn't come out quickly, he assumed I wasn't home and drove away. Mother finally made me tell him at least to come to the door and knock. I couldn't explain to her why we didn't want to sit in the living room, or go down to the pine-paneled basement at the Harbingers', or swing on the Harrises' front porch. We might not have been bothered at any of those places, but we really wouldn't have been alone. Cars were our private space, a rolling parlor, the only place we could relax and be ourselves. We could talk, fiddle with the radio if we didn't have much to say, look out the window, watch for friends passing by. Driving gave us a feeling of freedom.

Most of my memories of important moments with Peter center in that old black Ford. One balmy summer evening I remember particularly because my friend Emily said I would. Emily and Ted were out cruising in his rusty two-tone Chevy, the lawyer's son Jim and his girl had his father's shiny Buick, and Peter and I were out driving in the Ford. As we rumbled slowly down Main Street, quiet and dark at night, Peter saw Ted's car approaching. We stopped in the middle of the street so the boys could exchange a few laconic grunts while Emily and I smiled confidentially at each other. We were all in a holiday mood, lazy and happy in the warm breezes that swept through the open windows. One of us suggested that we all meet later at Camp Canwita, a wooded park a few miles north of town. Whoever saw Jim would tell him to join us too. We weren't sure what we would do there, but it sounded like an adventure. An hour or so later, Peter and I bumped over the potholes in the road that twisted through the woods to the parking lot. We were the first ones there. When Peter turned off the motor, we could hear grasshoppers thrumming on all sides of us and leaves rustling in the dark. It was so quiet, so remote, I was a little frightened, remembering one of my mother's unnerving warnings about the dangerous men who sometimes preyed upon couples who parked in secluded places. We didn't have long to wait, though, before Ted's car coughed and sputtered down the drive. Soon Jim arrived too, and then we all pulled our cars close together in a kind of circle so we could talk easily out the windows. Someone's radio was turned on, and Frank Sinatra's mournful voice began to sing softly of passing days and lost love. Someone suggested that we get out of the cars and dance. It wouldn't have been Peter, who was seldom romantic. Ted opened his door so the overhead light cast a dim glow over the tiny area between the cars. Solemnly, a little self-consciously, we began the shuffling steps that were all we knew of what we called "slow dancing." Peter was not a good dancer, nor was I, though I liked putting my head on his bulky shoulder. But he moved me around the small lighted area as best he could, trying not to bump into Ted and Emily or Jim and his girl. I tried not to step on his toes. While Sinatra, Patti Page and the Four Freshmen sang to us about moments to remember and Cape Cod, we all danced, one-two back, one-two back. Finally Emily, who was passing by my elbow, looked significantly at me and said, "This is something we'll be able to tell our grandchildren." Yes, I nodded, but I wasn't so sure. The mosquitoes were biting my legs and arms, my toes hurt, and I was getting a little bored. I think the others were too, because before long we all got into our cars and drove away.

Not all the time we spent in Peter's car was in motion. After several months, we did begin parking on deserted country roads, side streets, even sometimes my driveway, if my mother had heeded my fierce instructions to leave the light turned off. For a while we simply sat and talked, with Peter's arm draped casually on the back of the seat. Gradually I moved a little closer. Soon he had his arm around me, but even then it was a long time before he managed to kiss me good-night. Boys must have been as scared as we girls were, though we always thought of them as having much more experience. We all compared notes, shyly, about how far our boyfriends had gone; was he holding your hand yet, or taking you parking, or . . . ? When a girl finally got kissed, telephone lines burned with the news next day. I was getting a little embarrassed about how long it was taking Peter to get around to it. My sixteenth birthday was only a few weeks away, and so far I had nothing substantial to report. I was increasingly nervous too because I still didn't know quite how I was going to behave. We girls joked about wondering where your teeth went and did glasses get in the way, but no one could give a convincing description. For many years I never told anyone about what *did* happen to me that first time. I was too ashamed. Peter and I were parked down the street from my house, talking, snuggling, listening to the radio. During a silence I turned my face toward him, and then he kissed me, tentatively and quickly. I was exhilarated but frightened. I wanted to respond in an adequate way, but my instincts did not entirely cooperate. I leaned towards Peter, but at the last moment I panicked. Instead of kissing him, I gave him a sudden lick on the cheek. He didn't know what to say. Neither did I.

Next morning I was relieved that it was all over. I dutifully reported my news to a few key girlfriends who could pass it on to others. I left out the part about the lick. That was my last bulletin. After a first kiss, we girls all respected each other's privacy. What more was there to know? We assumed that couples sat in their cars and necked, but nice girls, we also assumed, went no farther. We knew the girls who did. Their names got around. We marveled at them, uncomprehending as much as disapproving. Usually they talked about getting married to their boyfriends, and eventually some of them did. A lot of "nice" girls suffered under this distinction. One of them told me years later how she and her steady boyfriend had yearned and held back, stopped just short, petted and clutched and gritted their teeth. "When we went together to see the movie *Splendor in the Grass*, we had to leave the theatre," she said ruefully. "The part about how Natalie Wood and Warren Beatty wanted to make love so desperately and couldn't . . . Well, that was just how we felt."

My mother worried about what was going on in the car during those long evenings when Peter and I went "out driving." She needn't have. Amazing as it seems now, when courting has speeded up to a freeway pace, when I wonder if a man who doesn't try to get me to bed immediately might possibly be gay, Peter and I gave each other hours of affection without ever crossing the invisible line. We sat in his car and necked, a word that was anatomically correct. We hugged and kissed, nuzzling ears and noses and hairlines. But Peter never put a hand on my breast, I wouldn't have known whether Peter had an erection if it had risen up and thwapped me in the face. I never got that close. Although we probably should have perished from frustration, in fact

I reveled in all that holding and touching. Peter seemed pleased too, and he never demanded more. Later, I suppose, he learned quickly with someone else about what he had been missing. But I remember with gratitude Peter's awkward tenderness and the absolute faith I had in his inability to hurt me.

After Peter graduated and entered the university, our relationship changed. Few high-school girls I knew went out with college men; it was considered risky, like dating someone not quite in your social set or from another town. You were cut off. At the few fraternity functions Peter took me to, I didn't know anyone there. I had no idea what to talk about or how to act. So I refused to go, and I stopped asking Peter to come with me to parties or dances at the high school. I thought he didn't fit in there either. When I was honest with myself, I admitted that romance had gone. Already planning to go away to college, I could sense new vistas opening before me, glowing horizons whose light completely eclipsed a boyfriend like Peter. When I got on the Chicago & Northwestern train to go east to Smith, I felt with relief that the train trip was erasing one problem for me. I simply rode away from Peter.

On my sixteenth birthday, Peter gave me a small cross on a chain. All the guys had decided that year to give their girlfriends crosses on chains, even though none of them were especially religious. It was a perfect gift, they thought, intimate without being soppy. Everyone's cross cost ten dollars, a lot of money, because it was real sterling silver. Long after Peter and I stopped seeing each other, I kept my cross around my neck, not taking it off even when I was in the bathtub. Like my two wooden dolls from years before, I clung to that cross as a superstitious token. It meant that someone I had once cared for had cared for me in return. Once I had had a boyfriend.

Girlfriends

Scrunched behind the closed kitchen door, my daugher is on the telephone. From the living room, where I am grazing through the evening newspaper, I can hear her whispers. I suppose if I listened hard, I could even gather her conversation, though I do not try. It is her business, and she can conduct it by herself. What I do hear are snatches of "I did not," "You did too," bits of stories about other second-graders, giggles. Lying on the sofa, I smile to myself. I am pleased that my daughter already has a girlfriend with whom she can giggle on the telephone.

She is entering the woman's world already, I tell myself, though I don't want to be overly sociological about it. I lay my newspaper on top of an unread Ms. magazine and think about my women friends. It has been a rich and sustaining network for me, those meandering telephone conversations, often interrupted abruptly by a child's cry or by a doorbell and always terminated by a man's entrance. "What are you gals gossiping about now?" I can hear a husband say indulgently, before his wife hangs up. If she tried to tell him, he'd shake his head and look puzzled. "How could you get worked up about something like that?" he'd ask, and his wife would probably smile, hug him, and pour him a drink. If a man has arrived at my door, I hang up even more quickly. I would be uncomfortable if he were listening; he might be too. I can say things to two, maybe three, of my women friends that few men would understand.

Being single, I depend on my women friends. My closest friends check up on me, know how I am feeling, come for emergencies. They ask the man in my life to dinner, and they refrain from offering criticism until it's all over. They invite my daughter for an afternoon or dinner or all night, often just at the time I feel the frayed bonds of motherhood are about to snap like a rubber band. They make sure we have somewhere to celebrate Thanksgiving, Christmas, Easter dinner. One recently insisted on spending all night on my uncomfortable sofa, in case she was needed, after I had tremulously called her and asked, "Have you ever vomited blood?" We all compare health histories; reassure each other that we had that too, only worse, and got over it eventually; suggest to each other jogging, roller-skating, afternoon naps, or not thinking about it so much. We share recipes, garden seeds, and ways of coping. I have a shamefaced fondness for posters with moral tags, and one favorite hangs in my kitchen: "I get by with a little help from my friends."

So it surprises me to remember that all through my years of growing up, boyfriends seemed more important. It is my old boyfriends who occupy my memories, who play the starring roles in the lavishly decorated romances and nonromances of my imagination. Though I had passing crushes on girls, it was boys who haunted my dreams, sometimes for years or until I had a chance to get to know them. That, of course, may be the key: I didn't really know the boys I dreamed about. "Boyfriends" weren't friends at all; they were prizes, escorts, symbols of achievement, fascinating strangers, the Other. It is simpler to regard people as the Other; it means you don't have to think of them as human beings like yourself, with any hopes, fears, or vulnerabilities. They can be pasted into position like movie stills or pictures into an album.

My old snapshot album, ending at my marriage, is a jumble of boyfriends and girlfriends. But the boys all seem posed and rigid; Peter Stone in his tux next to me at the prom; Peter's gang of friends standing stiffly before my camera, disliking my taking their pictures; boys behind desks or caught at parties, always looking serious or making awkward

*faces. I only find one picture, at the very end, of a young man look-
ing relaxed. Len was a friend my first year in graduate school, easy-
going, interested, uncommitted. Len leans against a Berkeley pillar,
arms akimbo, grinning. We would stride across campus together, laughing, talking of myth and metaphor and his fundamentalist background.
Soon I became engaged to someone else, and I don't know what happened to Len. But his casual friendliness in that picture announces that
he wasn't a boyfriend, wasn't intending to be; finally boys could be
"just friends."*

*Snapshots of my girlfriends over the years are much more various,
often comic as we clowned unselfconsciously for each other's cameras.
At a seventh-grade slumber party all of us form a cancan line in our
baby-doll pajamas. My friend Peggy, trying to row a boat for the first
time in her life, grins with triumph. Kristy and I, arms entwined, pretend to be drunks at an all-night Presbyterian religious retreat. As I
turn these pages, I can almost hear our high, clear, and infectious
laughter.*

*But our group pictures tell me something else about girlfriends. Our
annual class portraits fascinate me now in a way they didn't then,
when I only cared whether I looked plump or bug-eyed or silly. Now I
see how carefully we girls placed ourselves on that front cement step,
the boys ranged behind us according to height. In the center are the two
prettiest, most popular girls in that sixth-grade class, Marcie and Debbie, smiling at each other, hair tossing casually, radiating self-assurance.
Surrounding them, like courtiers, are my friends and myself. I am sitting next to Joyce Schwartz, who was usually my best friend, though
friendships were very fickle. She was coveted as a best friend by my
other friend, Kristy, who sits in the picture just behind Joyce, her hand
possessively on Joyce's shoulder. Over all these years I notice those rival claims being staked. At the edge of the picture are the other girls,
the ones who didn't count: a few from outlying farms, who rode a rural
bus and stuck together; one rather overdeveloped girl with not much
wit; a very brainy girl who wore saggy socks and ugly homemade
dresses. The bosomy girl smiles bravely into the camera; she was used*

to jokes and taunts. The brainy one stares to the side, looking unhappy, even sulky. She wasn't really unpleasant. Just not much fun to have around, and she knew it.

I see now in that simple sixth-grade class picture our sharp-edged social gradations, the cutting cruelty of our assumptions about acceptability, our jockeying for position and our uncertainty of its lasting. Perhaps the boys standing behind us suffered all this too; but since I didn't know them as real people, I can't be sure. I can only speak for us girls: we giggled together, we knew each other's secret wishes and fears, but we used each other too. We needed to find our places, and we had only each other to measure ourselves by.

Girlfriends were as essential as mothers. I could survive weeks, even months, without a boyfriend, although I did need to be able to produce one in those endless circular conversations of "Who do you like best?" "Do you think he likes me or Celia better?" "Don't you agree with us that Herb is a nerd?" "Would you ever sit next to Jim if you didn't have to?" But I always had to have a best friend.

A set of girlfriends provided a sense of security, as belonging to any group does. But having a best friend was more complicated: using a friend as a mirror or as a model, expanding your own knowledge through someone else's, painfully acquiring social skills. What little we learned about living with another person in an equal relationship, outside our own families, we learned from our girlfriends. It certainly wasn't a full preparation for marriage, but it was the only one some of us ever got.

My earliest memory of a best friend is a humiliating one. After spending a year in California in third grade, I returned to Ames to skip a grade and suddenly enter fifth. We had just moved to a new house in a different neighborhood, so I also had to switch to the other elementary school on the campus side of town. But schools joined at Welch Junior High, where we children remained together, a relatively unchanging group, until we moved downtown to merge with Central Junior High in Ames High School. By then our social alliances had been firmly forged.

My year away had erased a lot, and I was a new kid in fifth grade, suspiciously smart and a year too young. I felt lost and lonely, and the only girl who would consent to spend any time with me on the playground or after school was Margie Dwyer. Margie, though rather pretty, was shy and awkward. Her dark hair was twisted in old-fashioned braids on top of her head, emphasizing her sallow skin. I seem to remember she wore one dark plaid jumper all the time. Her father was a janitor somewhere at the college, and they lived in a basement apartment in an old building not far from our house. I don't remember visiting there, or her parents, but I do remember how grateful I was to hold hands with Margie, who smiled at me as we skipped in unison down the sidewalk. But I clearly knew then and remembered with shame later that Margie, like me, was a social pariah. She had no set of friends, no status. After we stopped being best friends the next year, she became best friends with "Sappy" Strickland, the dumbest girl in class. Years later Margie dropped out of high school and married an older man, an auto mechanic. No one noticed.

What humiliates me about my memory of Margie is how quickly I dropped her when, in sixth grade, I was suddenly adopted into an acceptable set of friends. There weren't, in fact, many sets to choose from. With two sections of each grade, about thirty students in each, we had a "pool" of sixty; roughly half of those were boys; so thirty girls had to divide themselves into appropriate groups. Six formed the elite, a group so tight, so deliberately exclusive, that they earned themselves the name of "the Society Six." They were the prettiest, most sophisticated, and stylish girls and naturally included all the ninth-grade cheerleaders. They chose the boyfriends they wanted from the homeroom presidents, athletes, and other "neat" boys.

Needless to say, with my plumpness, brains, wicked tongue and awkward uncertainties, I did not belong to the "Society Six."

Years later, so many years I had not heard of or seen any of the "Society Six" for two decades, I was talking at dinner to a psychiatrist about our junior-high social groups. I had never been a cheerleader, I told him self-effacingly, but then I added, "You know, they didn't end up all that well. One of them, Delaney Deere, lost all her popularity when she got to high school. She started going with an older man from Des Moines, quit school, and left town. I wonder what ever happened to her." He smiled with that knowing look a psychiatrist acquires, and said quietly, "Still hurts, doesn't it?" "What?" I said. "I mean, your not getting to be a cheerleader. Not being one of that High Society, or whatever-you-call-it. Why do you still take such satisfaction in what happened to that Delaney girl?" He smiled again and went to find another rumaki, while I stared speechless at my plate.

But if I couldn't be a member of the Society Six, I was delighted to be accepted into the next group on the social scale, a larger and more fluid one, ten or fifteen girls, democratic enough at least to be nameless. One of its leaders was Kristy Harbinger, whose parents were good friends of my mother's. On the day Kristy asked me to come over to her house after school to play "Sorry," I knew I had made it. Kristy and the other girls in this group were from various backgrounds, some with faculty parents, others with fathers who included an insurance salesman, a banker, a plumber, an oil-company representative who toured the state for Mobil. What your father did wasn't important, though you needed to have a house where you could bring friends home without embarrassment.

Most of us attended the nearby Presbyterian, Methodist or Baptist churches, but by ninth grade, when parochial schools ended, we had two Catholic friends as well. I'm not sure on what grounds we admitted others as friends, how we made up the guest lists for our slumber parties or Valentines or birthdays, how we knew whom to call to go to the movies. Most of us went on to college, but we certainly didn't base our friendship on intellectual merit. Most of us were moderately attractive, but one or two of us didn't date at all for years. Most of us were "popular," but I don't know exactly why. Perhaps we merely defined ourselves in relation to the Society Six and to all the other girls below us, the loners, the stupid ones, the fat ones. We had absorbed already by sixth grade a set of careful and cruel distinctions.

Whatever the sociology of our group, it was large enough to absorb newcomers and to permit trading best friends. When Kristy Harbinger asked me to her house to play "Sorry," I was already involved with Joyce Schwartz. For almost a year Kristy, Joyce and I uneasily maneuvered to see who would be whose best friend. I liked Joyce because she was more mature than I. Her body already rounded nicely, and when she wore a sweater, it had real bumps. When she turned a corner, Joyce flounced, her skirt swirling in a flutter of pleats. Even her hair seemed bouncier than mine, a neat cap of natural waves, while mine hung relentlessly straight in a long ponytail. Though I knew a little about teasing boys, Joyce actually flirted, her eyes flashing and her sparkly teeth dazzling the bewildered boy who would lean his bike awkwardly on the sidewalk while he tried to keep up with her jokes and jibes. To me Joyce represented self-confidence; my mother, who didn't like her much, said she thought Joyce was "tough" and "a little mean." We were probably talking about the same thing.

Although Joyce hadn't started to date then in sixth grade—no really nice girl did till seventh or eighth—she seemed to me to know more about boys, about life, than I did. For one thing, her parents fought. Since my mother had been widowed when I was just seven, I couldn't remember much about my parents' marriage, though my mother said they had been very happy and she still wept when she spoke of my father. None of my other friends' parents ever argued in front of me, except in brief, unthreatening exchanges of mild displeasure: "Oh, George, I *told* you to pick that up!" "How can we be out of beer *again?*" "No, I do *not* want to go out to dinner." But the Schwartzes really fought, yelling loudly and banging doors. At least Mr. Schwartz did. He was a large, flabby man with quick, shifty eyes—like Joyce's, only hers were set in a pretty face—and he had a quick, loud temper. When he came home he always had a few pleasant words for us—Joyce openly flirted with him as she did with the boys on the streets— but then he would ask us to leave, go outside, play upstairs, and soon we would hear his booming voice as he argued with his wife. Joyce's mother was pale, brown-haired, washed-out, with so little personality that I wondered if Mr. Schwartz shouted at her just to get some response. I never heard her answers from behind the closed doors. Sometimes, Joyce said matter-of-factly, her father hit her mother. "Not real hard," she added. I was shocked, not only by this disclosure of violence but by my knowledge that Mr. Schwartz was a leading deacon in his church. I was sure my own Collegiate Presbyterian wouldn't have stood for it.

Visiting the Harbingers' after school with Kristy was a complete change. Mrs. Harbinger, who was warm, friendly, and still poignantly beautiful, presided over a house filled with comforting sounds and smells: chocolate-chip cookies fresh from the oven, a ringing phone, the padding of active feet, shouts and laughter from Kristy's older brother and his friends. Doors slammed, but the sound was a happy one of activity, not the warning prelude it was at the Schwartzes'. Joyce Schwartz liked to come to the Harbingers' too, but she preferred to be asked by herself, not with me. Kristy Harbinger, understandably flattered by our jealous attentions, played us against each other. I remember dragging home heartsick, running to my room to cry, because Kristy and Joyce, whispering and giggling together at recess, had hurried off after school before I could catch up with them. Once I asked Joyce if she wanted to go to a Saturday-afternoon movie, only to be told, snippily, that she was already going with Kristy. "But if you want," she said, with a wide smile that made me seethe, "I'll find out if you can go with us." Whenever Joyce had something particularly nasty to say, she smiled. Her self-control always enraged me. Speechless, I turned away. We both knew that the three of us couldn't go together. Who would sit next to whom in the theatre? Who would get the prized middle seat? Whose house would we go to afterward? If we went to Schwartzes', would Joyce ignore me? If we went to Harbingers', though, couldn't Kristy join with Joyce in playing Ping-Pong while I waited disconsolately on the sidelines? If we played "Sorry" and I lost, wouldn't Joyce smile widely? And if we went to my house, didn't I know for sure that Joyce would complain there was nothing to do and leave early, probably with Kristy, so I couldn't follow?

Exactly how this triangle of tension sagged and lost one side I cannot now recall. But by the end of sixth grade, with subtle shifts in the social quicksands, I had risen and Joyce had fallen. Her flirtatiousness had come to seem brazen, her stylishness a bit cheap. She had begun to date, a sluggish, heavy football player who had almost flunked fifth grade; despite his athletic skills, he wasn't a boyfriend many of us wanted. Joyce's choice seemed to confirm a growing sense that she wasn't, in fact, quite the right sort. Meanwhile I had been elected homeroom secretary and probably shown other signs of promise. When Kristy showed me her latest list of friends, I had moved to the top. I quickly put her at the top of my list, too, and we were finally best friends.

Most memories of girlfriends lose their bitterness after sixth grade. Though Kristy and I did not remain best friends, I settled comfortably for the next six years into her gang. When I remember my desperate scrabbling in fifth-grade darkness, clinging to Margie Dwyer, and contrast it to my sailing with relative ease through junior high and high school in a convoy of friends, I am frightened for my own daughter. What will be her source of support? If she has to hang onto the edges of a group longer than I did, can I help her? Should I? What can I do about the other little girls, the ones *she* rejects, won't ask to her birthday parties, doesn't want to play with? Would life at the edges develop qualities I missed? If she doesn't have the girlfriends I did, will she be content? Will I?

Once the relentless search for a "best friend" merged into group acceptance, the tenor of my life depended not so much on family or on boyfriends as it did on girlfriends. My mother was always there in the background, of course, a quiet support. Boy-friends drifted across my skies, dreamy clouds, fierce thunder, dramatic lightning: they passed, and the weather changed. But my girlfriends filled my days with the steady pulse of constant companionship. When I remember what I actually *did*, outside of school and evenings at home, I always see myself with one or more girlfriends.

What did we do? Mostly, I think, we talked. We talked on the buses, in the halls, at our lockers, in the classrooms, between classes in the toilets, after school at the bus stop. Once home, we called each other up almost instantly and talked on the phone until some parent couldn't stand it any longer. Then we hung up for a while with promises to call back later. What on earth, our parents asked us, did we find to talk about? But it wasn't so much the topics we found engrossing, I think, the boys, teachers, clothes, gossip. All that talking built up a steady confidence that the trivia of our lives were worth discussing, that our *lives* were worth discussing, that we as individuals were worth someone's attention. "Do you think I ought to get my hair cut?" was a question that asked not only "How would I look with my hair shorter?" but "Do you *care* how I look?" Teachers snapped and lectured; parents discussed and argued; boys teased and muttered; but the steady hum of girlfriends, punctuated by laughter and whispers, was a reassuring continuo.

Besides talking, girlfriends went places with each other. No self-respecting boy would ever be seen shopping with a girl. We girls usually shopped in twos or threes, after school or on Saturday afternoons, not only to approve new purchases, but for the sheer fun of trying on new clothes. We were all known in Younkers, and although Mrs. Corter, the no-nonsense saleswoman, would tell us firmly to leave if someone else wanted the dressing room, until she did we could use the store as though it were a costume shop and we were actresses trying on different roles. Some afternoons we slipped into formals, very carefully, while Mrs. Corter hovered disapprovingly nearby, eagle-eyed for any rip or tear. We floated before the mirrors in layers of pink tulle or swooshes of yellow satin, admiring how much older we looked with bare shoulders and boned-in strapless bodices. We tried on the new cotton spring dresses as soon as they arrived in midwinter, assuring Mrs. Corter that we were already "looking for an Easter dress." She wasn't fooled and whipped the dresses back to the racks as fast as we slipped them off. We giggled to each other, crowded into the tiny dressing room together, knowing her irritation.

Drifting up and down Main Street, we had regular rounds. We'd browse quickly through Penney's and Ward's, if we were really killing time, and maybe pause at Marty's, a collegiate sportswear shop. We didn't feel right yet in the Shetland sweaters and matching pleated skirts that Marty's sold to Iowa State girls. But we stroked the cashmeres, sorted through cocktail dresses, and tried to imagine ourselves older and shapelier. We would only "look in" at Carole's, not daring to stay too long under the snooty, hard stares of the two saleswomen with pouffed lacquered hair, bright lipstick and shiny nails. Then we'd wander toward the library, or stop at Edith's Gift Shoppe to see whose new wedding patterns of silver and china were on display, maybe drink a Coke at the Rainbow Cafe before catching the bus home. And all the time we talked, talked, talked.

On weekends we went to the movies. By high school many of us dated, and sometimes we'd go with our boyfriends. But, with the bolstering company of two other girls—one wasn't enough—we'd go in a gang together, not caring whether we had dates or not. Sometimes the boys would come in their gangs, too, and we carefully arranged to sit so there'd be an empty row behind us for them. Couples migrated toward the back or the balcony, detached from our noisy, laughing, poking crowd, and we pretended not to notice them as we streamed down the aisles.

Since I was easily embarrassed on movie dates, fidgeting when a boy and I had to stare at a love scene side-by-side, I was happiest going to the movies with the girls. Then I could whisper whatever I wanted, unafraid of sounding foolish, surrounded by friendly elbows and nudging knees. Engulfed in the comforting blackness of the theatre, we could sometimes ask each other questions that would have been impossible elsewhere. One Sunday afternoon at the movies I briefly glimpsed the limits of my knowledge about sex. We girls had gone to see *The Barefoot Contessa*, a murky but dramatic love story in which Ava Gardner, a sexpot who verges on nymphomania, eventually marries mysterious but handsome Rossano Brazzi. On their wedding night, however, he appears at their bedroom door and announces that he cannot sleep with her. The words escape me after all these years, but not their doom-laden import. I vaguely remember Rossano telling Ava, who lay there visibly panting, that he was "wounded in the war." What I acutely remember is the dialogue that then took place in the New Ames Theater. Seated next to me was Leslie Gerard, a girl who was, everyone agreed, thoroughly nice. Her pleasant personality had led her to the presidency of Y-Teens, leadership in her church youth group, membership on Student Council. Sturdy and forthright, she would have been our captain if we'd had any girls' athletic teams. But Leslie did not date yet, and her mother did not let her stay overnight at slumber parties. So perhaps I shouldn't have been surprised when Leslie leaned over to me, puzzled, and said, "What does that mean, he was wounded in the war?" While I paused, one of the boys in the row behind us guffawed loudly. He had heard Leslie's question too. Leaning forward, he stuck his face between our heads and stage-whispered so that both rows could hear, "He had his balls shot off!" The boys collapsed in laughter, while a few of the bolder girls giggled and the rest blushed and looked straight ahead. Under cover of the laughter, Leslie, still undaunted, leaned toward me again and, barely audible, whispered in my ear, "What are balls?" "Tell you later," I hissed back quickly. But the fact was I didn't know. Someone else came to Leslie's and my rescue after the show was over.

Besides shopping and going to movies together, we girls herded together to attend dances and parties, those where you didn't need dates, as well as football and basketball games and track meets. Small towns in Iowa had girls' basketball, but Ames was too sophisticated for such pastimes. Girls who liked sports could swim or play tennis. But otherwise we watched the boys, cheering and caring so intensely whether they won or lost that we regularly wept or shouted ourselves hoarse. When the Ames High football team swept down the field, or a center dunked a difficult jump shot, we shared the boys' triumph; it was one of the few times we thought of us all belonging together and working for a common goal. Since I was a clumsy athlete, I was perfectly happy to sit in my black skirt and orange jacket, blending into the cheering section, a small but vital part of the whole. Even Leslie Gerard, whose skill at basketball amazed our gym teacher, and who regularly pleaded, usually vainly, for one of us girls to "shoot a few baskets after school," never murmured the wish that we could have a girls' team. She sat in the front of the section, captain of the Pep Squad, and cheered more loudly than all of us.

Even when we had boyfriends in high school, we spent our spare afternoons and weekend daytimes with girls. Boys had jobs, cars, athletics. Mostly we saw them at night under artificial lights. Boys were dates; girls were friends. We girls went sledding or skating together in the winter; swam, roller-skated and rode bikes in the summer. With other girls we took dancing, swimming, tennis lessons; we accompanied each other on family picnics and even vacations. A girlfriend was as close as the nearest telephone.

A girlfriend wasn't someone for whom you had to plan activities. My closest friend in high school, Peggy O'Reilly, and I always knew what the other felt like or wanted to do, and we usually wanted to do the same thing. Sometime during our Saturday mornings downtown, one of us would always ask the other, "What about going into Eschbach's?" In the late fifties, few of us could afford the expensive new long-playing records. Eschbach's Music Store, with two small glass-enclosed listening booths, tolerantly allowed us to take one l.p. at a time into a booth, sit on the floor, and lose ourselves in the music. Plugging one ear and holding the other close to the speaker, you could almost get the sensation of hi-fi. We never had any doubt about what records to listen to, since Peggy and I shared a terrible crush on Frank Sinatra. Those were his revival years, when his lean face, slouched hat, and hunched shoulders proclaimed on album after album, "How I need someone to watch over me!" Peggy and I felt he was singing to us, discerning our inarticulate fears of being lonely and rejected. Frank Sinatra knew that we weren't always sure life was going to be wonderful. We didn't know whether anyone would ever love us. He understood, and he told us how we felt. So we mooned and dreamed in Eschbach's glass booth, until, like Mrs. Corter in Younkers, an impatient clerk tapped at the window and motioned us out. Sighing, we left our melancholy in the stuffy little room and wandered out into the sunshine. "You know," I said to Peggy, "when I'm twenty-one he'll only be forty-six. Don't you think that would be all right?" Peggy smiled, nodded reassuringly, and linked her arm with mine. She was sure it would be all right. She was, after all, my best friend.

The spring we graduated from high school, we girls began to feel the first twinges of separation. Though some of us were planning to go to Iowa State, many of us were scattering east and west, to New York, Pennsylvania, Massachusetts, California. We couldn't believe that we wouldn't still keep in touch, stay close and spend our vacations together; but we also knew that something was ending. More deliberately than usual, we organized "girl parties," after-school and weekend get-togethers where we tried to pretend that nothing had changed. During the summer, while we sewed and shopped for college, we even practiced giving "luncheons," baking casseroles from our mother's cookbooks and entertaining each other with tunafish and noodles, deviled eggs in white sauce, and almost anything based on cream-of-mushroom soup. We "dressed up" and came at twelve-thirty for grape juice and ginger ale. Our mothers looked on tolerantly, helping in the kitchen, tactfully disappearing when "guests" arrived. Perhaps they could see what was happening. They may have remembered their own graduations and losses, old friends who had married and disappeared forever under other names in other towns.

We didn't hear anyone tell us about the process of sorting out, about how, over the years, friendships wax, wane, and disappear. After all, I sadly admitted years later, when I had to face the fact that a once-close friend and I had so completely lost touch that I no longer knew her job, address, or phone number, if I kept truly close to all the friends I've valued in the places I've lived, I would not be able to do anything else. Keeping up a friendship does take conversation, letters, phone calls. There is never enough time.

As we sat around a crowded luncheon table that summer of graduation, comfortably gossiping, ostentatiously drinking coffee like grown-ups, many of us had known each other for as long as we could remember. We would not have believed that we would never sit together like this again, that in two or three years some of us would have seen each other for the last time, that twenty years later only one or two of a whole table of ten would still have news of any of the others. Our mothers didn't warn us. What good would it have done? They joined us for dessert and laughed when Leslie Gerard tried, unsuccessfully, to smoke a cigarette all the way through.

By September the splintering was impossible to ignore. The first girls left for "rush" at Iowa State while those of us going later to our colleges hung around, took hurried phone calls that announced "I'm pledging Gamma Phi" or "Tri Delt wants me!" and pretended knowledgeable interest. One by one we waved each other off as the family car, loaded with suitcases, turned toward Lincoln Way and the road out of town. I was one of the last to leave. Late in September, a few days before I was to take the train east, I decided to attend the opening Ames High football game. No one else was free that night, and I went alone. I was a little late. When I walked onto the cinder path that led to the lighted bleachers, I knew I had made a mistake. Another Pep Squad sat in the stands, wearing the same trim orange-and-black jackets senior girls got from the Kiwanis Club every year. Though most of the faces in the crowd were familiar, they weren't my friends. A few waved. One girl called out curiously, "Hey, Sue! Haven't you gone yet?" When I stood for the school song, I felt for the first time as though it didn't sound quite right on my tongue. At the half I left, telling some of the new seniors who brushed by me that I had to go home to pack. They looked polite but uninterested. Moving in a huddle toward the refreshment stand, a blur of orange under the pole lights, they chattered excitedly to each other. Hurrying past them, I almost ran to my car.

That particular kind of belonging was over. My close friends in college didn't cling together the way we girls had in Ames. After I was married, my women friends had even less in common: one was single and gay, another married to someone my husband didn't like, a third didn't like my husband. We certainly never got together in a group. After my divorce, I had to learn how to do things alone, to stand in a movie line on Saturday night, to swim happily by myself in a public pool, to drive to a strange town and stay alone in a strange hotel. It wasn't easy, and there are times when I'm still not as good at it as I'd like to be.

But the joy of girlfriends wasn't over. Growing up with girls who talked, laughed, and shared together gave me a precious resource I have never lost. When I sprawl in a friend's sunny kitchen, drinking coffee and comparing notes about when and where we'll plant our sugar snow peas; when, paring carrots, I cradle a receiver to one ear and ask urgently, "But what did you say to your mother *then*?"; when I'm invited to a friend's for Sunday-night pizza because, she says, "We haven't seen you for a while" but I know she really means, "You're sounding blue"; when my college roommate from twenty years ago calls from Vancouver, anxious over the tone of my last letter; when another friend, even busier than I am, yells over the shouts and screams of four children, "I'm just calling to check in"; I feel a link that goes back to Margie Dwyer. The hand that reached out to me in fifth grade is still there.

Science

When my daughter was born, I didn't buy her Barbie dolls. I wanted her to know how to take things apart and put them together, to be fascinated by how things worked, to construct and to invent. So I have tried to tempt her with Tinkertoys, Lincoln Logs, and even those expensive Legos. But Jennifer has always had a mind of her own, and she ignored my efforts at encouraging what I hoped would be her scientific impulses. She set up schools for her stuffed animals, but she didn't want to build houses for them. She followed me around the kitchen when I baked bread, but left the bathroom in boredom when I struggled to disassemble a leaking faucet. The Tinkertoys stayed in chaotic heaps on the table where I'd helpfully laid them out.

It was the Tinkertoys I minded most. When I was young, I wanted desperately to build a Ferris wheel like the picture on the carton. It had two wheels, one big and one little, and real seats you could have filled with walnuts and pretended they were people. My instructions didn't say how to build it, though, and I think my mother told me we would probably need a bigger kit. She wasn't very good with Tinkertoys either.

As I grew older, I thought I might be able to remedy my lack of scientific know-how with the help of a junior chemistry set. My mother was uneasy, but she bought it and let me set it up in the basement. I took all the warnings on the box very much to heart and never dared to try anything dangerous. Instead I made vial after vial of soap, a simple *glycerine compound that did indeed have a greasy, soaplike feeling but didn't suds as well as our Cashmere Bouquet. When I was bored with soap, I prepared a solution to turn blue litmus paper pink. Or was it pink paper that turned blue?*

I am beginning to give up hope that my daughter will penetrate the mysteries of sciences I never mastered. I bought a set of children's encyclopedias on time payments, but she never opens the volumes that tell how and why. She just wants me to read the stories about dogs, the St. Bernard who saved his mistress from a grizzly bear or the Dalmation who leaped two stories from a burning building. Those adventures hold her interest more than the secrets of the universe.

Sometimes Jennifer asks me questions I know I should be able to answer. Maybe the answers would whet her scientific imagination. "What makes the leaves turn color, Mommy? Where does the wind go? Why is it cold in winter?" Wait, I tell her urgently, I'll go look it up. I don't know. I think it has something to do with chlorophyll, or air currents, or the way the earth moves. She looks at me patiently and says, "Never mind, Mommy." Sometimes I retreat into the simplest answer of all: "Because God made it that way, Jennifer." I feel guilty when I say that and glance mentally over my shoulder. If somewhere up there He heard me, I don't think He'd like that. He is probably a scientist too.

Even the name of the Synchrotron was ominous. Whatever men did there formed part of the coldly rational future being prepared by Science, and I feared and distrusted Science.

Surrounded by barbed wire, the Synchrotron stood at the end of a dusty road in the country just beyond town. A group of shapeless, gray buildings huddled together there in a small clump of trees. Isolated though it was, no one dared to park near the Synchrotron. My friend Emily's older sister and her boyfriend had once pulled up beneath those trees, and a guard in uniform appeared from nowhere to warn them to get out, fast. Behind the closed buildings ran railroad tracks, seldom used now that World War II was over, although some nights as I lay in bed I could hear the faint whistle of an occasional Chicago & Northwestern freight, rumbling toward the west. Gentle hills dipped behind the Syn-chrotron to a small creek, forming a little basin that was supposed to be a hoboes' hangout. I knew a boy who said he had seen flames and heard voices there. He went down the hill next morn-ing, but all he could find were some empty pork-and-bean cans.

One unlikely story I heard about the Synchrotron confirmed my belief that the men behind those windowless walls held ab-solute power. Emily, whose father knew someone who had been there during the war, told me in those days research had been so top-secret that the faraway Government had given orders to all suppliers to approve without question any request from the Ames Lab. The Lab scientists had been puzzled about how to dispose of radioactive waste, stuff so dangerous, she told me, that it glowed in the dark and killed anyone who saw it. The lab had decided to use empty oak whiskey barrels for this waste, and so they sent out a requisition, which, however, accidentally omitted the word "empty." No one dared to inquire why the lab needed a trainload of whiskey, and so it arrived on schedule. For months the tramps gathered in the hangout below the Synchrotron, fighting for the drops of liquor that were left in the bottoms of the emptied bar-rels. Emily said this story was funny, but I wasn't sure. Whiskey, government orders, radioactivity: all were part of the same man's world that lay, secret and protected, behind barbed wire fences. To a young girl growing up in the Midwest then, all men were po-tential scientists, just as all scientists were men. I had watched Orwell's 1984 on "Studio One," and I had screamed when they shoved rats into Eddie Albert's face in order to break him. Scien-tists knew exactly what to do, and if necessary they were going to do it.

I asked Mother what they did at the Synchrotron. Men smashed atoms there, she told me. Already in ninth grade we had begun to learn about atoms and molecules, though I could still not figure out how a solid wood table could possibly be made up of whirling particles. Anyone who not only could visualize atoms, but could smash them, was terrifying. I momentarily pictured serious-faced men with huge hammers, standing in white uniforms, pounding away inside antiseptic chambers.

Outside my window I could sometimes watch fathers in our neighborhood walking to work on the college campus. One of them, I had heard Mother say, was a solid-state physicist. Although I knew he worked at the Synchrotron, he didn't look very different from the others. All of them wore seersucker jackets in the summer, heavy overcoats in the winter, and rubbers if it rained. They all came home for lunch. Mr. Zachias was tall, skinny, with pale blond hair that barely covered his shiny forehead, and a preoccupied expression on his face. I watched him for signs of the immense knowledge I knew he must carry in his head, but I never noticed anything. (Not so long ago, I asked a class of Macalester College women to list men's professions in decreasing order of virility, as an exercise in uncovering sex-role stereotyping. All of them put "hairdresser" at the bottom, and most agreed on "physicist" at the top, but no one knew exactly why. Though these students were thirty years removed from Science in Ames, Iowa, I knew how they felt.)

Some fathers carried briefcases back and forth to their college offices, but they didn't seem to bring much work home with them. Whenever I played at one of their houses, the physicists or chemists or engineers were never surrounded by papers as my mother always was at home. Since I didn't know exactly what all these scientists did, I assumed that it only took place deep inside their laboratories. I knew what my mother did. She graded freshman themes, high piles of them that were stacked in our living room, spilling onto the rug at the slightest breeze. Sometimes she let me help her. Giving me the official list of errors, each with its separate number, I could look over the awkward, pained writing on ruled theme papers and spot misplaced commas, missing semicolons, ingenious spellings. I marked each error with a light pencil, so Mother could erase it when she checked the page later. I felt important, like a teacher myself, when I was allowed to make those little checkmarks in the margin. I was as comfortable with

English, which I associated with common sense, as I felt alien-
ated from Science.

Only once in my life did the Ames educational system seem to
link the worlds of Science and English. That was in Mrs. Gosselin's eighth-grade Science and Literature classes. For two weeks
we studied Literature, mostly in a big green book, marked and
spotted, with lots of Whittier and Longfellow and stories like
"The Man Without a Country." Mrs. Gosselin liked to read aloud
from the poems, thumping firmly on her desk, "Booth led boldly
with his big bass drum/ (Are you washed in the blood of the
Lamb?)" Then for two weeks we studied Science. Every time Mrs.
Gosselin announced that it was time to take the Science books
out from our scratched wooden desks, I felt a little quiver of anticipation. I kept hoping I would find somewhere in the flat, dull
paragraphs and labeled diagrams something that would explain
exactly what the magic of Science was all about.

What I mainly remember was not mystery, however, but projects. For every "unit," astronomy, or biology, or botany, Mrs. Gosselin devoted most of her energy to assignments that we could
work on both during classtime and at home. Our grades would depend both on how original and how neat our projects were, she
told us sternly, smoothing back her blued hair and tugging at her
dark purple crepe dress. Mrs. Gosselin knew nice, neat projects
would keep us in order.

With each project, I thought that perhaps this was my chance
to become, however briefly, something of a scientist. Never mind
that women weren't ever scientists, except Madame Curie once a
hundred years ago, just science teachers. I brought enthusiasm,
patience, and determination to the task of painting star charts or
sprouting plants from potatoes in glass jars and hoped that somehow I would be found worthy.

My favorite "unit" was leaves. In the middle of the fall, Mrs.
Gosselin assigned us to gather as many different leaves as we
could, mount them carefully on posterboard, and label correctly
the tree from which each had fallen. This meant you had to

persuade your mother to buy a cheap, colorful handbook showing blurry pictures of all the North American trees. Then you had to match your leaves to the minute illustrations. I remember worrying for days about whether a leaf with an enticingly strange shape might be a ginkgo; my *Little Golden Book of Leaves* didn't have any ginkgoes in it, and the big book on Mrs. Gosselin's desk didn't say the ginkgo's range included central Iowa.

Leaf hunts took many after-school afternoons, from four o'clock until after dusk, much to my mother's irritation at holding supper. I prepared as though for a long, dangerous expedition, arming myself with a paper sack, pencil, pad, *The Little Golden Book of Leaves*, and a Hershey bar. When I started, the sun would usually be shining with the brisk brightness of early October, a warmth that gently seeped through my poplin jacket but disappeared with the slightest breeze. As it grew dark, I could feel my ears tingle and my toes would curl a little into my thick white cotton socks as I walked along the quiet sidewalks, kicking up small storms of dead elm leaves.

Trying to find enough different leaves was difficult. Walking down block after block of elms, with a few oaks and maples in front yards, I scanned the horizon for signs of a truly significant leaf. Usually I ended up on the sprawling college campus, a world I seldom penetrated, where the people and the trees were equally foreign. Students jostled past me on the worn paths, laughing and talking together. Sometimes I would see a face I knew, someone's father or a neighbor, and I would stop and ask him if he knew of any special trees nearby. He never did.

Once I had gathered my leaves, most of the fun was over. Then I had to find heavy books to press my leaves flat without telling my mother, who didn't like to open her *Literary Tour of England* and find the pages damp and wrinkled. Sometimes I forgot which books I'd put my leaves in. For years afterward, I might open a book in my mother's house and have a brown dusty leaf rustle into my lap. Even then I didn't know what leaf it was. Once the leaves were pressed, I tried to stick them with heavy white paste on my empty piece of posterboard. Finally I got to print the name underneath: "elm," "maple," "oak," "ginkgo?" I drew lines with a ruler from each edge of the posterboard so I could have the tops of the letters even. But when I stood back to survey the final product, I was always unhappy. My leaves had ripped or crumpled; I hadn't found as many as Kristy Harbinger had; none of my leaves was really special; and Mrs. Gosselin never hung my poster on the bulletin board for display.

Something about the classification and order required in the leaf project appealed to my inner sense of what the world should be like, however. As I searched for leaves, I noted other possibilities for future collections: different shades of purple in the creeping phlox on a granite wall; the oddly shaped black cinders in our back alley; brown drying plants in a vacant lot, with fluffy milkweed and thistles and dying dandelions. But I never knew how to organize them.

My only success in the world of Science was when we studied fibers. I chose cotton, and I was supposed to collect examples of how it was used. Mrs. Gosselin said that this was a good project for a girl. So I spent a long afternoon inside Bellston's yard-goods store, begging samples from the patient clerk. She snipped and snipped, bits of Bates Disciplined Cotton, muslin, seersucker, poplin, chambray, and other names she had to tell me. When I had assembled all the bright small squares, floral prints and polka dots and pinstripes, I thought they looked dazzling on the white posterboard. Up at the top I pasted a big wad of Johnson & Johnson's sterile cotton from our medicine cabinet, just to show the raw product. Mrs. Gosselin loved it. My mother still has a picture of me, standing in my corduroy jumper and Peter Pan blouse, ponytail hanging down my neck, holding up my poster for the eighth-grade class to admire. I don't remember who took the picture or why, but it is tangible evidence of my brief triumph as a woman of Science.

I secretly knew, however, that even this successful Science project was a bit of a fraud. My research had, after all, taken place in bright daylight, during sunny afternoons while I dawdled after school in a fabric store, and my deepest instincts warned me that true Science only happened in the dark. In my mind the Synchrotron was illuminated by the flickering lights of night trains and hobo campfires, a fluorescent laboratory surrounded by darkness. I remembered the gloomy tower in which Snow White's wicked stepmother muttered over her charms and potions. So I wondered about Mr. Zachias as he walked along our shadowy street to "check on his lab" after dinner. Mrs. Zachias once complained that he often stayed until dawn. I couldn't imagine what he did there.

Science was never darker or more mysterious, however, than when I glimpsed it at the Institute of Arcanology, an aging campus crammed into the midst of a run-down section of Des Moines, thirty miles away. When we drove past the Institute late at night on the way home from a road show or a basketball tournament, it loomed suddenly out of the darkness. My mother didn't know much about it, but my Aunt Lily, whose deep contralto voice thrilled me with her intimations of secrets she was almost ready to tell, said she knew what went on behind those locked wrought-iron gates. The cluster of old brick buildings, once an unsuccessful small college, now housed a society whose disciples, she said, had to enroll for life. They also had to swear never to reveal the knowledge that would be imparted to them. As she talked, I stared out the closed car window at the few spots of light that escaped the dark blinds. Someone was working late in a subterranean room just inside the fence, but the light flashed by before I could make anything out behind it. Aunt Lily said that men in those hidden rooms were probing the secrets of human life. Death too, she whispered, and then my mother, who was sensible, would clear her throat and change the subject. I looked at the iron fences, the unkempt bushes and the shuttered buildings. We probably passed the Institute in daytime too, but I only remember how it looked at night.

As I grew older, I began to think that perhaps the best guide through the murky depths of Science was to grip tightly the cold security of numbers. At first I felt they were well within my reach. "Math" had no magic in sixth grade, it was just arithmetic, and even in junior high I could still master its simple formulas. Add, subtract, multiply, divide: these four functions had a neatness and simplicity that pleased me. No matter how long the column of numbers, or how protracted the terms, every problem had a clear answer. Only when a sum of long division came out odd, stretching into an uncomfortable infinity, did I dislike math. I preferred a world that came out even.

In beginning algebra, I still felt at home. X on one side, a solid number on the other: this was just another matter of perseverance. An answer might be hidden, but it lay there waiting somewhere, like an Easter egg. However, once our teacher gave us a theoretical problem, with no numbers at all, only letters, I was immediately lost. Xy plus cd divided by f equals what? I began to swim in a sea of possibilities. All abstraction bothered me. When confronted with "story" problems, I always paid more attention to the stories than to the numbers. If A rows up the river at x miles an hour, and B rows down the river past him at y miles an hour, and z is the speed of the current, how much faster is B going than A and when will they pass each other? I couldn't help wondering where they were heading, what sort of boats they were rowing, and why they were going in different directions anyway. Was one a boy and one a girl, and had they fought? Were they running away from home, going to visit relatives in nearby river towns, or delivering groceries? I got into the habit of drawing little pictures in the margin to clarify the issues, small crooked boats marked "A" and "B" with stick figures inside them, vigorously rowing. If I could somehow see them, I told myself, I could figure out what was going on with all the x's and y's.

When I signed up for second-year algebra in high school, I felt very daring. A few girls did enroll in Algebra II, since it was suggested as part of the college preparatory program. But we all knew that Miss Martin, the high-school math teacher, liked boys better.

She twinkled even as she scolded Jack Holmgren for throwing a spitball across the room, and when greasy George Pitkin grinned at her insolently, she actually smiled back. After Algebra II, her classes of "solid" and "trig" were reserved, we knew, for the boys. I wasn't at all resentful, though, because somewhere between the simplicities of plain arithmetic and the beginning complexities of algebra, I'd been lost from the equation. I didn't worry that the words *geometry* and *trigonometry* sounded foreign on my tongue, because I knew they were meant to. Although one or two girls each year could "do trig," it was tacitly understood that they were either abnormally brainy or dismally unattractive. If the former, they had no chance to hide their intelligence and would just have to pretend they enjoyed it. If the latter, they had to excel at *something*. Since I was alarmingly competent in English, social science, and other talky subjects, I was rather relieved not to have to perform well in math.

As I watched Miss Martin's senior boys stroll down the halls, slide rules hanging from their belts like masculine totes, I did sometimes wish I could handle the symbols of scientific power so easily, so confidently. It was as close as I ever came to penis envy. Later I was taught how to decipher the tiny numbers through a plastic square that glided up and down the slide rule. But I never really trusted the answers I got. I wanted instead the plain immovable figures I had once been able to add in columns.

By the time I was seventeen, Science seemed as remote as the moon. I knew instinctively that I could not live long in an abstract world, which was what Science seemed to be. I had already been caught and held fast by sensuous detail. I did not have the words then to express my distrust of what I thought was scientific method, but I had developed a deep reliance on intuition and feeling. Could Science help me understand what I felt about what I saw?

What I saw was quiet, unobtrusive beauty. Ames was still a small enough town to have a kind of country flavor, and the Iowa countryside was always beautiful, though in subtle ways that escape those who have not been seasoned by many winters and summers there. Even today, when I speed along the bald new freeways that have been slapped down across the state, I still catch my breath a little at the winter trees, intricate black strokes against a swirling gray sky, and I crane my neck to see a bright red barn or a purple silo standing near silvery weeping willows. I turned to poetry, not Science, to learn to see more clearly.

I thought of Science as lines, measures, and rules. How could they apply to Iowa, where the seasons changed everything so rapidly and completely? Midwestern weather, then and now, confounded prediction and evaded control. Though I eventually learned to complain about the violent extremes of Iowa weather, as a child I reveled in them. I loved the heavy damp snows that seemed to be waist-high every winter and the jagged icicles that we sucked like candy. As soon as the flakes had stopped falling heavily, my sister and I would dash into the backyard to lie on our backs and make snow angels, flapping our arms into giant wings. The few days of spring, warm with promise and wet with melting snow, sank so deep into my bones that when I first read a poem about April as the cruelest month, I felt sure T. S. Eliot had spent some time in Iowa in the spring. When summer steamily settled on Ames, I waited for the crackling thunderstorms sure to follow the breathless heat. If I left my bicycle standing in the sun, its metal seat seared me, and when I pedaled down concrete sidewalks, they sent up waves of heat, like a griddle. Sometimes the black dividing line down the center of an asphalt street would melt and waver, zigzagging crazily like an Abbott and Costello drunk. Another line, another exactitude destroyed by Iowa intensity.

Inside Ames, as well as in the countryside, color, texture, and fragrance reached out for me. A small town has time and space for the appreciation of minute differences, and in Ames I noticed, absorbed and savored the character of each store, restaurant, dry cleaner, and bank. Downtown I learned to distinguish the new smells of Penney's, with its starchy piles of blue jeans and antiseptic tile floors, from the air in the old Ward's store, dust drowsing over dark racks of rayon prints that gave off a strong odor of sizing. We had only one ice-cream parlor, and I remember it as though I had just gratefully opened its door on a hot afternoon after school. Inside Moore's Dairy, a cool damp mustiness seeped under the metal doors leading to the coolers, where I heard the clanging of large milk cans being unloaded. As I sat on a slick oilcloth seat at the counter, waiting for my chocolate cone, I admired the shiny spigots reflected in the mirror facing me and listened to the fizz of soda, the whirr of malted milk, the slosh of Coca-Cola. It was almost an ice-cream laboratory. That was what I wanted Science to be like.

When I left home at eighteen for college, graduate school, and, I assumed, marriage, I hoped that I might find somewhere a man who could understand my passion for specifics. I didn't think of my search in quite that way, of course. I simply wanted to meet someone who could understand all the things I cared about, who knew what held them together, who could explain them to me. I thought what I needed was a scientist.

Finding the right sort of scientist turned out to be difficult. Friendly, giggly, and exuding a bright Iowa innocence, I was often asked to go out with someone's lonely brother or cousin, since I was sure to cheer them up. Many of these blind dates were engineers, who seemed to have more trouble finding girls than history or psych majors did. I could see why. They had trouble talking; though eager to answer questions, they never seemed able to think of any. They wore awkward bow ties and ill-fitting hairy jackets, and most of them had receding chins or twitches. Yet I knew that the ones who went to M.I.T. or Yale must be smart, or they wouldn't have been admitted. So I tried my best, but we never exchanged more than a few sentences about Science before my date would founder and stop. I learned to switch quickly to possible comparisons of Iowa with Massachusetts, or Amherst with Wesleyan, or the Dekes with the Theta Xis. I usually went home early.

My mistake, I finally decided, was in not sticking to the "pure" sciences, an adjective we all took for granted. Anything not directly useful, like chemistry, physics, or biology, was "pure"; anything "applied" was mechanical, dull, and somehow second-rate. I was sure they practiced "pure" Science at the Synchrotron. I envied Marcia Hayter across the hall, who was pinned to a premed chemistry student named Tom. Once, when they had fixed me up with Tom's roommate, who was a lonely electrical engineer, we all four walked over to Tom's chem lab. I was entranced. The apparatus that covered several rows of long tables would have excited Snow White's stepmother. Test tubes bubbled, liquid coursed through curlicues of glass tubing into other test tubes, lights flashed and machinery hummed in unexpected places. At the end of the table a student in a white lab apron was bending over a particularly complicated set of intertwined tubes, which reminded me of the dizzying dreams I used to have of completing the most advanced construction in my Tinkertoy set. He was so engrossed in his manipulations that he didn't even notice us. I wished I knew who he was.

When I finally fell in love, for what I thought was forever, I was disconcerted to find that the man I had chosen did not have a lab like that. He was a scientist, but not the "pure" kind. His first degree was, in fact, in engineering, though he told me that I could think of him as a sort of solid-state physicist if I liked. He did the same kind of stuff with atoms that they did, he said, and he was probably right. I asked him about his work at first, but he didn't usually like to talk about it, and I didn't really understand when he tried. So we went to lots of movies instead.

After we were married, Lawrence embarked on a long, complicated set of experiments. He did much of his work at home, with a slide rule, making pages of calculations which were transformed into hypothetical formulas to be carried out in his lab. He called it a lab, but it didn't seem like one to me. It was just a room filled with a few large, expensive instruments, boxes with dials that had to be kept at a difficult temperature under impossible conditions. He put pieces of metal into these boxes, made them very cold, and then measured their conductivity. Nothing gurgled or whirred, no lights flashed, in fact nothing as far as I could see happened at all. This equipment kept breaking down, soundlessly, and then I wouldn't see Lawrence for days.

After a few months, Lawrence came home excited by an idea for an experiment he thought I could understand and even help him with. His adviser had suggested that he try to deduce something about the random diffusion of atoms by rolling some small steel balls in a pan of Jell-O, then letting them harden into whatever configurations they would. This seemed a sloppy way of conducting an important experiment, I thought, but Lawrence was already out the door on his way to buy three boxes of Jell-O. I had three cookie pans, and Lawrence thought we might as well fill them all. When he returned, I dutifully mixed all the red raspberry goo and ladled it carefully over the dozens of little balls now knocking about in my warped aluminum pans like berserk pinball machines. Lawrence, who had never even cooked an egg, wanted to put the pans in the oven. I argued that Jell-O wouldn't jell except in a refrigerator, but Lawrence insisted. If we left the pans alone long enough, he was sure the Jell-O would eventually coagulate. There wasn't enough room in the fridge anyway, he said, and he was right. I could never argue very long with Lawrence, because he was always so positive I was wrong that gradually I began to believe him. So I gave in about the Jell-O. Though I was the cook, I knew he was the scientist.

For three days I didn't bake anything in our oven. Several times a day I would open the door, peer at the sticky red mess that covered every shelf, and close the door again. Once I touched one of the little steel balls with my finger to see if it would move. It did. I wondered if I had altered an arrangement of atoms. Each night when Lawrence came home, he walked into the kitchen to see for himself. He never said anything as he stared at the experiment. The third night he grabbed one of the trays from the oven, stomped to the back door, and threw it open. From the window I could see him at the edge of the lot, where the weeds grew thick and high, as he emptied the contents of the tray with one fling. Later that night I washed the pans, scrubbing hard where the Jell-O had dried in crusty blobs.

That was the last experiment Lawrence tried to do at home. Afterward, he spoke even less about his work than before, but I no longer minded. I had somehow lost interest, and I soon stopped asking to go along to his lab when he went there to check on his equipment. I even gave up trying to read *Scientific American* in the bathroom. We stayed married for eleven more years, but I sometimes think our Jell-O experiment was the beginning of the end.

Every fall, when students at the college where I teach begin to pour back on campus, and they sit inside my office to ask about their schedules, I feel an urge to sign up for courses myself. Something about my discussion of the merits of introductory anthropology versus beginning Latin, human geography or Latin-American history, stirs in me that same feeling of anticipation, of knowledge waiting just around the corner, that I used to have in Mrs. Gosselin's eighth-grade science class. I briefly wonder whether I could audit a course in biology without taking the labs, or sit through all the lectures in "Physics for the Non-Physicist," or study vertebrates in zoology. But I never do.

Bookworm

"I'll make you a deal," I said craftily to Jennifer. "If you'll go to the grocery store and dry cleaner's with me, I'll take you afterward to the library."

"But I don't want to go to the library, Mom," she said, waiting for a better offer. "You can't keep library books. You have to take them back. I don't think libraries are any fun."

Libraries not fun? I looked unbelievingly at Jennifer. How could a daughter of mine not want to go to the library? When I was pregnant, I had a hard time picturing myself as a mother, doing the things they all do, baking brownies, sewing Halloween costumes, concocting vaporizer tents. But I comforted myself with a vision of reading to my child, the two of us tucked up under a quilt, as I enthralled her with stories I had once loved, Babar, Millions of Cats, Make Way For Ducklings. Some soon-to-be mothers go out and buy Carter's Jamakins; my first purchase was a hard-bound copy of The Little Engine Who Could. Alas, Jennifer never liked it. Babar bored her, and once through the Millions of Cats was enough. She did like some stories: Cinderella, Sleeping Beauty, Snow White, anything that ended with a beautiful maiden marrying a handsome prince. Unfortunately, I easily tired of all that happily-ever-after, not to mention the insipid heroines who could only faint and wait. I wanted to read to her instead about monsters, genies, flying horses, and bewitched frogs. They were the magical creatures who had lived, I thought, in the library of my childhood.

When I do take reluctant Jennifer to the library near us, we enter a shiny new building with a pop-art plastic sign outside. Inside it is brightly carpeted, well lit, hung with carefully lettered directions about where to find everything you need. This library is always busy, two or three people taking most of the room at the magazine table, others clustered at the almost-bare new-arrivals shelf, a short line waiting at the checkout counter. I am sure this pleases the library board. But I can see why Jennifer does not respond to the lure of this place and why she does not see it as a secret cave to which I have given her the key.

It is so unlike the library I remember. That was a marble sanctuary, ruled absolutely by a white-haired high priestess, whose initiates, also women, found themselves sworn to whispers and lifelong devotion. In the Ames Public Library we learned to worship the world of books. I gave myself to it so completely that I came to believe it had to correspond, if sometimes obliquely, to the world of real life. Sisters ought to be loving and playful, like the March girls; nurses were selfless and devoted, like Sue Barton; dogs were nicer than people, like Lad of Sunnybank; unhappy children found rich protectors, as did Sara Crewe; somewhere around a corner anyone might stumble upon her own secret garden. I was convinced that every locked door would open to a magic password. Even today, when I see a certain kind of Oriental rug, I can feel a momentary belief that at night it flies. So when I enter a library, even a commonplace one, I still have a reassuring sense that it is going to tell me all I need to know.

Whenever I hear the words *inner sanctum* I think of the Ames Public Library. It was a massive stone temple, with imposing front steps that spread on either side into two flat ledges, overhung by evergreens. Waiting for my mother to pick me up, I could sit almost hidden on the cool stone blocks, surveying passing cars with a removed superiority. Safely perched on my pedestal, surrounded by my stacks of new books, I always felt unusually serene, bolstered by the security of the library behind me and the anticipation of the books beside me. Even to the moment of leaving it, my visits to the library were high occasions.

Entering the Ames Public Library I could feel its compelling power immediately. Inside the front doors a split staircase climbed elaborately to the main entrance on the second floor, and trudging up the marble steps I was enveloped by the cavernous space. A chilly breeze always seemed to be blowing up my back. Few buildings in Ames had such grandeur; the only one that reminded me of the library was the college's Memorial Union, which had an entrance hall dedicated to the dead of World War I and inlaid with tablets of granite you weren't supposed to walk on. The library, and the Union Hall, seemed to be places where things lay precariously at rest, just below the surface, waiting to be summoned up again.

I always worried when I went to the library that I might have to go to the bathroom. That meant getting a key from the front desk and descending the staircase again, but turning this time down one more flight of steps into darkness. The locked toilets were in the basement, a storage area known to no one but the janitor and Miss Jepson, the head librarian. Shadows lurked everywhere down there, steps echoed noisily, the light switch was impossible to find. Once I felt the door and fumbled with the key, it didn't always turn right in the lock, and I often had to go back upstairs, embarrassed, to ask an annoyed librarian to come down and try. When the heavy door of the ladies' toilet finally swung shut after I got inside, I was afraid that it might lock itself again. As the day wound on, no one would hear my cries for help behind that wooden block, and night would find me alone and helpless in the dark bowels of the library. I tried to avoid all this by not going to the bathroom. Sometimes I had to cross my legs and pinch myself in the car in order to make it home safely.

But if I didn't have to go down to the basement, I was seldom as happy anywhere as I was at the library. It was a place in which you always knew exactly where you belonged. At the entrance stood a circular wooden enclosure, only entered by librarians, who flipped up a small wooden shelf. There all books were checked in and out. When you came in the door, the librarian on

duty glanced up and mentally checked you in as well. Directly behind the librarians' sentry post was adult fiction, both on the
main floor and on a dark mezzanine above. For a long time I wasn't
allowed up there. To the left was the map, newspaper and pe-
riodical room, where I seldom ventured either. Grownups who
worked downtown sometimes came and ate their lunches at the
big tables there, surrounded by spread-out newspapers whose
rustlings blended with the quiet sounds of munched lettuce. My
world lay to the right.

The west wing of the library was divided into sections for Children and Juniors. At first I nested happily in the Children's
Room, with its small round tables and equally small chairs. I liked
knowing that adults looked ridiculous trying to squat on those
chairs, though of course that was also why a few years later I was
ready to escape to the Junior Room, which had adult-sized chairs
that didn't make you feel as though you were a baby. Besides its
coziness and small scale, the Children's Room held two of the
most important places in the whole library. One was the curtained door to Miss Jepson's office, which you never entered unless you were going to have a Serious Talk with her. The other
was a window, a three-sided display case at child's-eye level that
held a changing miniature diorama. It always rushed to see it before I went anywhere else in the library. All children did. Usually
it was a scene from a familiar book, like *Goldilocks* or *Rumpelstiltskin*, though sometimes I had to guess. Nobody I knew had miniatures like the library's, tiny kettles, braided rugs, hand-knit doll
aprons, and I could stand for fifteen minutes admiring the elaborate sets. It was like a small theatre with the actors all frozen into
a single moment. Like a theatre, it had a small velvet curtain that
was kept drawn when the scene was being changed. Its inner
doors, or backstage, were entered from inside Miss Jepson's office,
although she personally never had anything to do with the actual
changing of displays. That, like most menial tasks, was left to
Mrs. Erhard and her assistants.

The Children's collection was not a large one, and before long

I roamed through it confidently. I gorged myself on books, lugging home piles as high as I could carry, sometimes begging for Mrs. Erhard's permission because she was so sure I couldn't read them all in a week. But I could. At home I read before school, after school, with a book on my lap at dinner, and at night before I went to bed. I read with equal avidity about Horton hatching an egg and about East of the sun and West of the moon. I moved without pausing from Rabbit Hill to the tower of the Little Lame Prince. It was like having a box of assorted chocolates, all tempting, with unknown centers. I wanted to bite into each one right away to see what it was like.

About this time I first heard myself called a bookworm. One of the boys in my class saw me struggling off the city bus on a day when my mother hadn't been able to pick me up at the library. "Whaddya think ya are, a bookworm or something?" he said with a sneer. I had my chin on the top of my stack of books to keep them steady, so I couldn't open my mouth very far to respond. "I am NOT," I said defiantly, as the stack quivered. But I felt caught, labeled with something dirty and unpleasant. I didn't like worms. After that I looked around carefully when I was carrying a load of books, and if a friend was with me I made her carry part of mine. But not even the fear of being known as a bookworm could stop my reading.

As I looked ahead to the Junior Room, I could see that it held at least four times as many books as did Children's. I worried about how I was going to tackle such a task; I felt the order and serenity that emanated from the library dictated that I approach my reading in a suitably controlled way. So in third grade I decided to compile a miniature card catalogue, like the library's, for each book I read. My mother bought me a pile of index cards and a small metal file box. Now I felt official, part of the library itself, as I sat down at a polished maple table and importantly spread out my stack of cards. On each card I noted author, title, and one or two sentences of plot summary so I could remember what I'd read. Then I created an elaborate series of abbreviations, which today I can barely decipher, like "N.G." for "No Good," or "Exc." for "Excellent," as well as a series of numbers which must have been an attempt to compare each book with the others. I can no longer remember why *Caddie Woodlawn* might have been a "2," let alone "G," as opposed to *The Five Little Peppers*, which was "3" and "V.G." Soon I was spending more time making notes and inventing annotations than I was reading, a fact which Mrs. Erhard pointed out to me one day. She looked at a few of my cards and laughed. My feelings were hurt. I had thought of myself as preparing for a job like hers. Not long afterward I put the card catalogue away.

When I moved to the Junior Room, probably at the age of ten or eleven, I decided, like many omnivorous readers, to begin with the A's and read through to the Z's. I thought this was obviously the best way of making sure I didn't miss anything. Though three walls of this large room were lined with books, I didn't think it would be impossible to cover it all. The Ames Public Library did have a human scale to it. I might have done so, too, except I found somewhat to my surprise that I was developing tastes. I didn't really like books about horses. I wasn't very interested in boy detectives. I didn't want to read anything if the author was trying too hard to be educational. I was happy through the B's, where I found *Sue Barton, Rural Nurse; Sue Barton, Public Nurse;* and *Sue Barton, Superintendent of Nurses;* but after that I bogged down quickly. I skipped ahead to the L's, where I had discovered Maude Hart Lovelace's sequential adventures of Betsy, Tacy, and Tib, and promised myself I would someday return to the C's. But I never did.

When I abandoned my plan of methodically reading everything in the library, I was stimulated by new freedom of choice. I began to explore the nonfiction sections, which had never interested me before, and gradually I realized that within the walls of the Ames Public Library could probably be found the answers to any questions I would ever have. All my problems could be solved if I could only find the right book. At twelve, when *The*

Teen-Agers' Complete Guide to Beauty fell into my hands, I thought I had found just such an authority. It was written, its cover assured me, by a successful New York teen-age model named Barbie Betts, whose unfamiliar face and name didn't deter me from believing every word she had to say. I checked out her book and renewed it twice, until Mrs. Erhard said I would have to ask Miss Jepson to change the rules if I wanted to renew it again. Then I reluctantly released it back to the shelves.

My mother hated *The Teen-Agers' Complete Guide to Beauty*. It upset our home for weeks. I fervently believed that if I followed all its instructions, I would be transformed into the girl of my dreams, thin, graceful, well dressed and well groomed. Barbie Betts felt especially strongly about the importance of good grooming, a phrase I had previously connected only with horses. She suggested that I make my evening bath a beauty routine, buy a pumice stone for the rough skin on my elbows, soak my cuticles in olive oil, powder carefully between my toes. Although my mother muttered loudly that she couldn't see anything wrong with the way I looked, I disappeared each night for an hour into the bathroom with a tray of beauty aids and soaked, scrubbed, powdered. I got wrinkles from staying so long in the water and the places I scrubbed turned very pink, but I didn't look different at all. Nobody ever stopped to admire my cuticles or tell me how nice my elbows felt. I eventually gave up and only continued halfheartedly to brush my hair one hundred strokes a night.

Then I turned my full attention to the problem of being well dressed. Barbie Betts said that the key to a successful wardrobe was not money but organization. I tried to follow her directions about sorting my clothes, coordinating them into interchangeable outfits, and then color-coding each outfit with markers in the closet. This took days of heaped clothes on the floor, disastrous experiments with colored paper glued to hangers, and hours of frustrated weeping when I discovered I lacked several crucial essentials of the master plan, like a wide black leather belt and a white wool skirt, which my mother said we couldn't afford. Near despair, I thought perhaps I could transform my environment even if I myself remained a lump of raw material. I studied intently Barbie Betts's pictures of model bedrooms, which were frilly and feminine, and asked my mother if we could at least buy a headboard and make a canopy. She sighed. I wept again. I gradually realized that I could never carry out Barbie Betts's full-scale plans, and I was convinced halfway measures wouldn't work. I was doomed to a life of unmatched sweaters and tufted chenille bedspreads.

But when my dream of beauty failed, I retreated, as always, to other dreams. The Ames Public Library had an unending supply of them. I was too old by now for *The Blue Fairy Book* and *The Green Fairy Book*, but for solace I soon found Elizabeth Goudge. For at least a year I wandered blissfully through English cathedral towns and country inns, where I met benevolent grandfathers with spiritual secrets and freckled fun-loving boys who grew up into gentle sweethearts. If only I had lived a hundred years ago in England, I thought, how satisfying life would have been.

As I moved toward high school, I began to consider what I was going to be when I grew up, a question I felt it was time I took seriously. Despite my attraction to Sue Barton, I doubted whether I would make a good nurse. The only one I knew in real life was at school, a cross-faced tough-jawed woman who didn't believe you were sick unless you threw up copiously in the hall. Then she grumbled, took your temperature, and sent you home. I would have to be pretty lucky to escape that kind of life and find one like Sue Barton's, who married her Doctor Bill in the end. For a long while I thought I could be a foreign correspondent, since I liked to write and loved the idea of travel, but the career guides I began to read assiduously all seemed discouraging about a woman's chances as a reporter. My inevitable choice was the career I had been nurturing in my bones since my first trip up those marble steps. I decided to become a librarian.

Although librarians didn't make much money, my career guides warned me, they had something else that appealed to me as much as constant proximity to all those books. They had power. Not many women in Ames visibly wielded that, but Miss Jepson did. Even her deputy, Mrs. Erhard, had a derived air of stern authority. Miss Jepson, whose white hair and wrinkled pink skin made her seem agelessly preserved, was a definite-minded woman whose tongue had an almost audible snap. Whenever she submitted a budget request to the Ames City Council, she was able to get almost everything she wanted. No one dared to argue long with Miss Jepson. She personally selected each book the library ordered and gave the impression that she had read them all first. No detail of the library's operation escaped her inspection; she knew it so well I thought for a long time she must live there, in a secret suite connecting to her office.

The most impressive symbol of Miss Jepson's power was her locked glass case. This was a small cabinet in her office where she kept books whose literary or scholarly worth was unquestioned but whose text or illustrations she deemed obscene. Only Miss Jepson had the key. If you wanted to read one of Those Books, you had to knock at Miss Jepson's curtained door, enter when you heard her gruff voice, and then sit down facing her to explain why you felt it necessary to check out that particular book. If your reasons were unsatisfactory, it stayed in the locked case.

If I ever wanted a book in that case, I don't remember what it was. But I did have several uncomfortable conversations in Miss Jepson's office. One was the culmination of my struggles with her deputy, Mrs. Erhard, who had to enforce Miss Jepson's edicts. The rule that got me into trouble was the strict age limitation placed upon moving from the Junior to the Adult collection. Although sometimes Mrs. Erhard might stretch a year or two to let a child take something from Juniors', she was not going to yield so much as a month when it came to Adults'. I think the dividing line for Adults' was entrance into the downtown high school; whatever it was, it came too late for me. I was impatient to be exploring the stacks of novels on the mezzanine long before Mrs. Erhard thought I should. We would stand at the checkout desk and argue over my confiscated books, as I pointed out that my mother let me read everything in her library at home. Mrs. Erhard said what my mother did at home was her business, but in the Ames Public Library I was not yet an adult and could not check out adult books. Besides, she asked slyly, had I read every single book in the Junior section? I admitted I hadn't. With a triumphant smile, Mrs. Erhard lifted her wooden drawbridge and left. A few minutes later she was back, holding a small pile of Junior books. Had I read any of these? She could recommend them all highly.

I agreed ungraciously to try them. But I had no intention of giving in. Back home, I complained vehemently to my mother, until she agreed to call Miss Jepson for a little chat. Whatever my mother said must have worked. The next week Mrs. Erhard glared at me and told me to report to Miss Jepson's office. There Miss Jepson looked me up and down, asked me a few questions about books, impressed upon me the rarity of exceptions to the library's rules, and told me from now on I could check out three adult books a week.

After that I wandered freely among the adults, though I tried to choose checkout times when a student assistant was replacing Mrs. Erhard. I was afraid she might veto some of my choices. I remember trembling when I carried *The Empress of Byzantium* from its shelf to the desk, hoping Mrs. Erhard hadn't read it. I had already seen enough to know she wouldn't approve. *The Empress of Byzantium*, whose author I had never heard of, should have been in Miss Jepson's locked case. I discovered it by accident, as I often uncovered marvels in the library, pulling down books because of their elegant gold lettering or well-worn bindings or unusual color. Adult fiction was particularly suited for this kind of browsing, since the mezzanine had narrow aisles just wide enough to brace your back against one shelf while you sat on the rubber-tiled floor and ruffled through the books opposite. Whatever first attracted me to *The Empress of Byzantium* soon fled my mind when I saw what the book held inside: sex, sadism, and a graphic style that left little to my active imagination. I remember nothing

about the plot, but I do recall one particular scene that galvanized me. The heroine, who had recently given birth, was in bed
with her husband. He resented the child, I think, and they had
some kind of argument followed by what I could dimly recognize
as lovemaking. He grabbed her, began to nibble on her nipples
until little drops of milk leaked out, and sucked until she managed to push him away. She was shocked; so was I. I couldn't remember seeing anyone breastfeed a baby, but I thought husbands
were probably repelled by it. I read greedily through as much of
the book as I could manage that afternoon, brought it home and
hid it in my closet, and then carried it furtively back to the library the next week. I looked at Mrs. Erhard with a new respect.
If she had read all the books in the adult section, she probably
knew all about sex too.

Not only did librarians have access to all important knowledge, but in the Ames Public Library they had social power as
well. It was not that either Miss Jepson or Mrs. Erhard attended
coffee parties, played bridge, or belonged to the Country Club,
but rather that they carefully used their ability to select student
assistants. Miss Jepson's hand-picked band, chosen from high-
school applicants after a long screening process culminating in an
intensive interview behind her curtained door, were dedicated to
becoming future librarians. They had to be serious, devoted, and
of high moral character. The training they received from Miss
Jepson and Mrs. Erhard was supposed to be the equivalent of a library degree; in return the student assistants had to agree to work
a steady number of hours after school and weekends all through
high school. Like dedicating yourself to a convent, you knew that
to withdraw from this agreement after acceptance, and worse, after months of training, was to fail disgracefully.

When I was just beginning junior high school, I desperately
admired Miss Jepson's student librarians. One of them was Shelley McNulty, the oldest daughter of one of the most respected
families in town. Her dignified father served communion at our
church, and her mother played golf regularly with the wife of the

head of the Leichner Clinic. Shelley herself was gravely beautiful, with warm dark eyes and softly curling short hair. She was
quiet, graceful, assured, all the things I had given up hope of being after abandoning Barbie Betts's optimistic teen-age program.
Only the best boys were permitted to take her out, and she never
went steady with any of them, not because they didn't ask her,
but because her parents didn't approve. Everyone in high school
knew how special she was; Shelley had already been Homecoming Queen and was an obvious shoo-in for Senior Sweetheart
in her last year. If Shelley McNulty was going to be a librarian, I
could hardly have aspired to any career more socially sanctioned.

As I grew older, however, and Shelley eventually moved on to
college and away from the library, I found to my dismay that my
dedication to her model began to waver. My future had seemed
quite set. By the time I was in eighth grade, I had already had one
serious talk with Miss Jepson about becoming an assistant when I
was a sophomore. But as the time approached, although I still
loved the library, I was no longer quite so sure that I could give up
all my after-school hours and weekends. In ninth grade, I tried being a student helper in our school library, and I was disappointed.
Although I enjoyed shelving books, finding the infinitesimally exact Dewey decimal numbers between which to sandwich each volume, noting with pride the tidiness of the arrangement when I had
finished, I found that within a day all the books were messed up
again. Other people kept taking them out. I had always thought of
the library as a personal possession, and I wasn't altogether comfortable about sharing it. Since nobody asked me questions about
where things were, I didn't get a chance to show off my superior
knowledge either. Mainly I sat on a high stool behind the one-
drawer card catalogue and guarded the checkout slips. It was
against the rules to read while you were being a student helper. Not
many kids wandered back to the library to talk, and none of them
were boys. My volunteer hours became duller, and shorter.

When Miss Jepson called me into her office as a new sophomore, to check her list of promised disciples, I had to tell her that

I was too busy. I said I wanted to work on the high-school news-paper, act in some plays, and attend all the out-of-town football games. As I faintly concluded this feeble list, Miss Jepson's eyes seemed to crackle and give off small sparks of light. "All I can say is that I'm disappointed in you, Susan," she said, her firm mouth tightening even more. "I hope you have made the right choice. You know your decision will close the door here to you perma-nently. I'm sorry because I think you would have been a fine li-brarian." I had no reply. I backed out of her office and left the library that day without even checking out any books.

Although I tended to avoid Miss Jepson for a while after that, I certainly didn't give up the library. I continued my regular visits there during high school, and while in college I managed to squeeze trips to the library into my brief vacations home. I sought it out increasingly as a place of quiet more than as a source of knowledge. Although I was now aware that other libraries had more books and more impressive buildings, the Ames Public Li-brary was my own private refuge. If I had a difficult paper to write, I knew I could spread it out on the shiny maple tables in the Ju-nior Room. I would make notes, sort piles of paper, look out the tall windows at the elm trees, and take little breaks to wander past the familiar shelves, plucking out old friends that seemed like once-loved dolls carefully packed away for someone else. Few people came into the library when I spent my afternoons there, and I would be lulled by the soft padding of the librarians' feet, the gentle thud of the heavy front door, the rare whispers from the Children's Room next door. Sometimes during college vaca-tions I would just go there to write letters. Miss Jepson nodded at me then and asked me how I liked Smith; I smiled at her as one adult to another. Eventually I no longer even wondered about the books in her little glass case. Perhaps now I had read them all.

But although the Ames Public Library eventually became sim-ply a pleasant place to visit, I still think of it at odd times. When something troubles me, I feel an urge to go to the library to get a book on it, though now that I can afford to buy books occasionally, I sometimes go to the bookstore instead. My crowded shelves hold all the books I thought would help: advice and guidance on needlepoint, cats, England, loneliness, parenting, and antique jewelry. Last spring, when I decided it was time for me to get my body in shape, I went downtown in a self-satisfied glow to outfit myself for exercise. I had planned to buy some properly cushioned shoes. But I passed by a bookstore first, stopped to browse, and spent my money instead on *The Complete Book of Running*. I thought I had better read about running first to see whether I would like it.

Party Girl

*F*elicity had promised I could always go home early. As I lingered in front of the raised teak platform whose Marimekko bedspread was heaped with coats, I looked toward the noisy room beyond and wondered if I could leave right now. During my rare and fearful trips to New York, Felicity tries to make sure I have a good time. Tonight she had arranged for me to tag along to a loft party given by a lawyer with political aspirations.

As soon as we got out of the taxi, I knew this hadn't been a good idea. How could I leave early if I had to find my own taxi in an eerie place like this, with grates dropped over warehouse doors and everything shuttered up? It looked as though a plague had emptied the whole neighborhood. I didn't feel any better when we got out of the elevator on the top floor and walked toward an open doorway. No one came to greet us, but Felicity and her date Tom went right in, chatting together, and asked someone where to put our coats.

I looked around me and marveled as though I were in a modern museum. The loft had been subdivided with ten-foot-high partitions that looked like tiny egg-carton dividers in proportion to the soaring rafters overhead. I couldn't imagine how the different apartments had any privacy; sounds must drift over each partition into the next space. The white walls were sparsely hung with abstract paintings, a few Barcelona chairs and chrome pieces filled corners here and there, but mostly the apartment seemed very empty. I suddenly realized why. I couldn't see any piles of magazines, unanswered mail, cans of plant spray, wastebaskets. Nobody who lived here seemed to have any junk. I wondered where they stored things. I turned abruptly to a woman who was dumping her coat on top of mine and asked her, "Where do you suppose they put the tricycles?" She looked at me strangely. "I wouldn't know," she said after a moment; "I don't think they have any," and turned away from me.

Felicity and Tom had disappeared. I couldn't stay in the bedroom, if that's what it was, much longer. I decided to go to the bathroom. After a few minutes I found it, but it didn't have any door. It opened into a hallway behind the bedroom, so it was sort of private, but not private enough for me. I went back to the doorway leading into the main room and looked around for someone to talk to. I didn't see anyone standing alone. Everyone was in groups, smoking, laughing, and clinking ice cubes. After I had drifted in and out of a few conversations, I walked to the window wall and stared out at the night. Looming over the rooftops was the Empire State Building, bathed in blue and white lights that coldly blinked back at the chrome and gleaming plastic of the loft. I stared so long into the darkness I felt as though I had disappeared from the party behind me. When I turned back, I didn't see any group I wanted to join. I wandered about the room, ate some cheese, drank some wine, and went back to the window to watch the lights again.

After a while Felicity had Tom help me find a taxi, and I went back to her apartment. In the taxi I sat and thought about the evening. Why hadn't I liked this party? Why didn't I like most parties? Was it because I didn't try hard enough? Or was I tired of trying hard, of forced gaiety, of meaningless conversation? I certainly hadn't felt like this about parties as a child. They were fun then, weren't they? My own daughter reminds me of my past anticipation. "Please," Jennifer often asks, "can we have a party soon?" If I agree, she goes into a state of high excitement. She wants to discuss times, menus, guest lists. She gets out a feather duster and whisks it over the kitchen counter, the floors, the fireplace. "See, Mom, I'm going to clean everything up for our party." She tries on different dresses, asks me to make several sets of pigtails until they're just right, waits anxiously at the door for the first guests.

Although afterward she is not quite sure the party lived up to expecta-
tions, she is always ready for another one.

Growing up in Ames, I always looked forward to parties too. I loved
their implicit theatre, the costumes, the roles, the settings. Always a bit
of a gambler, I even enjoyed the tension of wondering whether I would
be a success. Most of the time I was lucky. But as I grew older, I
stopped believing in the magic of such performances. I began to notice
shadows backstage, dropped lines, and heavy makeup. Now as I evoke
those early parties, I am surprised to remember that I had a good time.

I must have enjoyed those first birthday parties, which I remember for frilly dresses, pin-the-tail-on-the-donkey, crepe paper
streamers, and of course the presents. Mostly we gave each other
paper dolls, stationery with little dogs printed on it, and colored
beads of bath oil in see-through plastic boxes. Even knowing
what to expect, I was always frantic with excitement when I sat
in front of my heap of wrapped presents with their gaudy tissue
papers and corkscrew-curled ribbons. Birthdays were better than
Christmas because I got all the attention as well as all the presents. I picked the flavor of ice cream, stuck the candy letters on
the cake, and got to cut them out of the frosting. I chose the
games and the paper napkins. I was the Birthday Girl: queen for a
day. All the rest of my life I've expected my birthdays to have
that same excitement, and when they don't, I'm childishly disappointed. If my birthday wears uneventfully on, and nothing
happens, I become cross and then self-pitying. Finally I go to bed
in a profound funk, haunted by a phantom party.

All the girls wanted to go on having birthday parties. After
kindergarten, boys stopped attending, but we girls conspicuously
observed each passing year. We felt we had special limits to our
lives, particularly a certain number of years, perhaps twenty-five
to thirty to get married. Birthdays all led up to marriage, when
life stopped. By late junior high school, when our mothers no
longer gave parties for us, we girls arranged them for each other.
To keep things fair, and cheap, we decided every year exactly

what identical gift to give each other and then pooled resources to buy it. Our senior year in high school, for our last round of birthday parties, we chose a blue satin garter with white lace in a padded white satin box. It was extravagant, from Carole's, an elegant store, and intended, as a fancily lettered card instructed us, to be "something new and something blue" to wear at one's wedding. Though none of us had weddings in the offing, we knew that at eighteen they were edging closer. After the birthday girl opened her garter, we shared some ice cream at the Rainbow Cafe and went off together to an afternoon movie. But this round, we felt self-conscious. Now that we were well into our teens, girls didn't usually have real parties unless there were boys.

Only one other kind of party officially excluded boys, even though we schemed how to sneak them in. That was the slumber party, which started in sixth or seventh grade, reached its peak of popularity in early high school, and then eventually disappeared. A high-school slumber party was a real treat. Only one mother liked to have her daughter give them, which was one of the reasons we knew she and her husband weren't quite like our own mothers and fathers. Stan and Josie Hayward were casual, jolly parents who didn't seem to care too much what their daughter Martha was doing. They insisted we call them "Stan" and "Josie" and when we watched t.v. at their house, they offered us little sips of sherry in shot glasses. Sometimes they sat and watched with us, just as though we were all friends together. Josie always liked to hear about everyone's boyfriend, who was chasing whom, who had just broken up, the sort of information most of our mothers never asked about or seemed not to understand when we told them. Whenever Martha asked Josie to let her give a slumber party, she not only said yes but started to plan how to move the furniture in the living room so everyone could fit on the floor.

Preparing for a slumber party was like preparing for a camping expedition. First I had to fix my bedroll, a complicated layering of sheets and old blankets. Those of us who were Camp Fire Girls had some practice, but it was still tricky to fold the ends and sides so I didn't find my feet freezing in the middle of the night. I then had to decide what pajamas to take and make sure they would be like everyone else's pajamas. Baby-dolls were "in" one year, the lacier the better, and no one wanted to be caught in last year's short-sleeved, snap-up, seersucker Penney's two-piecers. Since some boys were bound to show up outside the Haywards', I wanted to look my best as I screamed and clutched my bathrobe. A few unlucky girls who had to sleep in curlers brought along puffy curler-caps that looked like boudoir pillows. Poor Emily Harris only had a plastic shower-cap printed with pink flamingoes to fit over her bulky metal rollers. She always tried to stay in the rear when we crowded to the door to see who was standing on the steps.

Excited and giggling, we arrived at the Haywards' just before supper on the Friday or Saturday night of the slumber party, all a little nervous until each sleeping bag and bedroll was carefully placed. Sleeping arrangements involved delicate social issues, indicating who was your best friend and how many other girls liked you by who wanted to sleep next to you. You could placate a girl who couldn't be across from you by asking her to sleep at your feet, but she knew she was getting second-best. You could always sit up and talk to her, but you just couldn't whisper in the middle of the night as you could to someone a few inches away from your head. Once the living-room floor was laid out in an elaborate gridwork, ten or twelve blankets smoothed and pillows fluffed, vanity cases carefully arranged, we were usually ready for dinner. Afterward we separated into small groups, gossiping, watching t.v., listening to the Top 40. When it was finally and safely dark, we began to listen for the boys.

They weren't supposed to come, of course. Our mothers all inquired conscientiously whether we would be properly chaperoned at the slumber party, whether so-and-so's mother planned to be home, even whether boys might have been invited. At nine or ten, we wouldn't have dreamed of seeing boys. But by twelve or thirteen, we hoped a few might arrive unannounced. At fifteen or sixteen, when boys began to drive, we expected them. Once boys had been asked to the Haywards' for dessert, and mothers complained until Josie backed down and disinvited them. But we all knew that they would show up sooner or later, in groups of two or three, because we had made sure they knew exactly where and when the party was happening.

Sometimes the boys just drove by the house, slowly, honking their horns and yelling out the windows. Then a few brave girls dashed to the front porch, maybe even the sidewalk, and waited for the car to come around again. If it did, the boys pulled over to the curb and the girls advanced to the car window. Everyone laughed, the girls pretended to blush at letting the boys see them in pajamas and robe and fuzzy slippers, and finally after half an hour the girls, freezing, retreated back to the warmth of the living room. Sometimes a couple who had broken up patched things over in one of these curbside conversations, and then, if the mother in charge wasn't watching, the girl slipped into the car for a quick, private trip around the block. Patsy Jones almost got sent home one night because the mother caught her sitting in a car with her boyfriend at the end of the drive.

If the boys were really gutsy, they came right up to the back door. There they stayed on the other side of the screen, talking to whoever could crowd up to it on our side. If the mother came down, invited them in and fed them popcorn, she spoiled everything. The deflated boys then soon went sheepishly home of their own accord. If these clandestine meetings escaped the mother's notice, which they seldom did because of the tidal wave of hysteria that swept up the stairs to her room, they might go on for hours. All kinds of romantic connections and misconnections flowed through that screen. If a boy asked if a certain girl were there, she had to come, giggling self-consciously, to the door. That might upset another girl who had always thought of that particular boy as her own unclaimed property. Some nights the slumber party reached a climax at midnight or one A.M. with handfuls of weeping, heartbroken girls rearranging their sleeping bags in the living room.

Sometime in the early hours of the morning the boys eventually went home. A few girls were already asleep, deaf to the whispers and rustlings around them. Those of us still awake, determined to last until breakfast, began to tell each other ghost stories. My favorite was "The Monkey's Paw," which I'd read in one of my mother's books, and which, if I told it right, escalating the horror with dramatic knocks on a nearby table, would make everyone scream loudly enough to wake up the sleepers. We told about headless lovers, blood-soaked sheets, girls who found themselves embracing corpses, sweethearts who were buried alive, girls found frozen inside vaults, betrayed lovers who came back from the grave. When we ran out of scary stories, we told jokes, short ones we'd remembered from the *Reader's Digest* and more elaborate shaggy dogs we'd gotten from older brothers. Then the jokes got a little dirty. We scrunched down into our bedrolls, squirming deliciously, as some of the faster girls got more and more daring. Sometimes it was hard to get to sleep after hearing Gloria Wilder's honeymoon jokes.

In the morning we all staggered to the dining-room table for orange juice and glazed doughnuts. I always felt awful, bleary and nauseated, as I rolled up my blankets, packed my overnight case, and crammed everything into the car that was taking me home. As soon as I got there, I fell into bed and was sick for twenty-four hours.

While we knew all the rules of a slumber party, we were just beginning in junior high to learn about "boy-girl parties." Those were parties to which boys were invited where dancing took place. Everyone in Ames learned to dance in seventh grade. Someone, probably a group of socially conscious mothers, arranged "optional" dancing classes once a week after school, taught by strange ladies from the Des Moines Arthur Murray Dance Studio, and attended by all children except a few Southern Baptists. On dancing day we filed solemnly into the school gymnasium, which smelled sweaty but glistened with a shiny floor and rows of varnished bleachers. We took off our shoes and left them scattered on the bleachers so we wouldn't mar the finish on the floor. All dances in the gym were "sock hops," where we slipped and slid on the floor until our socks got dirty enough to pick up some traction. Our dancing teachers briskly organized us into two circles, one of boys and one of girls, and invented elaborate techniques to "mix us up," which was their way of saying we had to pair off, boy-girl. The easiest way was to have two circles whirling madly around each other until the teacher blew her whistle. Then you slid to a stop and took as a partner the boy who was facing you. Even if he was pleased, the boy always groaned. Boys weren't supposed to like dancing lessons.

I didn't like dancing much myself. I was always very slow at learning how my body worked, and my coordination wasn't very good. By the time I had figured out one basic step, the dance instructor had moved on to the next one, and I was hopelessly confused. In seventh grade we were supposed to learn the waltz, the foxtrot, and the two-step. The only one I mastered was the two-step because it was so simple: one-two back; one-two back. During "free dance" at the end of the lesson, when boys had to ask girls to dance, I begged my partner to two-step. That was hard on one flashy dancer who liked to whirl around the floor in a waltz, which I could see in my mind as a series of geometric figures but could not duplicate with my feet. If we could have danced in a straight line of boxes, maybe I would have been all right. But he turned and circled instead, and I often stepped on his toes.

Stepping on your partner's toes was one of the two unforgivable sins for a girl in dancing. Everyone expected boys to be a little awkward, so if a boy stepped on your toes, you both laughed; if a girl did it, she blushed and sometimes the boy yelled an exaggerated "ouch!" to embarrass her even more. The other sin, more serious, was leading. A girl was supposed to be as finely tuned into her partner's touch as a thoroughbred horse to the gentle press of a rein; I strained my nerves trying to read the secret messages being tapped into my back, but I never succeeded. Sometimes a boy would be gripping my waist so tightly I couldn't tell when he was changing pressure. Other times he would jab me in the ribs until I jumped and lost count of the beat I was trying to follow: one-two back, one-two back. At the party on the last day of dancing lessons, my partner, Johnny Prince, broke up the whole dance floor by stopping dead in the middle of the mass of churning couples and shouting, "Cut it out, Allen! You're *leading*!" Everyone laughed. I wanted to die immediately, but at the same time to hit Johnny hard in the stomach. Instead we kept on dancing.

Once we had all officially learned to dance, seventh-graders began attending the junior-high sock hops. Several of these were held each year in the gym from four-thirty to six o'clock, usually on the Fridays before Saturday-morning basketball or football games. For years I thought of parties as vibrating with the excitement of pregame pep rallies. We girls planned weeks in advance what to wear, since we had just enough time after school to slip home and change into party clothes. I usually tried to sew my outfits for the sock hops, but I never finished in time. The night before the dance, and sometimes the hour before, I would be weeping with frustration as my rattled mother tried to help me sew the infinite hem on a circle skirt. Once I had to go to a dance with safety pins instead of a zipper. I was never pleased with how I looked.

When I arrived at the sock hop, however, I usually had a good time. It was hard not to respond to the gloomy romance of the transformed gym, whose shades were now pulled so that the air seemed dusky, rather than sweaty, and whose stage now contained a disc-jockey's booth. There one of the older boys from ninth grade who had set up the school's big black record-player perched on a stool under a spotlight changing 45's. The teacher-chaperones called out each dance, mixers, ladies' choices, and free dances. Those free dances were the only ones to worry about. We girls hung together near the bleachers, pretending to be so busy talking and laughing that someone wouldn't notice a boy until his hand was actually on her shoulder. Then she started, looked surprised, and moved away with an air of assurance from the knot of rejected girls onto the dance floor. I was as popular as most girls, but I too sometimes had to stand self-consciously un-chosen through an entire record. After the party was over, I was always relieved.

The most important party in Welch Junior High School was the annual Box Social, held on a Saturday night and as far re-moved from an ordinary "sock hop" as the boys' state championship from an intramural basketball game. The Box Social was a nostal-gic farewell for the ninth-graders, who were about to move into the socially complex world of the downtown high school, and a sparkling introduction to the new seventh-graders of the alluring years of boy-girl parties ahead.

An old-fashioned Box Social, whispers of whose past we heard, was an open auction in which boys got to bid for the dinners pre-pared by the girls. The boys naturally knew whose box was which, though the auctioneer wasn't allowed to mention any names; the auction was a public test of popularity. In Ames, where parents prided themselves on being democratic, we didn't believe in such crass ways of determining social value. So our Welch Box Social was carefully rigged to avoid hurt feelings. Every boy paid a set amount for a numbered ticket, like a raffle. Then the teacher run-ning the show stood in front of a microphone on stage and pulled a ticket out of her basket as she held up each girl's decorated din-ner box. The boy whose number was called had to take that box, eat dinner with the girl who had made it, and dance the first number with her.

Even though who got your dinner box was a matter of chance, we girls nonetheless spent weeks planning, making and decorat-ing our boxes, while our mothers were expected to produce per-fect crispy chicken, smooth potato salad and moist chocolate cake to put inside them. Everyone had a tacit understanding about the menu, which varied only slightly. We were allowed considerable originality on the outside of the box, however, so we vied to see whose would be most ingenious. One year, when two girls could prepare a box together, my friend Emily and I decided

to make a merry-go-round. We talked her mother out of a round
hatbox and managed to cover its sides with glued-on animals,
stripes, stars, and odd bits of crepe paper. Then we spent a week
of after-school afternoons trying to construct a conical top that
would rise to a triumphant pennant. After two packets of construction paper and several disagreements, we at last waited till
suppertime to catch Emily's father, who was a mechanical engineer. Gruff and short-tempered, he still knew the importance of
the Box Social. So he spent his evening with our hatbox and
construction paper, and next morning before school Emily called
me with relief to say he'd graphed, cut, wired, glued and anchored
a perfect spread cone to the top of our merry-go-round. It was another triumph for a man of science.

Even though most of us had worked on decorating the gym for
the Box Social, we always oohed and aahed when we arrived
there at six o'clock. It was just turning dark outside, and the colored lights strung inside the gym twinkled like a carnival. Whole
boxes of crepe paper had been transformed into streamers, loops
tacked against the walls, arcades woven over the entrance, bands
wound around the bleacher banisters. On the floor of the gym
stood an army of card table, brought by each girl earlier in the day
and now carefully set up with white tablecloths, napkins, and
glasses. It no longer looked like a gym. In our eyes it had become
a supper club, like the elegant Jimmy and Lou's in Des Moines.
On this one night we were allowed to walk on the floor with our
street shoes, and we tapped on short heels busily over the waxed
floor looking at each other's tables and admiring the growing
heap of gaudy boxes on the stage as each girl arrived and handed
hers to the auctioneer.

We also looked carefully at each other's dresses. No single outfit in the whole year mattered as much as the dress you wore to
the Box Social. Most of us had spent many Saturday afternoons
downtown in Younkers trying on the whole rack of teen-size
dresses, comparing flounces, gathers, and pleats. We seriously discussed necklines, which were permitted on this one night to be

scooped, and sleeves, which might disappear entirely even though the spring night was apt to be windy and cold. A few lucky girls were even driven to the big Younkers in Des Moines, the one with escalators, to buy dresses no one else would have seen before.

On Box Social night our mothers let us wear Tangee lipstick and, by ninth grade, our first pairs of nylon stockings. Mine were Penney's Suntan Beige, a shade that Younkers called Nearly Nude. When I eased into my nylons for my last Box Social, wearing gloves so I wouldn't run them, they felt scratchy and loose. Though I fastened them carefully to my new garter belt, I was worried that somehow they might not stay up. I couldn't get used to the strange sensation of having something hang and rub where nothing had hung and rubbed before. I thought I could hear a rustling noise when I walked. After I arrived at the party, watched my box auctioned off to a scrawny seventh-grader who sat across from me, eyes averted, during dinner, and danced a few two-steps, I was so distracted that I forgot all about my nylons. But then, dancing with Johnny Prince, something terrible happened. I suddenly realized that I could no longer feel my nylons clinging to my legs. They must have come undone from those tricky garters. They must be about ready to drop to my ankles, here right in the middle of the dance floor. I was in agony. After a few minutes of panicky silence I decided to act. I stopped dead and looked helplessly at Johnny. "Excuse me, Johnny," I said in a whisper. "I have to go down to the locker room. " I paused for a moment. I didn't want him to think I had to go to the bathroom. "I think my nylons are falling down," I finally hissed and fled from the floor. Once near the girls' lockers, I lifted my skirt and examined my hooks, snaps and slides. To my surprise, everything was still tied up. My nylons bagged a little, which is probably why I hadn't felt them, but nothing else had happened. I was intact. But I was so shaken I waited for several dances before I ventured upstairs again.

Compared to the Box Social, most other boy-girl parties in junior high and early high school were pale and unexciting. The ones I remember most happily, without the trauma of the Box Social, were square dances. Even Baptists were sometimes allowed to come, and at our own Presbyterian church an ancient deacon served incongruously as caller, screeching and slapping his thigh with startling vigor on the occasional nights when our youth fellowship had a party. I liked square dances because I could follow the caller a lot more easily than I could wend my way through waltzes, and also because I didn't feel the tensions of constant choice. Square dances were relaxed: one partner lasted a long time, and as a bonus you got to do-si-do with several others.

The only difficulty with having a square-dance party was finding room to hold it. Few of us had basements big enough to accommodate more than one square, and even then we were cramped. At one not-so-successful party at the Pitkins', we all bumped into each other on every grande allemande, and whenever I dipped under my partner's arm I found my head disappearing into the washing machine. The Pitkins had made an attempt to disguise their appliances, decorating the hot-water heater with crepe-paper streamers, folding up drying racks, and hiding detergent boxes in the corners, but still we all knew where we were. When we had worked hard enough to earn our refreshments, we trooped upstairs to the living room, turned on the radio, and tapped our feet as we drank our cider, ate our popcorn, and flirted conscientiously. That was the part of the party most kids looked forward to. But I was afraid of whom I'd get stuck talking to, since I hadn't learned the art of extricating myself from the glassy stares of boys too shy to talk to anyone else. I often found myself wishing we were back in the basement ducking, bowing, and exchanging partners.

Since parties at home were tenaciously organized by anxious parents, we were delighted by the freedom of high-school social life. High school meant parties where boys could drive you home and, three times a year, real formal dances with tulles and tuxes. I remember much of Ames High School, in fact, as a series of parties punctuated by classes. Continuing the junior-high tradition of linking social and athletic competition, Ames High always scheduled postgame dances after Friday night football or basketball. Walking home from the blazing lights of the football field back to the high school along empty streets, filled with the euphoria of victory or the melancholy of loss, we were already emotionally in high gear by the time we arrived at the darkened building. Knots of students who had left the game early gathered around the front door, waiting for enough people to arrive so we could all surge upstairs together. There the study hall was emptied, a job that the last class on Friday always had to do before going home, piling up chairs and desks in a tangled forest at one end of the room. At the other end stood a small platform on wheels, holding a huge record-player, amplifier, table, stack of records, and one chair for the member of Audio-Visual Club who had volunteered to run equipment that night. One awkward, silent boy volunteered almost every party; he must have felt safely insulated from the social tensions crackling like electricity on the dance floor in front of him. He could exercise some power too, deciding when to play the soft, romantic ballads and when to put on the hard, loud rock-and-roll music that emptied the floor of clinging couples.

Except for steadies who were never separated anywhere, not many kids took dates to the after-game parties. Most of us clung to small groups of friends, darting back and forth to other groups until the music started. Unlike our junior-high sock hops, these parties were so dark that if I wasn't chosen for a particular dance I wasn't noticeable. I could hover in the gloom by the wall or sink into a desk pulled down from the heap behind me. If I began to feel conspicuous after several dances, or the group around me thinned out too much, I could always go to the ladies' room. That was another social center, where girls gathered to check lipstick, comb hair, pull down blouses, change Tampax, and compare notes on what was happening at the dance. It was bright and warm with fluorescent lights, noisy with the sound of flushing toilets and water running, jammed with people. It was never lonely in the ladies' room. If things got bad outside, you could even stay there all night.

At most after-game parties I danced confidently, since the floor was so crowded nobody could waltz. On fast dances, which I never mastered, I simply told my partner I didn't know how and he was usually just as glad to sit it out with me, watching the one or two flamboyant couples who could twirl, bump, and grind so wildly that other people would stop dancing just to watch them. Mr. and Mrs. Post, the history teacher and his wife who always served as chaperones, watched carefully too. They didn't know how to discipline wild dancers, so they saved their interference for the slow ones. If a couple seemed to be dancing too tightly interlaced, plump Mr. Post would waddle self-consciously onto the floor and tap them on the elbow. "Tut tut," he would try to joke, "light! Let there be light!" That meant, we all knew, Post's rule: he wanted to see some space between them. We all laughed at the Posts behind their backs as they tried to execute an old-fashioned foxtrot, weaving and dipping between the sluggish waves of slow dancers, but we had to obey them. Mr. Post had the authority to send someone home, and no one wanted to miss the end of an after-game dance.

Tension began to rise in the darkened study hall about ten o'clock. We girls then had an hour in which to find a ride home, and although someone's parents were always available in case of emergency, what we really wanted were boys to ask us. Not every boy had a car, but two or three might pool together, squeezing in their dates. Those rides were fun, because we ended the night with a noisy, laughing crowd at the pizza parlor or the Rainbow Cafe. The Rainbow was roomy, cheerful, cheap, and only four blocks from high school, one block from Main Street, and right on a bus stop. From its booths and stools we could see all important traffic. A tenderloin sandwich and a Coke earned us at least an hour of staring out to see who was staring in, and a quarter bought three hotly contested punches on the tableside jukebox. In such a crowd I never worried about conversation or about what might happen at my front door, since everyone was watching from the waiting car.

When the Audio-Visual boy put "Stardust" on his record-player, we knew it was the last number. Usually the boy who asked a girl to dance then also took her home. Making the tension worse was the fear that the wrong boy might ask me. It was hard to lie, because he might see me sneaking out with a girl-friend. I always had a lamentable compulsion to tell the truth, anyway, and could only lie with much forethought. So I often ended up riding home with George Pitkin, who would slam the car door after me when I wouldn't kiss him goodnight, or with Don Petrowski, who never said a word from the moment we left the dance until he said "goodnight" at my house. I didn't know which was worse. To this day when I hear "Stardust" my stomach begins to tighten.

Although the after-game parties provided almost weekly doses of anticipation, romance and disappointment, those were small quivers compared to the tidal waves of emotion that flowed toward the major formal dances of the year. Most important was the Christmas Dance. It completely overshadowed the spring Junior-Senior Prom, which was overorganized by watchful parents with an all-night program guaranteed to keep us all in plain sight from the gymnasium dance to the midnight movie in the auditorium to the early-morning games at the Country Club. The all-school Christmas Dance was much more private. It was held in the Great Hall of the Iowa State College Memorial Union, a room vaulted and wainscoted in dark oak, where some of us had peered past the bronze-studded doors to glimpse the splendors of the annual Iowa State Homecoming Dance. Just walking into the Union in our formals and tuxes we felt the reflected glow of those adult ceremonies. Not many college students hung around the Union during Christmas vacation, so before the dancing began we could swarm into the lounges, ladies' rooms and even the billiard room as though we belonged there, perching gingerly on easy chairs, leafing through old copies of *Time*, and watching our dates trying to act as though they shot pool every day. None of us felt really comfortable, but then you weren't supposed to be comfortable at a formal dance.

One reason for feeling awkward at the Christmas Dance had nothing to do with the place. A girl might be with a date she hadn't spoken to for months. Unlike any other social event of the Ames High year, the Christmas Dance was strictly ladies' choice. In theory this was fine, since it gave every girl a chance to attend. But in practice it didn't quite work out. For the other formal dances, boys asked girls only a few weeks in advance. We girls, on the contrary, began scheming in September about whom to invite to the Christmas Dance. We tried to keep a kind of union rule about not asking any boy until at least October, but enforcing this rule was difficult. Meanwhile we eyed each other suspiciously, sounding each other out delicately about our lists, comparing duplications of first, second, and third choices, bargaining to exchange one slot for another.

But in the end someone always jumped the gun. "Linda asked Jack Bolton to the Christmas Dance yesterday!" The excited whisper whirled up and down the study hall like a gust of wind. By noon that day, little enclaves of girls gathered in the hallways, buzzing and fretting. That afternoon several more prime boys would be picked off, and then there was a panicky rush to get what was left. By mid-October nearly every date for the Christmas Dance was set. Then, of course, grim things began to happen. Couples broke up, flirtations waned, an appealing boy began to look humdrum, a dark horse emerged too late. By December, many of us were gloomily contemplating an evening in the company of a boy we'd tired of, jilted, insulted, or vice versa. No one ever thought of switching dates. Once a choice had been made, it was immutable. So on the waxed oak floor of the Great Hall that December night, I could see couples dancing in sullen silence, others exchanging as many dances as possible, many standing at the edges looking bored. Only a few of us, lucky enough to have guessed right in October, were able to hum along truthfully with the band that we were indeed that night in my blue heaven.

If conversation dulled, we girls could always turn to discussing each other's dresses. Choosing a formal for the Christmas Dance was almost as serious as choosing a wedding dress. The year I sewed myself a bright red velveteen frock with a V-neck that plunged almost four inches below my collarbone I felt gloriously like a scarlet woman, though I probably looked more like an overripe apple. I envied the two or three girls who confidently held up strapless dresses. We also stared at each other's flowers, a heavy item of concern before Coe's Florists' truck arrived on the day of the dance. A boy was supposed to ask a girl what color dress she was wearing, but sometimes he didn't. If she had red velveteen, she lived in fear of clashing pink roses. Corsages came in three price levels, carnations, roses, and orchids. A date who wished he weren't going with a girl sent her carnations. Only a few lucky girls each year got orchids, but they wore them like medals of honor. We girls in turn sent our dates little boutonnieres, which most of them managed to pull off or destroy before the evening was over. Nobody spent much time admiring the boys.

Looking each other over carefully didn't always reveal the intricate planning that had gone into one's appearance at the Christmas Dance. Early that morning, I laid out on my bed all the paraphernalia I had painstakingly acquired for weeks: new Penney's nylons, still in their cellophane wrapper; new white lace garter belt; a padded Merry Widow we had driven to Des Moines to find, with bony ribs that were supposed to give me a wasp's waist and low-cut cups that were meant to push whatever I had up and out; shiny Capezio miniheels I would have to break in that night on the dance floor; and all the fresh makeup I could afford at Woolworth's. I had a new bottle of Evening in Paris, a jar of Cashmere Bouquet cold cream, a compact of pressed powder, a tin of dark blue eye shadow I would dab on sparingly so that no one would notice I was wearing it. By late afternoon I began a ritual of washing, shaving, curling, trimming, powdering, dabbing and creaming. I have probably never been so clean before or since.

Besides the initial effect in the Great Hall, girls had a second chance to dazzle that night. At intermission almost everyone was invited to refreshments at the Stewarts' house just across the campus. We bundled into our borrowed velvet wraps and, refusing to cover satin slippers with boots, tiptoed carefully across the snowy sidewalks to the Stewarts' door. Inside, a huge Christmas tree was lit with red, green, and blue blinking bulbs, and ribboned mistletoe hung everywhere. We sparkled too. The Stewarts' living room gleamed with rhinestone earrings, jingling charm bracelets, patent-leather purses, and moistened red lips. Most of us spent at least half the intermission upstairs in Sally Stewart's bedroom in front of her mirror, straightening seams and retouching makeup. I tugged ineffectually on my Merry Widow, which kept riding up so that the little white foam-rubber cups peeped over the edge of my red velveteen. At this point in the evening, my eye shadow smeared and nylons itching, I wasn't sure that everything had been worth it.

The second half of the Christmas Dance was an anti-climax. I knew already who was going to take me home, and the dance got out so late nobody could have a party afterward. Dresses and makeup exhaustively admired, we girls subsided into dancing. We were all feeling a little tired. The hired band, the only live music we ever heard except at the spring prom, played old favorites they had known for years. It may have been the late fifties for some musicians, but not for Tommy Flanagan and His Foolin' Fantastics and their versions of "String of Pearls," "Blue Moon," and "Mood Indigo."

The darkness of the high-vaulted ceiling seemed to descend slowly and fill the corners of the cavernous hall. It was too big a room for our group to warm. I now began to feel a cold draft blowing on the bare skin of my neck and shoulders. Not much of the evening was left. Anyone who hadn't signed my dance card yet wasn't going to do it now. Hopes dimmed. When the band came to "Stardust," I was ready to go home.

When I got home, I didn't bother to put anything away except my corsage, which went into the refrigerator. Next morning I would pick up the strewn nylons, pack away the red velveteen, clean up the messy bathroom. But tonight I just wanted to get into bed and lie quietly a while before I went to sleep, looking out the window at the streetlight shining on the snow. No one but me in the entire neighborhood was still awake. I thought back over the whole evening. I wondered if my date had thought I looked beautiful. I could still sense the faint paste of blue eye shadow on my lids and smell a lingering mist of Evening in Paris. It seemed incredible that the next day would be so ordinary. Turning on my side, I felt my body begin to relax in little quivers. Burying my cold nose in the pillow, I tried to remember the dim light in the Great Hall, the crooning saxophones, the touch of someone's hand on my waist. Then I fell asleep.

Preparation for Life

"**N**o allowance this week, Jennie, twice you didn't get your bed made," I say regretfully but firmly, in my best parental voice of authority and responsibility. "I know," she answers cheerfully. "That's okay. I don't really need the money anyway." She is probably right, I think gloomily as I chalk up one more defeat for the Protestant work ethic. With two grandmothers, a weekend present-giving father, and an indulgent mother, why should she feel the need to earn money? What, besides a dog, does she want that she hasn't got? My attempts at starting Jennifer on an allowance have been a failure. Current child-care experts offered me two opinions: give money but don't require chores, because children should simply expect to help around the house anyway; give money and require chores, because children need to learn the connection between work and money. Anyone who grew up in Ames when I did would have unhesitatingly chosen the second approach. But I have become out-of-date.

In Ames everyone worked. Fathers had jobs and mothers were homemakers, a word religiously observed in a town whose college was famed for its Division of Home Economics. Some mothers had outside jobs, not for pleasure but because they needed the money. Everyone knew that Mrs. McCallum clerked at the Hy Valu because her husband drank, Mrs. Olson managed the Dairy Dreme because her husband had deserted their family, my mother taught because she was a widow and had to support two daughters. A few other women, mainly faculty wives, worked even though they were securely married; but they were idiosyncratic individuals who somehow made their own rules and were not judged by ours.

As soon as I can remember, my friends and I wanted to get jobs. We looked forward to being sixteen, the magic age when most employers would be able to put us legally on their payrolls. Until then, we had to scrabble furiously for what summer and after-school jobs we could dig up in a small town whose work force did not usually expand at the times we were available. All girls baby-sat. Boys mowed lawns, raked leaves, shoveled walks and delivered papers. In junior high school, we all detasseled corn in the summer. But by high school, we began to look more seriously for jobs that might "lead to something," jobs that seemed more important, jobs that offered what our high-school vocational counselor portentously called "preparation for life." As a sixteen-year-old reporter on the Ames Daily Tribune, I did a photo feature on teenagers' summer jobs, ostentatiously lugging my large black box camera around town to interview my friends. Kristy ran the elevator between the basement, first, and second floors of Younkers; Jack washed dishes at the Iowa State Union cafeteria; Emily was a carhop at the A&W Root Beer Stand; Patsy clerked at her aunt's fabric store; Charlie was cutting and hauling sod on an outlying farm. Kristy told me, confidentially, that her job was numbingly dull; Jack was planning to quit in a few weeks, when he'd saved enough for golf clubs; Emily hated the rude jibes she had to endure with her tips; Patsy didn't get along with her old-maid aunt; and Charlie said his job was about as much fun as football practice, and a lot dirtier. But we were all proud of ourselves, and the Ames Daily Tribune was proud too: my pictures ran on the front page, a visible testament to the way the younger generation was absorbing the values of its elders.

Besides the prestige that went with holding a job, a public acknowledgment that we were almost ready to enter the grown-up world, we of course wanted the money. All of us had small allowances, and we sighed together with agonized desire when we window-shopped on Saturday afternoons. Most of us schemed and planned from junior high on how to stretch our baby-sitting money, detasseling pay, and allowances into an annual first-day-of-school outfit and a formal for the Christmas Dance. In August I both sewed and plotted about how to spend my summer's accumulated earnings. At first my atlas and guide was the August issue of Seventeen, then, by the end of high school, the college issue of Mademoiselle. Thick as catalogues, bulging with advertisements, they offered page after page of tempting photographs, models I knew I'd never really resemble but whose clothes might just make me passable at a distance. Ames had never seen such exotic outfits: Bermuda shorts with raccoon jackets flung over them, blazers, Chanel suits. Eagerly I read the copy, absorbing the ease, the self-confidence the models exuded. "Jenny Blair, a senior at Southwest High, will enter Penn in the fall. Here she dashes to a tennis date in a crisp skirted outfit in white pique. Note the casual fling of her silk jacquard scarf." I didn't know anyone who had a tennis outfit. Since I didn't play tennis myself, I was able to pass over Jenny Blair without too much envy. But the next page! "Scotty Wales will party tonight in this red striped jersey two-piece pull-on outfit. Later she can wear the top with her gray flannel slacks." Scotty, who was sixteen, according to the text, looked more like twenty: smooth, sleek, gleaming red lipstick. I noted the price of the red striped wool jersey: $35. Almost half my budget of $77.40, counting the bonus I'd get from having stuck the whole detasseling season. Over many long hot afternoons, I made notes, added figures, shuffled priorities, folded back pages until my fingers were black with newsprint. Occasionally I asked my mother's advice. "That seems awfully like the striped dress you have, dear," she'd say discouragingly. Or, "That is nice, but my, it's expensive. I wouldn't spend all that money if I were you." Finally, "Maybe you'll have time to make a new dress."

Money, money, money. How I wanted it then, as I tried to reduce my shopping list to the size of my budget. In the end I never bought anything from the magazines anyway. Their world was too remote from mine, and I settled for what I could find on sale downtown in Ames. Years later, when I was married, I suddenly had access to a joint income that was more than enough to permit an occasional extravagance. I soon opened a charge account at Peck & Peck, where I'd *vainly dreamed hours away on college afternoons. Browsing there one day, I saw a handsome plaid wool suit that cost more than I had ever paid before, and bought it. I never wore it much. It didn't matter to me like the orange print cotton dress with a tucked midriff I'd bought one fall at Younkers for $14.98. I'd tried on a whole rack that day, consulted my friends, thought my purchase over for two days; when I decided to take the orange dress home, I carefully paid out money from my small horde saved from clearing dishes at the Memorial Union, baby-sitting, and assisting at playground dramatics. I didn't have to ask my mother's permission to charge it. I wore that dress till deodorant rotted its armpits. It was a tangible proof of my earning power and my growing independence.*

Aside from basic money management, what did I actually learn from all my summer and after-school jobs? Each one may have given me some small skills, but the cumulative effect was to deepen my belief that work was the essential aspect of grown-up life. Even now, I am sometimes filled with anxieties at the prospect of stretches of free time. When I do not immediately rush to fill that time with work, I have to fight off guilt, struggling mentally against a picture of a Real Grown-up shaking a finger at me, someone with the droning voice of our high-school career counselor, but with firm overtones of former employers, teachers, even my mother. "This," the voice beats relentlessly into my ear, "is your preparation for life."

I wanted a paper route, but I baby-sat instead. Perhaps that disappointment was itself a preparation for life. All during grade school I longed to deliver the afternoon Ames *Daily Tribune*, but since our neighborhood had plenty of boys to do it, my applications were always turned down. No girls were allowed to carry the more prestigious morning Des Moines *Register*. But the undernourished *Tribune*, desperate for carriers, sometimes had to let a girl or two onto its list. My friend Shirley Conover was one of them. Although I didn't share Shirley's passions for softball, climbing trees, and dogs, she let me wistfully tag along many afternoons on her paper route. Making sure a *Tribune*, neatly rolled and rubber-banded, was carefully slipped inside every front door for blocks seemed the height of responsibility and importance. Sometimes, after careful instructions, Shirley let me take a whole block by myself. Shirley's route even carried us out of her neighborhood, on the edge of Campustown, into strange apartment buildings, where we crept down dark carpeted halls, and along streets where I didn't know anyone, up long sidewalks guarded by dogs, onto screened porches where the sound of an opening door made me jump. I felt as though we were being given privileged glimpses into unknown lives. The money, Shirley told me proudly, wasn't as much as her brother made from the *Register*, but it was lots more than she got baby-sitting. And it sure was lots more fun.

All girls in Ames, even Shirley, baby-sat. When we were eleven or twelve, old enough for our mothers to approve our staying out late at night, we were expected to accept baby-sitting jobs eagerly. Although I had no younger brothers or sisters, and knew nothing about infants or even toddlers, grown-ups evidently assumed that the mere fact of my sex qualified me to care for their children. They also assumed I wanted to. I had, in truth, no particular love for babies or young children, a passion I only later acquired, and then selectively, when I had my own child. Despite my popularity as a sitter, which was probably based mostly on my proximity, I suspect I had no particular talent either. Even today, I cannot quiet crying babies, and small children do not rush to sit in my lap. But since baby-sitting was often the only available money-making opportunity for me, I naturally seized it. Between my sister and me, the Allen girls had a monopoly for years on Oakland Street and Franklin Avenue.

Perhaps I felt inadequate as a baby-sitter because I was haunted by the memory of Marcia Fitzpatrick. When I was very young, she had been my favorite sitter, one I loved so much I used to beg my mother, "Can't you go out tonight, Mommy? Couldn't you get Marcia Fitzpatrick to come?" My mother tells me I even offered to take money from my piggy bank to pay for Marcia's visits. Although I barely remember how she looked, other than a kind and friendly face, what really enthralled me about Marcia was her story-telling. She had a genius for making up stories about a charac-ter called Snoopy Mouse, who was often threatened by a clever but villainous Reddy Fox, and her "Snoopy stories," as we called them, were long, inventive, and exciting. My mother used to urge Marcia to write them down, but, shy and self-effacing, she always blushed and shook her head. When I was ten or eleven, old enough myself to baby-sit, I tried to re-create her marvelous stories, vaguely recalling stray incidents, shamelessly plagiarizing what I could, haphazardly adding from my own small store of imaginative power. I felt I was trying to carry on Marcia's tradi-tion, but with woeful inadequacy. "Give us another Snoopy story!" my little charges would ask, and my heart would sink. Even my own attention would wander from my threadbare plot-tings, and I would find myself repeating, adding another chase or explosion, abruptly ending when I was too weary to carry on.

When I finally realized that I was apt to be a sitter for at least several years, I decided that I should approach the job in a more organized fashion. If all my resources were my small cache of patched-up Snoopy stories, I would run out quickly. So, adapting an idea from some project in my Camp Fire book, I made a baby-sitting box. With a small capital from my proceeds, I invested in several dime-store toys, tiny cars, inch-long dolls, rubber ball, new crayons, colored paper, blunt scissors, paste, a few cheap Golden Books. As part of my organization, I painstakingly let-tered a series of information blanks, asking my employer-parents to list their telephone number, name of family doctor, and so on. Armed with this box, I marched off to my assignments feeling somehow that I was prepared, not, perhaps, a Marcia Fitzpatrick, but at least a girl who looked as though she knew what she were doing. The mere appearance of professionalism, I learned early in my work experience, was sometimes good enough.

Even with my baby-sitting box, however, I had my problems. Having been gently raised by my mother, but having fought hand-to-hand battles with my older sister, I was never quite sure how to discipline small children. Should I coax or spank? I myself had almost never been spanked, and it seemed sadistic. Scolding, yelling, screaming didn't work. Other than threatening early bed-time, which was useless in the middle of the afternoon, I had to resort to pleading and bribes. This damaged my self-respect and also led me into playing many unwanted games of tag, hopscotch, or ring-around-the-rosy, most of which seemed both boring and beneath my dignity, and all of which I had to be careful to let my charges win.

I both feared and longed for the time when the children would go to bed. When the house was quiet at last, I would get to ex-plore, wandering among rooms furnished differently from ours at home, admiring velvet sofas or shell collections or silver tea ser-vices. Though I seldom touched anything I shouldn't, I felt a lit-tle like a thief. Even a promised snack in the refrigerator tasted like forbidden fruit. Mostly, though, I delved into libraries. At the Kendalls' I could always count on a collection of *Reader's Digests* and condensed *Reader's Digest* books, neither of which my mother ever bought. After avidly devouring all the true adventures, jokes, and poignant spiritual confessions in the *Digest*, I palpi-tated through the condensations of *Mrs. Mike*, *Anna and the King of Siam*, and dozens of other popular novels that Mrs. Erhard at the Ames Public Library would not yet let me check out. A night at the Smiths' was always a feast of romance too, with heaps of old *Ladies' Home Journals*, *Woman's Home Companions*, *Coronets*, *McCall's*, stashed in a basement corner where I soon discovered them. I was fascinated by the marriage-counseling articles, never fully believing that this marriage could be saved until the ab-solute last minute, and I thrived on the fiction. While movies formed many of my images of love and marriage, the stories in *McCall's* and the *Journal* confirmed them. Would a small-town girl (like me) be happy in a big city (no) until she met a lonely, sandy-haired, cheerful young man who turned out to be from a town near hers? (Well . . .) Would they fall in love? (Yes.) Would they return to Rock's Corners? (Yes, yes.) Would he be the town's new pharmacist, and would she love raising a houseful of children? (Yes, yes, yes.) At the end of such stories I tried not to compare the heroines' obvious virtues, their sweetness, good temper, and love of children, with my own irritation as I had finally salted away a runny-nosed little Smith in his rather smelly crib. One night, just after I had closed a *Journal* with a sigh of satisfaction, still blissfully seeing myself in the arms of my childhood sweetheart, who had forgiven me and taken me back after I had gone to the country-club dance with a black-haired, flirtatious, and dangerous young man who kept a pocket flask in his glove compartment, I heard little Tommy Smith cry. Dashed back to earth, I plodded dutifully up the stairs to his room. There he sat in his crib, wide awake, silent now, looking rather proudly at the corner of his crib. There, compact and irrefutable, was a large brown glob. It was several moments before I realized, with horrified amazement, that it was . . . "B.M.," said Tommy proudly. I ran for the bathroom and a piece of toilet paper, gingerly wrapping the glob for deposit and then with a fresh piece scrubbing away at the brown smear on the sheet. I felt shaken. Somehow I could not find a bridge between the world I had just left between those glossy magazine covers and the world of Tommy's poop.

My fear at the children's bedtime was simply that of being in a strange house after dark. Closely nurtured, sheltered by my mother in the safest of homes, I was ill-prepared for lurking dangers beyond it. Since Ames had a minuscule record of murders and molestations, I do not know what I was afraid of, though I could probably guess. All I knew was that I was scared of noises and of uncurtained windows, black glass that reflected back my own image but did not permit me to see what was outdoors. I wondered who might be hiding in the backyard, looking in. As I lay curled on the sofa, every gurgle of a water heater or click of a refrigerator made me jump. In one new house, heated by a fancy arrangement of hot-water pipes running along the walls, I was driven into near-terror by the constantly changing liquid murmurs. At most houses, though, I eventually drifted into a groggy som- nolence, ready to leap up when I heard the front door open. Though parents assured me I should go to sleep when they stayed out late, I never felt quite right about leaving my job unattended. Baby-sitting was an uneasy business.

Besides baby-sitting, young girls in Ames could sometimes get part-time jobs housecleaning, another skill most grown-ups as- sumed came with gender. Most grown-ups, not all. My first house- cleaning job was with an exception, old Mrs. Werdle, a crotchety widow who lived next door to one of Mother's friends. This friend, a kindly neighbor, knew Mrs. Werdle, crippled from arthritis and rheumatism, badly needed help. She called my mother, who asked me, and next Saturday, cheerful and willing, I arrived at the Werdle house. My cheerfulness soon waned. Old Mrs. Werdle, it seemed, did not trust me. She didn't think I knew how to vacuum or dust properly, and she wanted to be sure I didn't cheat her out of her twenty-five cents an hour. Much of that unpleasant morning has disappeared, but I still can see my- self, crouched on hands and knees, washing the floor, while Mrs. Werdle sat a few inches behind me, doubled over on a small stool, peering over my shoulder to make sure I scrubbed all the way into the corners. I don't think I minded the hard work, the dark and musty house, or even Mrs. Werdle's snappish tongue, as much as I was wounded by her assumption that I didn't know how to work. "A good hard worker" was a phrase of highest ap- probation in Ames, and I knew I was one. I was so angry with Mrs. Werdle that I refused to return to her house. Even baby- sitting held less indignity.

Some time after the Werdle incident, my mother asked me if I would consider one more cleaning job. A colleague of hers, a bachelor who sometimes took Mother to an occasional party, needed a replacement for his cleaning lady for a few weeks. He would pay fifty cents an hour. And, my mother added, he would be at work himself while I cleaned; I'd have the apartment to myself. I multiplied fifty cents quickly several times and accepted. Work conditions seemed ideal, and in fact they were: privacy, a chance to work at my own pace, good pay. The only problem with cleaning for Mr. Sanders was that I couldn't find anything to clean. A meticulous man, he kept his apartment so tidy, dusted, and swept that I felt real frustration when I vacuumed. I couldn't tell afterward what I had done except by watching the fine marks the vacuum wheels left on the carpet. If I managed to find a stray crumb under a sofa pillow, I was delighted. In the bathroom Mr. Sanders had showed me how to use Jonny Mops, a refinement we didn't have at home. But while I dutifully scrubbed around the toilet bowl, I never found a ring to erase or a spot to remove. Though Mr. Sanders seemed pleased with my work, I was relieved when his cleaning lady returned from vacation. I was tired of creeping carefully backward out his door so I wouldn't disturb the telltale vacuum wheel marks on the floor. They were, I felt, the only sign I had been there at all.

At about twelve or thirteen, I was old enough for a uniform. That was one of the few rewards of clearing dishes from the Grill at the Iowa State Memorial Union. In summer not many college students used this large dining room that sprawled like an underground auditorium in a windowless basement. Jammed full of people during the school year, the heavy dark oak tables and chairs were mostly empty now, a sea of shiny surfaces stretching across the floor. Often I was the only clearing girl on duty in the deserted room, watching from a distance until two or three girls scraped their chairs back, strolled out the door, and left their coffee cups and pie saucers waiting for me. I was supposed to carry the dishes to the kitchen and wipe off the tables with a greasy rag, whose mildewy, sour smell can still waft acridly under my nose if I close my eyes and pretend I'm wearing my yellow cotton uniform and dirty white apron. The Union allowed only one apron a day.

Working at the Union made me realize how lonely you feel

when you are invisible on the job. Sometimes older high-school kids I recognized wandered into the Grill for a Coke or a hamburger, but I couldn't go over and talk to them. Once in a while someone would nod at me and wave, and from my corner by the dishtrays I nodded and waved back. The supervisor was very firm about clearing girls mixing with the customers. I was often bored, too, waiting idly for some table to empty. Late in the afternoon, when I often worked, I would sometimes sneak a quarter into the jukebox so I could listen to music, trying to stay near the machine till my three records had ended, hoping the supervisor wouldn't suddenly march through the Grill and notice an uncleared table at the other end. Slowly wiping down the dark varnished surfaces, watching my rag make greasy circles, I swayed a little in time to the music. I always played mildly sad love songs, Sinatra, Perry Como, the Four Aces, so I could pretend the echoing Grill was just a garden in the rain, a dance floor where someone was playing the Beguine, a mountain top where love was a many-splendored thing. Anonymous in my uniform, moving around the quiet room, I felt as though I were an unseen ghost in an echoing empty space. I was living in the midst of the world of college, but the world had vanished. Leaving this cave, with its heavy oak furniture and gleaming dark surfaces, and emerging into the late-afternoon sunlight, I always experienced a kind of time warp. I was suddenly free and thirteen again, stretching cramped muscles, racing home happily on my bicycle to dinner and a movie with my girlfriends.

My only excitement at the Grill came from foreign students. By the 1950s, many young men from developing or war-torn countries were drawn to Iowa State to study agriculture, industrial arts, or engineering. Lonely and at loose ends in the summer, they would often congregate in the Grill for card games and company. Unlike the regular Iowa State men, who ignored me, the Indians or Germans or Filipinos tried to flirt with me in their broken English, rapidly commenting in their own language, poking each other if they thought someone had gotten a response. My mother had taught me never to strike up conversations with strange men, and I usually confined myself to polite smiles and shakes of the head. Eventually they would give up and go back to cards, only glancing occasionally in my direction. After they had left, I would sometimes find a few nickels and dimes scattered for me under their plates. Those were the only tips I ever got.

One summer clearing tables at the Grill was enough to convince me that I needed another job. Stacking dishes, I knew, wasn't going to lead to anything; I should be exercising my talents, such as they were. So I was delighted to be asked to serve as assistant to the Ames Playground Drama Director, who happened to be a neighbor, friend and faculty colleague of my mother's. A vivacious, assertive woman who frightened me a little by her sheer energy and organization, Dorothy Mae Frankel would certainly teach me something.

What I learned that summer may have been, in retrospect, preparation for certain aspects of college teaching: the ability to perform under unfavorable conditions, the instant tailoring of material to fit the audience, the necessity to keep going no matter what. Every weekday noon, just as the sun shone hottest, Mrs. Frankel honked her car outside my door. Sleepy from the heat, thinking longingly of our cool dark basement with its old rocking chair and a pile of books, I hurried out, slid gingerly across the hot plastic seat, and squinted my eyes as we barreled toward the concrete and brown grass of the city playgrounds. Mrs. Frankel crisply outlined our schedule for the afternoon: Whittier, Welch, a longer stop at Roosevelt.

When we arrived at the first playground, its harried director, relieved to see us, blew long blasts on her whistle to assemble the children in whatever shade we could find. Hurrying behind Mrs. Frankel, I lugged with me a bulging laundry basket filled with old costumes and a few props, a fancier version of a "dress-up box" intended to keep some of the smaller children amused. Older children could be given scripts, dittoed poems, or short stories to act out. But first they all needed to be warmed up, and I was the crowd-pleaser. After everyone had more or less quieted down, settling haphazardly into the dirt or forming into rows under the nudging of the playground director, I stepped determinedly forward. Mrs. Frankel had taught me a simple narrative, "Bear Hunt," with sounds and gestures about an Indian, a journey, his fright and his sudden retreat. It must be an old camp favorite, and any summer now I expect Jennifer to come home with her version of it. The trick was to get the crowd of restless children to copy my actions, join in, and then, reversing the narrative, speed up as fast as possible for the Indian's return trip. This led to a wonderful hulla-baloo of sounds, hands drumming on knees, growls, screams, general shouting and hallooing, ending in a hysterical collapse of giggles, shoving, and war whoops. If I had done well, hurrying fast enough to get everyone thoroughly excited, Mrs. Frankel waited a few moments and then told me to do it once more, "now that everyone's got it." If the group was quick and lively, I improvised and added a little new material, evoking squeals of glee. By this time our audience was hooked. Hoarse but game, I began beating on my knees once more. After three playgrounds, and eight or nine Bear Hunts, I was exhausted. Bear Hunts rang in my head at night. But I had done them well, Mrs. Frankel assured me, and I could do them again tomorrow at a new set of playgrounds.

Following the Bear Hunt, Mrs. Frankel divided the children into groups for instantaneous versions of "Hansel and Gretel," "Rumpelstiltskin," or improvised plays based on the costume basket. If too many children had drifted away, we would combine into one group, and I took some of the parts myself. Then Mrs. Frankel directed me too, which, I felt, threatened my shaky position of authority, but I knew we had to keep the show going. So I only grumbled inwardly, wrapped an old velvet skirt over my head, and cackled, as directed, like a witch or a wicked step-mother. It might be humiliating, but it would pass the time: half an hour more, and we could all go home.

Promoting Bear Hunts to hot, restless children was only one of the ways I learned about salesmanship, which I grew up intuitively recognizing as the backbone of the Ames work ethic. Selling a product and selling yourself were inextricable. My earliest lesson in this axiom was during the annual drive to sell Camp Fire candy. Even as a young Bluebird, I was eligible to peddle my boxes of candy at fifty cents a box, and I responded eagerly to the challenge. Whoever sold the most boxes would be awarded a free week at Camp Hantesa, a resident camp on the Des Moines River, with real cabins, tents, and teepees. I was beside myself with anxiety and ambition. Most of my friends were Camp Fire Girls too, and they had first dibs on their own neighborhoods. That didn't leave much free territory, though I was out knocking on doors the very afternoon the sales sheets were distributed. After covering a mile around our house, and often discovering a particular block had been picked clean by some nearby Camp Fire Girl, I had a brilliant idea. I shared it with no one but my mother, who could be trusted to keep it safe from my rivals. I would peddle my candy in Pammel Court.

Pammel Court, which still stands amazingly more or less intact, was a cluster of prefabricated metal buildings hastily thrown up at the edge of the Iowa State campus after World War II to house the flood of returning veterans and their families. "Married student housing" is a dingy-sounding phrase, but it was almost too glamorous a description for Pammel Court. The rows of silver barracks looked like a prison camp, only it lacked barbed wire and guards. In summer, the corrugated roofs baked their inhabitants like ovens; in winter, wind blew through the uninsulated walls lined with cardboard. Tiny squares of worn grass were sometimes cultivated into foot-long gardens, but mainly children played in the Pammel streets, which were dirt tracks running between the barracks, or in a small playground somewhere in the middle of the complex. Years later, when I was older, I was told that Pammel residents had a wonderful community spirit, but when I was only ten, all I could see were battered screens, running noses, tiny rooms, and tired-looking women at the door.

Pammel Court, however, had two distinct advantages for the

candy-seller: a compact population and plenty of mothers. I knew that I could cover many more families in an afternoon at Pammel than I could by trudging up long sidewalks or crossing endless lawns. The women who opened their plastic storm doors to me in Pammel were young enough to remember their own Camp Fire days, sympathetic to a friendly child, ready with a smile if not always with money. So I filled my old red wagon with boxes of candy, asked my mother to drive me to the entrance, and began a long tour of Pammel Court, dragging the wagon behind me. My only difficulty was in remembering which rows I'd already traveled, since they all looked alike. The candy sold quickly. When my wagon was empty, I took future orders, noting names and addresses on my sales sheet. Though it seems to me I spent weeks and weeks in Pammel, feeling the hot sun beat down on my unshaded back, hearing babies crying from inside the dark little rooms, kicking the early-autumn dust with my sneakers, it was probably only several afternoons after school. When I had filled several sheets with orders, I was exhausted, both from my long tramps around Pammel and from the energy my salesmanship required, the cheerful smile, polite inquiry, eagerness. My list was impressive, though, and I dreamed of walking up to the podium at the annual Camp Fire Fair, where awards would be announced.

But I didn't win a prize. Worn out from my exertions, perhaps susceptible to the first flu bugs of the oncoming winter, I got sick. I had to stay in bed for days, and even when I got up again, Mother wouldn't let me out of the house for long. Home from school, I collapsed in a tired little heap on my bed; outside the weather had changed, the wind howled, rain poured. No trips to Pammel Court. When the last call went out to our Camp Fire troop for ordering boxes from the supplier, I wasn't there to hear it. After I was well again, a girlfriend and I practiced bedrolls so we could do a team demonstration at the Camp Fire Fair. Mother said she thought she could afford to send me to Camp Hantesa for a week anyway. The next year I didn't try to sell much candy, and I never went back to Pammel Court. I was afraid some of the women whose orders had never arrived might remember me and ask what had happened.

I didn't give up the idea of selling, however, since I could tell I had a certain persuasive skill. Perhaps what I needed was a more secure home base, I thought, none of this door-to-door stuff. Somehow I learned that the supermarket across from Welch Junior High needed an after-school salesgirl in its bakery department, and I applied. Tying on a white apron, cleaner than the one I'd worn at the Union Grill, I presided over a small corner of the store, tucked behind the checkout stands, just inside the large plate-glass window that faced Welch School. There I could sit on the window ledge, looking onto the sidewalk and playgrounds, or I could burrow back against the wall to read or do homework on a small stool. It was like having a window on the world, which passed me by a few inches away. My friends hammered on the double-paned glass, made funny faces, tried to shout through; but, afraid to break the silence of the store, I only gestured back. I had withdrawn into a kind of cocoon, sweet and sticky, with only the buzz of shoppers and the rattle of shopping carts for company. For two hours all I said, like a recording, was "May I help you?" "Here you are." "Thank you."

Few customers drifted to my corner of the Hy-Valu, since the bakery department was small, its goods delivered twice a week and often stale. Sometimes the same decorated cake would wait in the case from one Monday to the next. After four or five days, I was allowed to label items "day old" and sell them at half price. Uneasy at this shady practice, I often whispered advice across the counter: "I'd skip the bismarcks today," or "I think those cookies have been around a while." I alerted the pleasant-looking customers, and let unpleasant ones take their chances. Mostly I sat, read, ate glazed doughnuts and tried to stay awake. At least when I was bored at the Union Grill, I could move around, wiping tables or adjusting salt shakers. Here I had no space, just a window ledge, a stool, and hot afternoon sun warming my back through the window. When I had cleaned empty trays, stacked rows of cookies more artistically, shooed stray flies out of the case, and dusted the countertop, I had nothing else to do. Eventually the boredom, sleepiness, and general heaviness of the job weighed me down so much I quit. I had gained five pounds.

If drowsing my way through a dull afternoon was not my idea of a good job, neither was hard physical labor. For two summers, at thirteen and fourteen, when I was too young to do anything else, I detasseled corn, a job that lasted only three or four weeks, but one so strenuous and numbingly exhausting that it later seemed to have stretched over the whole summer.

During that brief time, hordes of teen-agers were hauled into the local seed farms, where half- or quarter-mile rows of corn alternated, one male row to four female rows. In order for the plants to crossbreed correctly, the tassels had to be removed from the female cornstalks. A swift tug at the tall silky stem, a toss to the ground, another tug at the next tassel. Repetitive, numbing work, but it was good money. White's Hybrid Seed Farms, the biggest employer, offered a bonus: fifty cents an hour if you quit, but sixty-five if you stuck the whole season. Both summers I worked to what I thought was the limit of my endurance to earn that fifteen-cent-an-hour bonus.

Signing up for a detasseling crew didn't take much: a phone call, then a written statement of age, address, and height. A few very tall girls were put into special foot crews, but most of us were automatically assigned to machines. No boys worked on machines; we understood that it was tougher to do the work on foot. A day detasseling began at six A.M., when my alarm went off, so I could be dressed and waiting at the corner gas station by seven for a pickup truck. The driver didn't wait; he had to gather teen-age girls all over Ames. We all wore varieties of the same uniform: swimming suits, over which we pulled jeans or shorts, shirts, and large floppy hats. Early mornings in the field were cool and dewy, and we'd shiver a little as the wet stalks brushed our thighs. But by midday we'd be so hot and sweaty that we'd gratefully peel down as far as possible, hosing each other off in the farmyard where we took our lunch break. Now we huddled in the truck, keeping out of the cold breeze that whipped our faces if we stood up too far. I loved the ride into the country, jouncing in the box, watching the morning brighten on the fields around us. I wished we could just keep driving.

Once the truck dropped us in the White Farms parking lot, we waited for other trucks or cars, bringing girls from outlying farms or from small towns farther away. On the first day we were quickly divided into crews and assigned to machines. We would keep the same driver, always a man, for the whole season. He was our field boss, who reported if we slacked off or caused trouble, who could queer our bonus, who reigned as absolute dictator from his metal seat high above us. One lucky crew drew Ben Bowie, a handsome older Ames High boy. At lunchtime one of my friends on Ben's machine would always tell me whom he'd flirted with that day. My crew, however, got Pancho, so christened on our first day by someone who was struck by his fat red face under an enormous Mexican sombrero. He was much older, perhaps in his twenties, crude and ignorant, as well as paunchy. We had to humor him constantly, laughing at his dirty stories, many of which I didn't understand, answering his questions, smiling pleasantly. Fortunately we couldn't hear him often over the roar of the machine. If only, I thought, I could have gotten Ben Bowie.

Describing a detasseling machine to a college roommate was once so difficult I was finally reduced to drawing a picture of a sort of mechanical spider. I think of that picture now, seeing Pancho as the two beady eyes at the spider's head. From a tractor-like seat, Pancho drove a machine that consisted of an engine, with two platforms on each side of it, and four branching metal arms that were suspended from the center at distances adjusted to the corn rows, each with its own platform. We girls stood on the platforms, leaning over metal encircling rods that prevented us from falling, and pulled the tassels from the cornstalks as the machine huffed along. Pancho was supposed to cover a certain amount of

territory each day, and he set the speed we had to follow. Relentlessly, inexorably, the machine moved down the rows, while we
plucked, yanked, pulled. If Pancho speeded up too much, we
started to miss stalks, and then he swore loudly, stopped the machine, and waited for us to dismount, hurry back on foot, and get
the missed tassels. He slowed then for a while, but before long he
speeded up again. Of course he couldn't always see every tassel, or
watch all of us at once, and sometimes we let a tassel slip by un-
noticed. I was too squeamish to grasp the stalks that were covered
with insects, or the ones distorted by smut, a fungus that makes
the stalk swell and rot. If Pancho caught me shirking a bloated
stalk, he shouted, stopped the machine, and I angrily stomped
down the row, grabbed the stalk by its roots, and just pulled the
whole plant out. As long as the tassel wasn't going to pollinate,
Pancho didn't care. Otherwise the machine didn't stop until we'd
reached the end of a half-mile row. Then we dismounted, drank
from the lukewarm cooler of water strapped to the machine,
stretched our cramped muscles, applied more suntan lotion, and
climbed wearily back on board for another row.

Row breaks and lunchtime were our only real chances for conversation, though you could sometimes shout to the girl standing
on the platform next to you. At lunchtime we had chatted briefly
while eating our gooey peanut-butter or soggy cream-cheese
sandwiches, splashing in the hose, or stretching prone on the
green mown grass of the Whites' front yard. I remember broken
bits of talk with other girls on my machine as part of my education. Usually three or four were girls I didn't know, from farms or
small towns I never visited, girls who seemed older, with bigger
busts, redder lipstick, real swearwords. They often understood
Pancho's dirty jokes and could top them. One girl even told me
she thought Pancho was "kind of cute." These girls talked of
dances, beer, cruising, necking. They were tough, unafraid of smut,
mildew, or insects; grasping an infected stalk firmly, they'd simply
wipe their slimy hands on their shorts. "For God's sake," one

called after me as I ran back to bend over a mildewed stalk, "what the hell are you scared of? Them things won't bite you." Pancho grinned in approval. "You know," he said several times a day, usually when we were slowly rolling back and forth to different fields, "you Ames kids are sure picky. Real snotty. Hey, Sue! Emily! Whaddya think? Are all Ames girls snotty?" My friend Emily and I looked at each other, reddened, and were silent. The other girls laughed. One, older at fifteen than I'd be at twenty, was engaged, she said, to a man who was taking over his father's farm soon. Then they'd get married. She didn't own a swimsuit, so when the sun glared directly overhead, she stripped off her shirt to a dingy gray cotton bra, sagging from the weight of her heavy breasts. It was so thick and laced with elastic that it hid her body better than a swimsuit might. Even Pancho, after a few wolf whistles and lewd remarks, which she ignored, didn't seem to find the sight very exciting and soon turned his attention to someone else. I was embarrassed for her, and glad that she pulled her shirt on again when the machine turned onto the road to head back to the farm at the end of the day.

Piling into our pickup truck, carrying our wadded clothes and lunchpails, we lay back for the hot, dusty trip home. After being dropped off, I dragged myself the few blocks to my house, and a long tepid bath. Dirt caked the sides of the tub. After dinner I was too tired to go out, even to a movie. Falling into bed like a stone, my reddened back stinging, my face flushed from too much sun, I tried to think of the wonderful tan I'd have, the money I'd make if I stuck the whole season. I was asleep even before it got dark outside.

After two seasons of detasseling, I was through. I had earned my bonus and a sense of survival with it. Now finally old enough for real summer jobs, I wanted glamour. Aided by persistence, luck, and perhaps a mention of my father, whom he said he'd known, I persuaded the general manager of the college radio and television station to hire me at fifteen as a courier and part-time receptionist. As courier, I'd carry mail back and forth from the television station to the third story of the nearby communications building. As receptionist, I'd answer the phone and type simple letters for secretaries who were taking vacations. I was thrilled. To work inside WOI-TV! Mingle with celebrities! Watch live shows! Every day I dressed carefully, my prettiest circle skirts, fresh ribbons around my ponytail. Every day something magical might happen, though I wasn't certain exactly what. Being so close to the entertainment industry, who could tell?

What I mainly saw, however, were closed doors. No one was allowed into a studio when a show was on. What I heard were tired, irritable voices, hassling over timing, guests, and the deadline of another show tomorrow. I particularly admired a young director from Chicago, Len Finkelstein, who came to WOI-TV that summer and left the next year; black-haired, sharp-nosed, and wiry, he snapped out commands to everyone around him, including the old-timers who had been with the station since television came to Ames. They didn't much like his arrogance, I could see, but he had a convincing big-city air about him: "We did it that way in Chicago," he'd say, or "Ed Murrow once told me, confidentially, of course . . ." Sometimes he wandered into the cubicle where pretty Liz Woods perched, when she wasn't planning her morning women's show. "Liz," he crooned, "geez, I miss that city so much. How do you all *stand* it here? I mean, year after year?" She laughed and their voices sank to a low murmur I couldn't hear.

Beauty, polish, and self-confidence floated around Liz like an expensive perfume. All the men in the station scrambled after her, finding excuses to sit on her desk, ask her if she wanted coffee, offer to run her home. She was careless of them; of her desk, piled high with mail and packages; of her expensive wardrobe, which even I could tell hadn't been bought in Ames. Once in the women's room, where Liz changed clothes, leaving some on hangers, others strewn on the floor, I saw in a corner a bundle that looked familiar. I unrolled it. It was a matching cashmere skirt-and-sweater set, in a lovely powder blue, which I'd admired the previous week as Liz had sailed around the offices, her hand patting her slim hips. I had never owned a cashmere sweater. This one had a smear of makeup on it now, as did the soiled skirt. They lay in the corner, waiting for someone, not Liz, to take them to the cleaners or perhaps even give them up for good. I carefully smoothed and folded them and put them back in the corner. When I quit my job a month later, they were still there. As I think now of my brief introduction to the mystique of television, my first image is a dirty, crumpled cashmere sweater.

I didn't quit WOI because I didn't like my job, but because I got one better. For several years, probably since I was ten or eleven, I had timidly knocked on the glass door of the Ames *Daily Tribune*'s publisher, an old man with a sharp wit and good business sense, and a fondness for enterprise in young people. He laughed at first when I explained I wanted to work on the newspaper, I was going to be a reporter someday, I could write well already, I was editing the junior-high paper. But he treated me seriously too, listened to my whole application, then patted me on the shoulder as he dismissed me. "Come back in a year or two," he said, "and we'll see." I kept coming back, he was encouraging but noncommittal, until that summer I was fifteen. Then suddenly the society editor got sick and needed an operation. Mr. Skaggs called my mother. Would I like to come to work as soon as possible, just until the society editor got back? She was sure I would, I had a talk with the station manager next day, and I left for the *Tribune* offices the following morning.

From that summer on, all the way through college, I spent my summers filling vacation spots and doing odd jobs at the *Tribune*. My first editor, Clarence, a gentle, quiet man, spoiled me; pleased at what he kindly said was my quickness and rapid progress, he taught me a few basics about type, headlines, and layout and then left me to do what I wanted. As long as I clocked forty hours a week, I could go out evenings on a feature assignment, come in late next morning, leave early in the afternoon. He encouraged and praised me. The second editor, Rob, who arrived my second year, was a much younger and tenser man, who thought I had become an office pet; he wanted me to go back and start from the ground up. I learned from both of them, though not always what they thought they were teaching me. Of course I acquired some basic journalistic skills, memorizing the right questions, compiling data, editing and proofing, juggling headlines. I also began to understand for the first time how one could be passionately committed to a job well done. Most of the day our small newsroom was in chaos, five of us elbow-to-elbow, phones ringing, old typewriters clacking, doors constantly swinging open to the business office on one side, the back room and presses on the other. But when the first paper rolled off the presses, and our editor carried in five copies and flung them down on the one big desk we all shared, suddenly the room was silent. Except for the flap of turning pages, small grunts of approval and whispers of dismay, we were all studying our work, adjusting our expectations to results, quietly noting what we might do differently next time. I always felt a certain amazement at seeing a whole paper, neat and finished, emerge from our slapdash, frantic efforts of the hours before. There it was until tomorrow.

Although moving relentlessly down a row of corn on a detasseling machine held its own tension, until my summers on the *Tribune* I never really understood what working under pressure meant. Despite my love for the work, that pressure may be the main reason I eventually decided newspaper life wasn't for me. At first I mostly worried about typing. Just before I came to the *Tribune*, I bought a typing book and managed to learn the keyboard. But faced with a crotchety, oversized machine, and a story to be retyped within an hour, I quickly had to get a steady rhythm, and get it fast. As work piled up on my share of the desk, I was constantly aware of the huge clock on the wall above us, its minute hand sweeping by. If I looked too long at it, it mesmerized me, until someone else at the desk poked me. Then I'd snap back to attention, and bury myself in my rewrites again. I had always been a perfectionist in my writing, toying with my English essays, adding flourishes to my poems, rewriting and finally printing them all carefully by hand. Now I had to pick words quickly, not always wait for the right ones to appear, ignore unanswered questions if I couldn't find solutions right away, read quickly and make as few corrections as possible. When my galleys came back from the shop, I could sometimes sweet-talk Harley, the gray-haired, grandfatherly typesetter who liked me, into making a few cosmetic changes, but if Rob, the editor, caught me, he was furious. "Harley's got other things to do than pretty up your prose," he'd say. "Get your picture caption on my desk right now and let that story go." When I left the office in the afternoon, I was exhausted, my stomach in knots, my shoulders tight from having hunched over my typewriter.

Much of the fun of my job, aside from the daily delirious pleasure of seeing my writing, and sometimes my by-line, in print, came from faking a certain professionalism. From my first summer, when I filled the women's page with recipes (when I didn't cook), articles on child care (when I didn't have a child), fashion (when I read only *Seventeen*), and marriage (what I knew least of all), I took great glee in posing as a grown-up who was an expert in all these matters. Scissoring out syndicated columns, clipping from the wire service, and even fabricating some stories myself, I applied what I thought was my own superior intelligence and common sense. One of my mother's friends, upon hearing of my new job, laughed and said to me, "Oh, don't worry, Susan, you'll do fine. Nobody reads the women's page anyway." I was a little hurt, but I knew she wasn't entirely right. Once in a while a reader would call in to complain that I'd missed a typesetting error, slipping two cups of salt into a recipe instead of two tablespoons. And all the women in outlying small towns read their local "correspondence columns," filled with items about baby showers, bridge clubs, out-of-town visitors, and birthdays.

Families, down to the last cousin, always read the detailed wedding stories it was then the *Tribune*'s principle to print in full:

I had to ascertain whether the soloist sang "I Love You Truly" or "The Voice That Breath'd o'er Eden," if the bride wore pearls that were a gift of the groom, whether she carried a bouquet of stephanotis or white roses, the length of her veil and the style of her bridesmaids' gowns, who cut the cake, what the bride wore as a going-away outfit. Most of these details I merely copied from the *Tribune*'s standard wedding form, but sometimes deciphering handwriting or unscrambling description led me into omissions or vague generalities: "The bride, in a white scoop-necked gown, wore pearls." Then I might have to confront a critical mother, who had driven all the way from a little town an hour away, storming into the newsroom, demanding to see the Society Editor, and blinking, open-mouthed, at a fifteen-year-old with intense self-possession that I fought hard to keep from slipping. I wore heavy earrings in those days to balance the flippancy of my ponytail. With my swishing crinolines and round-collared blouses, and a furious blush when I was upset, I must have been a strange sight in that clacking, ringing, little newsroom. If I couldn't soothe my angry critic, Rob usually stepped in; I was always surprised at the iron quality he could suddenly assume. After the mother had left, he would turn to me, the iron only slightly softened, and snap, "Next time, Allen, get it right." Years later, when I was married in Ames, I made sure the organist played Handel, the wedding cake was chocolate, and nobody gave me pearls.

So I knew I had an audience, even if it wasn't my mother's friends. Most of them depended for news on the Des Moines paper and claimed they only read the *Trib* for grocery ads. "Too big to line your drawers and too small to wrap the garbage in," wisecracked our neighbor Mr. Ball. I had the freedom to make mistakes without fearing that I would damage either my or the *Tribune*'s reputation forever.

Since I was so young, the other reporters and even the subjects I was sometimes sent to interview took an amused interest in me and offered me all the help I wanted. When my job eventually involved filling any gap or need in the editorial department, I found myself by turns society editor, religion editor, farm editor, and general reporter. The only department no one trusted me with, quite rightly, was sports. As farm editor for three weeks the summer I was sixteen, I only had to copy-edit news releases and prepare the layout of the weekly farm page, which my editor supervised closely. But I did have to make several trips into the country, nervously driving the *Tribune* staff car, which, since I barely knew how to shift, I usually kept in first or second gear. My most important job was to interview the Mystery Farm of the Week. An aerial photographer was hired to zoom over surrounding farms and snap pictures, one of which appeared on Monday, with a Mystery Caption. Readers were invited to send in their guesses about whose farm it was. On Friday, farm-page day, the *Tribune* ran a long feature, with lots of pictures, about the family who lived there. It was my job to do the feature.

On my first visit to a Mystery Farm, I tried to do it alone. Now sixteen, I wanted to carry off my job like a pro. Since I constantly ground the old Plymouth's gears and killed its engine at every stop sign, I was already shaken by the time I crawled up the long dirt drive to the Janacek farm. Once safely inside the Janaceks' kitchen, I felt more at home; Mrs. Janacek, kindly and talkative, chatted easily with me about her life. I was able to understand something about her routine and ask fairly intelligent questions about her baking, sewing, church circle, and prize-winning honey. But when Mr. Janacek stamped in from the barn, his heavy boots and overalls thick with mud, I was daunted. Pleased with the idea of a newspaper story, he was eager to help too. But I didn't know what to ask him. "How are the crops?" I ventured weakly. He answered, and I took copious notes, but he might as well have been speaking in Greek. He took me around the farm, where I snapped dozens of pictures with my heavy box camera, having no idea what I was photographing or why. "What kind of pigs are those?" I occasionally managed, or "Isn't the corn unusually high for this time of year?" Mr. Janacek either assumed I knew more than I let on or pretended not to notice.

When I had returned to the office, and my developed photographs lay scattered around my desk, I felt utterly defeated. I had no idea what to write under any of them. Then, like a deus ex machina, John Crawford, the county agent, appeared in the newsroom door. Soon I was to learn how important and respected a man he was in the countryside around Ames; now I was merely grateful that someone with answers could help me with my story. He was easy to ask, a friendly, open man, with sandy hair, a sunburned face, and ready jokes. My editor always took time for a cup of coffee when John stopped by the newsroom. John took a quick look at my rough copy and began to laugh, checking himself only when he saw my wounded face. "Next week, Susan, why don't you let me come along with you?" he asked gently, sliding into an empty chair and grabbing a pencil. I could see him choking down laughter as he made notes on my copy.

I must have learned something about farm life from those weeks as farm editor, including two afternoon trips tagging behind John Crawford. I even have a graying snapshot John took of me standing in a cornfield; I am wearing huge organdy earrings shaped like butterflies, a full-skirted summer dress, and high heels. I look hot, plump, and out of place. My editor stuck this snapshot on our bulletin board with the label, "Our farm editor: Iowa raises corn and pork," and I immediately went on a diet. Yet only last year, when a friend who had given up teaching Latin for farming began talking about his heifers, I let slip that I didn't know cows had to give birth in order to give milk. For almost four decades, I had assumed that when female calves grew up, they simply became cows and began to give milk nonstop. My own breast-feeding experience had never suggested to me anything about other animals. John Crawford would have been amused.

When we were short on local news, the editor often suggested topics to me for long pictorial features, usually about Ames residents with unusual hobbies or exotic travel experiences. One day he assigned me to interview Willie Tallman about the pipe organ he was building in his basement. For three years I'd taken organ lessons myself, and I was confident I could do an informed piece. I talked to Willie at his real-estate office one afternoon and then spent a long evening in his basement, taking pictures and scribbling notes. Though the story wasn't as promising as I'd hoped, I turned in several pages of typescript to my editor next afternoon with the feeling of a job well done. After spending a half-hour in the back room checking on my pictures and captions, I returned to the newsroom to find my managing editor, the women's editor, the sportswriter and the general reporter all convulsed in laughter. "What's so funny?" I asked innocently. "Nothing, nothing," breathed the sports editor, trying to suppress his snorts. Even Rob had a grin on his face when he said, "Here's your copy, Susan. I've made a few changes. Run it back to Harley now."

Changes? In *my* copy? I snatched the manuscript and glanced over it. Everywhere I'd written the word *organ*, he had inserted the prefix "pipe." I couldn't understand why. "Hey, Rob," I said complainingly, "this sounds funny. How come you want me to repeat 'pipe' all the time?" The sportswriter began to snort again. Mary Ann, the women's editor, beckoned to me. "Come on, kid, let's go to the ladies' room," she said firmly. I followed, still puzzled and irritated by the laughter behind me. Once we were squeezed into the tiny dark room, she said, "Susan. Listen. You just can't print the sentence, 'Most nights Willie plays around with his organ.'" "Why not?" I asked belligerently. She paused, herself evidently puzzled about what to say next. "You know what organ means, don't you?" she finally asked. "Of course," I said, getting even angrier. "Does it mean anything besides pipe organ?" "It's his thing," she said, looking embarrassed. She gestured vaguely toward her crotch. "Didn't you know?"

I was struck silent. That had never occurred to me. How stupid, I thought. Grown-ups have such dirty minds. None of my friends would laugh at something like that. But I blushed anyway at my innocence. Mary Ann thoughtfully left me alone in the ladies' room, and I stayed there for some time, splashing my cheeks with cool water. When I walked back into the newsroom, everyone was bent assiduously over his work. I snatched the revised copy and carried it out to the typesetter. But for weeks afterward, the sportswriter would ask me if I was going out that night and if my date was planning to play a little on his organ?

From gearshifts and pork production statistics to double-entendres, my summers on the *Tribune* were educational. But probably the *Tribune*'s most important contribution was to show me day after day how wildly various life was. Poring over a wire story about famine in India, or correcting a local correspondent's excesses about a golden wedding in Zearing, I was exposed to overwhelming trivia inflated to importance and overwhelming importance reduced to trivia. I began to acquire a fledgling ironic sense, a perspective that permanently altered the way I looked at things. So much was funny, even absurd, and I had to pretend it wasn't; or it wasn't funny at all, but I had to refuse to take it too seriously. One long hot summer, the last I worked on the *Tribune*, a really big story broke in Ames. In one of the steaming tin bungalows of Pammel Court, a young husband had gone berserk and killed his three small children. His wife had escaped. Writers and photographers alit from Des Moines, our editor himself went out to the college to handle the story, and I was the only one left in the newsroom when Rob returned, sober-faced late in the day. "Okay," he said shortly, "there's only one thing I want you to do before you go. Call Mrs. Johnson and talk to her." "You mean his *wife?*" I asked incredulously. "That's right," he said, and banged the door into the back room. I sat numbly and stared at my telephone. What in the world would I say? Would I ask her if he was crazy? Had he always been crazy? How did she feel about it? My stomach began to sicken. Twenty minutes later Rob walked in. "Well?" he asked. "Is the story ready?" "I can't do it, Rob," I said. Tears trembled in my eyes. "I just can't do it." He looked at me. I looked at him. The he sighed. "No, of course you can't," he said. "I can't do it either. Forget it." He took the typescript from the desk and disappeared.

That's the way I like to think it happened. Remembering that hot afternoon, my shock at the murder, the shiver with which I drove by Pammel Court on my way home that night, I feel the incident strongly but am uncertain of its details. Although I can recall many of the minutiae of my childhood, I have had to invent the dialogue between Rob and me. Somehow I've drawn a curtain over that afternoon. Eager as I was to prove myself a real reporter, curious, shut out from the scene of the crime, it might well have been I who suggested to Rob that I call the wife, not the other way round. He may have rejected *my* request. Since I like to remember myself as sensitive and tenderhearted, I may have constructed this dialogue in self-defense. All I am sure of is that the idea of calling the wife came up and that it was rejected.

But if my last vivid memory of working at the *Tribune* is shrouded in moral confusion, that in itself has a truth of its own. All the lessons I learned in my jobs as I was growing up in Ames now seem to me ambiguous. I wonder about the hypocrisy with which I approached babysitting, the intensity with which I hustled Camp Fire candy, my brooding melancholy as a Union Grill waitress. Only my summers in the cornfields have a kind of awful simplicity. When I left Ames, I took with me an underlying sense of a work ethic that highlighted dedication but left much else in shadow. Perhaps that inconclusiveness was a most important preparation for life.

Holidays

Holidays light up the sky of my daughter's life like dazzling sky-rockets, briefly cascading before her eyes before disappearing into the darkness of time. When one star has gone out, she looks for the flash of another on the horizon. "Mommy, what special day will May have?" she asks, disconsolate but hopeful, after the Easter eggs, greenish with age, have been ground up in the disposal. "But what do we do special on Memorial Day, Mommy?" Sometimes she makes me recite the full litany of the year's holidays: New Year's, Valentine's, St. Patrick's, Easter, Mother's Day, Memorial Day, Father's Day, her half-birthday, my full birthday, Fourth of July, Labor Day, her father's birthday, Halloween, Thanksgiving, Christmas, her real birthday two days later, and back to New Year's. She recites them after me, an alphabet of anticipation. "It won't be long now till Christmas and my birthday, will it, Mommy?" she asks after Labor Day. "It'll just be Halloween and Thanksgiving first."

I wonder at the continuous sparkle of my daughter's year. Not only does she want to celebrate all the holidays, she is incited to presents for each one—at least a trip to a store to buy something appropriate, an inflatable Easter bunny, a small flag, cardboard skeletons to hang in our windows. When I was growing up, Ames did not pay much attention to most holidays. The stores didn't bother with window displays of shamrocks or Irish coffee mugs in March, though some of us school-children reminded each other to wear something green on St. Patrick's

Day, hoping to trap with embarrassment those who forgot. Nobody bought cards for Father's Day, and we didn't worry much about Mother's Day presents either. Even Christmas didn't begin to appear in the downtown stores until well into December, when the city fathers draped Main Street with a few red paper bells and evergreen loops, put some lights on a tree or two, and considered the season adequately announced.

Although we Iowans certainly considered ourselves patriotic—we knew we were the heart of the country—we didn't get very excited about the Fourth of July, Armistice Day, Lincoln's or Washington's Birthday, or Memorial Day. On the Fourth Ames always managed some kind of city celebration, a band concert in a park, perhaps a small parade, free fireworks after dark, and for several years a traveling carnival parked on an empty lot near the center of town. It wasn't much, just Tilt-a-Whirl cars, a merry-go-round, a Ferris wheel and lots of stands where you could pitch dimes into glass dishes or try to knock milk bottles over with three softballs. Some families drove to the Ledges State Park and picnicked.

On Memorial Day, a small religious service was held in the college cemetery. A brass band played "Taps," and then a rifle team fired blanks, while we children held our ears and quaked with excitement. Afterward a lone bugler stationed in the woods below the cemetery echoed the "Taps," distant and quavery in the cold spring morning. My mother often wept. My father was buried at the edge of the carefully mown grass near the woods, and we placed some fresh flowers on his stone before going home. But we obviously didn't look forward to Memorial Day as any kind of treat. It was a solemn occasion tinged by the sadness of the grown-ups' faces around us. To my daughter Jennifer, it is simply another day off from school, and thus cause for celebration.

Perhaps one reason Jennifer looks forward to holidays so eagerly is that she does not have one holiday that Ames observed weekly. Ames sank on Sunday into a special quiet. Almost everyone went to church in the morning, children to Sunday school and parents to the eleven o'clock service. We walked, so the sidewalks on our side of town were filled with a procession of families, or children walking alone, all dressed up in "Sunday best." My daughter has party clothes, but they are not the same thing. "Sunday best" was your new dress, something you were supposed to save as though it were an investment, with shiny shoes, perhaps even a little flowered hat. One's whole Sunday outfit had a sanctimonious air. After church, we children hung around on the steps or church lawn, admiring each other, waiting for the grown-ups to stop visiting. We were hungry, but we'd have to wait; dinner was late on Sunday, because mothers couldn't get it on the table until an hour or two after church was over. Not long ago Jennifer and I were invited for Sunday dinner with some friends my age who live in a nearby small town, where they have kept up Sunday traditions. When we sat down to roast beef, mashed potatoes with gravy, peas, Parker House rolls, strawberry jam, cottage cheese salad with a pineapple ring, red Jell-O, and lemon meringue pie, I was in ecstasy. "Look, Jennifer!" I cried. "This is a real Sunday dinner. Look, look!" She stared at me. She had no idea what I was talking about. After Sunday dinner, my friends' children and Jennifer scattered to the television, and I left to do some shopping at the Red Owl before we headed home. That was not what happened on my childhood Sunday afternoons. Children read books, thought about homework assignments but didn't do them, maybe wandered over to friends' houses. Grown-ups leafed through the Des Moines Sunday paper and napped. When we were in high school, we sometimes went in groups to the afternoon movies, but my ninth-grade Sunday-school teacher had disapproved so strongly of Sunday movies that a residue of guilt crept into the movie theatre with me and took the edge off my pleasure. Nothing else in town was open, not a gas station or a grocery store. Sunday night we all ate light suppers, soft-boiled eggs or Velveeta sandwiches, and went to bed early, hushed into sleep by the slowed rhythms of the day.

No, my year was not a restless search for holidays. Time seemed like a gentle wave, a long slow sweep of months moving toward summer, peaking in August during our annual trip to my mother's family home in Minnesota. Then the wave rose again, briefly crested at the opening of school in September, and finally broke with a joyous crash *against the Christmas holidays. After Christmas began the long slow movement again toward summer.*

I try to join in Jennifer's celebrations. When she wants an Easter-egg hunt, I arrange one. I hang the skeletons on our window and blow up the inflatable reindeer or bunnies. I ooh and aah at what her art class made for Mother's Day, and next year, I promise, maybe next year we can go downtown in St. Paul and watch the St. Patrick's Day parade. Yes, it is true, I tell her, here in the Twin Cities we also have an Aquatennial and a Winter Carnival, but we are not going this year. I am too busy, and that is part of the truth. But the rest of the truth is that I cannot sparkle so often for so many occasions. My spirit rises on schedule for those few joyous days when school lets out for a summer vacation and again when the Christmas tree is decked in December. Otherwise I prefer to stumble into holidays by accident and celebrate in surprise.

What I remember about most traditional "big" holidays, particularly Thanksgiving and Easter, is my sense of anticlimax. As a child I saw Norman Rockwell's large families, grandmothers, aunts, and cousins, all gathered thankfully around laden tables or shining trees in the *Saturday Evening Post*; from Louisa May Alcott to Laura Ingalls Wilder to the *St. Nicholas Anthology* I read about old-fashioned feasts, returns of prodigals, sleigh rides through the snow, joyous reunions, last-minute miracles and thanksgivings. But by the late forties and fifties in Ames, most of the families I knew hung on to vestiges of tradition with a determination that, if one listened closely to what the mothers said to each other on the telephone, came close to weariness.

Although the parents of my friends had always lived in Ames, as far as I could remember, *their* parents had not. A grandparent in visiting distance was rare, let alone a relative living in the same house. Most of us had aunts, uncles and cousins, but they were scattered in unlikely places, far enough away so that it wasn't a simple matter of a sleigh ride to bring them home for Christmas. Home, in any case, was indefinable; no one I knew lived in a house where their grandparents had lived before them. I had plenty of relatives, but aside from one set in Des Moines, thirty miles away, and another in Osage, a three-hour drive, they lived in Minnesota, North Dakota, Oklahoma, Idaho, Illinois and Colorado. There was no old homestead, no one place we could all converge.

So, early in my life, I do not remember when, my mother linked our little family to two others, the Harbingers and Kramers, who also had far-flung relatives, and together we created the illusion of family reunions on holidays. Although the Harbinger and Kramer children were close in age to my sister and myself, most of us were separated by different school grades and didn't see each other often. Coming together for holidays was indeed a kind of reunion, an oasis of time when we could enjoy each other without the pressure of remembering Freddie Kramer was only in seventh grade and his sister Lucy a mere fourth-grader, while I was already in eighth grade and practically in high school.

Thanksgiving, Easter, Christmas dinner all blend together in my mind, year after year, the same ritual of celebration. We salvaged some old traditions and managed to make our own as well, focusing mainly on food. Holiday dinner was served in mid-afternoon, when everyone was hungry from long-ago breakfast. The men relaxed for a half hour with martinis or sherry while, with a flurry in the kitchen, the women unpacked their pies or salads or rolls. We all joined the men in the living room briefly. The hostess of the day kept her apron on, a ruffled badge of responsibility. We children, dressed self-consciously in Sunday best, then wandered into each other's bedrooms, taking games off the shelves for later, poking at books, climbing on double-decker beds, trying to lose the younger children who padded eagerly behind us. When we heard the call for dinner, we scurried to find seats near the children we currently liked and far from our own parents, who might regulate what we were allowed to eat.

Dinners were long, and we ate like gluttons, stuffing as many helpings of everything into our groaning stomachs as possible.

Since none of us ever stuffed from real hunger on ordinary days, I
have often wondered how we all acquired the subliminal message
that on holidays we should eat, and eat, and eat. It was almost a
moral duty. The Allen-Harbinger-Kramer menu was never exotic, but it was always superbly prepared. Basics seldom varied:
turkey at Thanksgiving and Christmas, ham or roast beef or,
rarely, lamb at Easter. Mrs. Harbinger's gravy, brown, savory, and
creamy, was ladled over her hot potatoes, mashed with milk by
hand moments before in the kitchen. Her stuffings were moist,
nutty, soaked with warm juices. Mrs. Kramer's specialities included spicy cheese sauces on unusual vegetables like limas or ar-
tichokes, marinated mushrooms that of course we children never
ate, green grapes frosted with sugar. She was one of Ames's noted
gourmet cooks, and the first person to tell me how to use grape
shears. "Don't just pick off the grapes like that, Susan," she said
with some asperity. "It makes such a mess. Can't you see that's
what the shears are for?" I reddened. I had seen the silver scissors
lying on the table but had had no idea why they were there. "You
see how much neater?" she asked a few minutes later. I nodded
and munched my grapes with great care. I hoped no one would
notice the ugly bare branch I had unwittingly plucked clean.

We always had at least two desserts, my mother's hot apple pie
made with cinnamon, nutmeg and lemon juice; Mrs. Harbinger's
fudge brownies; maybe Mrs. Kramer's caramel custard with wine
sauce. Mrs. Kramer used colored liqueurs for her desserts, char-
treuse or red or cocoa-colored, and we children wrinkled our
noses as we rolled them on our tongues.

The dining room was always warm, filled with wonderful
smells, buzzing with talk. What did we talk about? The grown-ups
told jokes, sometimes from the *Reader's Digest*, sometimes about
us, and we said things like "Mother, don't tell them *that*," and
"Dad, that simply isn't *true*!" We exclaimed over the food, teased
each other about our boyfriends and girlfriends, asked someone to
please pass the gravy or butter or salt. Someone was always getting up to get something else from the kitchen. We groused about

our teachers, and our parents groused about us. "I wish Freddie would practice the flute more. Sometimes I think it's just a waste of our money." "Donald's paper route may be good training for him, but it's hell on my sleep." "Where did Karen learn to do those wonderful sketches I saw in the library last week? I can't seem to get Lucy interested in art at all." We children made faces and kicked each other under the table.

After coffee, the afternoon stretched sleepily before us. The grown-ups retired back to the living room, and we older children cleared, scraped, and took turns washing or drying dishes. It seemed hours before we could leave the steamy kitchen, the piles of plates, the cut-glass water goblets that had to be dried by hand with rolled corners of the flour-sack dishtowels. But then we had nothing to do. We sat for a while in the living room, listening to the grown-ups, who talked about Democratic politics, books, or college business. If we hung around too long, they roused themselves, looked at us, and someone suggested that maybe Freddie could play the flute now, or we could sing carols, or put on skits. So we children usually retired to a back bedroom or a den or even to the basement, where we brought out Chinese checkers, Scrabble, Monopoly, Sorry, or Chutes and Ladders. One year we played endless Canasta, another it was Ping-Pong. When the older children reached junior-high age, we begged our parents to drop us off at the movies. Ordinarily, given our age differences, none of us kids would have attended a movie together. But holidays were different. On this long afternoon we were prepared to see anything: Westerns, Ma and Pa Kettle, Francis the Talking Horse. Our parents almost always agreed to let us go, even on Christmas afternoon, perhaps anticipating a few hours of quiet. Sodden with food, we sat happily for two hours. Then it was dark, someone picked us up or we walked home together, finding our parents packing up leftovers. We thanked the hostess and then grinned shyly at the other children, whom we might not really talk to until the next holiday. When we got home, my mother seemed tired. We had had a good day together, hadn't we, she asked us, and we agreed. Our stomachs felt a little funny, but we knew we had celebrated.

Although we dressed up for Thanksgiving and Christmas dinners, we paid close attention to our clothes on only one holiday, Easter, that odd mixture Ames concocted from fading religious fervor and materialism. None of the families we knew was particularly religious, but we all did go to church on Easter Sunday. Most Protestant children even attended an extra service, called "sunrise," held at seven A.M. at a different church each year, followed by juice and rolls in the church basement. Perhaps because it was a rare chance to see boys from the other end of town, by the time we were eleven or twelve we paid special attention to our Easter outfits. Since Ames had no Easter parade, I still do not know why an Easter outfit seemed so important. After church we went home or to the Kramers' or Harbingers' for Easter dinner. Who could have noticed what I wore? Who could have cared? But, from some deep instinct, perhaps the putting on of new plumage for spring, most of us girls and even our mothers spent weeks in February and March sewing, or selecting, a spectacular Easter outfit, complete with dress or suit, hat, gloves. Except for an occasional wedding, Easter was the only time I wore gloves or a hat. Because Easter in Iowa often fell on a cold, even snowy, day, and our Easter outfits were by definition springlike fabrics like pink cotton piqué or organdy or linen, we shivered and chattered with cold on the dash from car to church, church to car. Abandoning our winter coats, we wore perky little toppers of light yellow fleece or navy tissue wool. They didn't keep much warm. Even when sleet rained on our beribboned hats, we held our heads high. Easter was supposed to be a spotlessly white holiday of lilies and cotton gloves, colored perhaps by the greens of plastic grass in egg baskets or the flaring spears of potted tulips. Mixing the colors of religion, nature, and vanity, we did our best to bloom.

Though I never got too excited about Easter, and considered Thanksgiving mainly as a brief school vacation devoted to gorging myself, I did store up enthusiasm for Christmas. Other holidays in Ames had a halfhearted air, a sense that people had done better in the old days. But Christmas remained intact, as exciting a holiday as any child could wish. Ames was often beautiful at Christmas, its neat rows of white and yellow clapboard houses framed by heaps of white snow, its dark evergreens lit by extravagant displays of outdoor lights. Night skies were cold but clear, and the stars seemed to dance like the lights on the trees. Once during the season, Mother would drive us around the town after dinner, circling downtown neighborhoods we seldom traveled, so we could admire the outdoor lights, the twinkling trees blazing through living-room windows, the wooden deer or makeshift sleighs or snowmen decorating front lawns.

On Christmas Eve our neighborhood children caroled, gathering at one house and ending at another for cocoa and Christmas cookies. No grown-ups were allowed to come along, only children old enough to be out at night by themselves. Even during the handful of years I caroled, I was aware of the passing of generations. At first I was in a younger middle group of children, following the lead of a few college students who chose the songs, struck the chords, and always kept in a key too high for my faltering alto. I hung at the rear of the crowd, flirting a bit with Tim Melgaard, who lived three blocks away, stamping my toes to keep out the cold. But in a few winters, those older students had gone, gotten jobs, married, settled in other parts of the town or state or country. Tim, my sister and I were suddenly at the front, deciding whether to do one or two verses of "It Came upon the Midnight Clear," pitching the key lower. Purposefully we led the group door to door, giving a few more carols at the homes we knew and liked, knocking noisily at windows if we felt we weren't being noticed. Even when we went away for college, we of course rejoined the Christmas Eve caroling, greeting each other with glad cries and hugs. We ignored the sullen stares of the high-school and junior-high kids, so recently too young to be allowed out this late. Tim had acquired a pitchpipe. "Wait!" he commanded, and hummed loudly. Karen and I picked up the vibration and turned to the group with a loud refrain. From the back sometimes I heard a rebellious effort at another carol, "O Little Town" attempting to drown out our "Good King Wenceslas," but by sheer volume and moral force we carried the tune.

My first year out of college was the last Christmas I caroled. My sister was sick that night, and I went alone. I was the oldest one in the group, and I didn't even recognize some of the small children who must have been from new families in the neighborhood. We stopped at the Melgaard house. At the opened door, where listeners were supposed to stand to hear us, I could see not only Mr. and Mrs. Melgaard but my old friend Tim. He had been married a year ago to a girl I'd known in high school. He and Patsy stood in the doorway together, next to his parents. Patsy was holding a small wrapped bundle, a baby so new and tiny it was completely hidden in the folds of blanket. They all beamed at us, and I waved vigorously. That night I skipped the cocoa and cookies party and went home to read late into the night, thinking murkily about life, marriage, babies, and how fast everything seemed to happen.

If the religious element of Easter was uncomfortably mixed with fashion, Christmas in Ames miraculously managed to keep material and spiritual fairly separate. Our church, modest enough in its celebrations of other seasons, palm branches for Palm Sunday and Easter lilies on Easter, but no other foolishness, went into a most un-Presbyterian frenzy of activity around Christmas. Along the upper stuccoed walls of the sanctuary were arch-shaped bronze plaques, closed and flat against the wall all year. But for a few Christmastime Sundays, they were opened to reveal small niches, where, draped in real evergreens, real candles burned brightly. To a child looking upward, they shone with a mysterious and reverent light. Banks of poinsettias were piled high around the altar, sometimes mixed with evergreen boughs or amaryllis. Even the choir loft was decked with greens. All this color was a setting for the annual Christmas Eve pageant. The church doesn't have a pageant like this anymore; but for a few years it was the highlight of our Christmas at church, with costumes, lights precariously poised on the upper balcony, and real makeup troweled on everyone's faces by those of us who had taken high-school drama class. We had hordes of angels, incorporating any Sunday-school children who could persuade their mothers to fashion robes from sheets and wings from cardboard and aluminum foil. We had a Nativity Scene, with beautiful Shelley McNulty the natural choice for Mary, a younger Joseph whose beard kept coming unglued, and various Shepherds and Wise Men who were not anxious to participate. It was unfair, I thought, that there was only one good female part. Who wanted to be lost in a crowd of trampling angels, all stumbling over their sheets, the small ones crying? The Virgin Mary, or nothing. Only boys could be Wise Men or Shepherds or even Herod the King, and most of the boys I knew didn't even want to be. Unfair, unfair. I comforted myself by taking charge of all the makeup one year, and forcing all the boys to wear eyebrow pencil and rouge. It was all in an actor's job, I told them, and powdered lavishly until they choked from the clouds.

After many tense, tearful evening rehearsals, with the director shouting, cajoling, moving props and calling to someone to dim or focus or change the lights, the show finally went on. The church was jammed with proud parents, curious friends of the angel hordes, and the old members of the congregation who never so much as missed a potluck supper. The candles on the wall flickered their magic light, and in the sudden hush of the church for the opening prayer I felt the Christmas spirit unfold, an angel's wing brushing over the congregation. We sang all the old hymns, the youth choir bravely chirping "Away in a Manger," the fathers booming out "Hark! the Herald," my mother's strong soprano with its piercing clarity soaring into the high notes of "sleeeeeep in heavenly peace." The angels paraded properly to their stations, the few stragglers tugged into position by their elders. Shelley McNulty sat serenely by the creche, looking so lovely in her blue robes and white mantle that I barely suppressed a most un-Christmassy envy. Everyone remembered his lines, and only one Wise Man stumbled over his frankincense when he put it down. It all passed quickly to the moment when we lit our small wax candles, sang a last chorus of "Silent Night," and bent our heads for the benediction.

The excitement of Christmas morning was not entirely greed. Like all children, my sister and I shook boxes, peered through tissue paper, guessed and argued about what was in whose present, anxious to know if we really *had* gotten what we wanted. Mother always saw to it that we did. But she had taught us that Christmas meant the joy of giving, and we were almost as concerned about what we gave as about what we got. Sometime in November I began to worry about what to put in Mother's stocking, which my sister and I always stuffed. Our choices in Ames were limited. I was happiest shopping in the Fastco Drugstore or in Woolworth's, where a dime or a quarter went a long way. Woolworth's was gaudier at Christmas, with its long counters of decorations, multicolored glass balls laid delicately like eggs in their sectioned cardboard cartons; boxes of silvery tinsel; strings of Christmas-tree lights that bubbled or blinked or just shone steadily in blue, red, green; red cellophane-and-cotton Santas; shiny tin stars; fluffy Fiberglas angels. Usually my sister and I went to Woolworth's together, hovering at the cosmetics counter or notions or kitchenware to find some special treat for Mother. For my own private forays, I preferred Fastco Drug. There everything was jammed into dark, narrow aisles, heaped high on towering shelves or pushed into open boxes on a crowded counter. No one ever waited on me in Fastco. I took a little basket at the front, wandered among the treasures, found what I wanted, and threaded my way back to a front cash register where a bored checkout girl was usually sitting on a stool reading a magazine. I never knew what I would find at Fastco, but it would always be unexpectedly just what I wanted. One Christmas, when my mother still smoked, I discovered a white plastic ashtray in the shape of a toilet whose lid flipped up and down to hide the ashes. I loved it and was sure Mother would enjoy using it for guests. In fact, for several weeks after Christmas that year, I ostentatiously brought it out whenever someone lit up a cigarette in our living room. On various other Christmases, I gave Mother a note pad with pencil glued on a rough piece of redwood carved like a birdhouse, to hang at our front door for friends to leave messages, though they never did; a folding yardstick to carry in her purse; an eyelash curler, rubber-tipped, guaranteed to make her lashes longer and sexier; a plastic flowered envelope to store nylons; heart-shaped guest soaps; and off-color lipsticks, deep magenta or bright orange, that I had found in a box marked "Reduced." I entered Fastco anxious, afraid that Mother's stocking wouldn't be full this year, and I left, like Santa, with a bulging sack. Watching Mother's surprise on Christmas morning as she pulled these unexpected items from her stocking was as much fun as opening my own presents.

Not all the presents I gave at Christmas came from Woolworth's or Fastco, however. About the same time that I began to rummage in Mother's dresser drawers, to see if she needed handkerchiefs or thimbles, she would begin saying what she *really* wanted this year was something we girls had made. "Not bought, *made*," she repeated. "It would mean so much more to me." Like what, I asked dispiritedly. "Oh, like some nice decorated paper napkins, or a calendar, or perhaps some paper place mats?" my mother suggested brightly. My sister and I groaned. Karen, who was artistic, soon cheered up and started work on some hand-painted vase made from a Ma Brown jelly glass or an appliquéed cigar box begged from the local pipe shop. I remained dispirited. Nothing I made ended up like the pictures in *Better Homes and Gardens* or *Family Circle*. My paper napkins ripped when I pressed hard with my crayons, I could letter the names of the months neatly but I could never draw interesting pictures to go with them, and I had never seen *anyone* use colored-paper place mats. I would much rather have bought some plastic mats I'd seen downtown, white with loud red and blue windmills stamped on them, scallops on the edges, four for ninety-nine cents. But thought was what counted, Mother said, and I knew I was stuck. So I stenciled and crayoned, cut and glued, and if what I made seemed tacky, as it usually did, I comforted myself with one last foraging expedition to Fastco.

My mother was not the only person in Ames who felt that giving was the essence of Christmas. At school our teachers encouraged us to fill Red Cross packages with Band-Aids, socks, Kleenex, and rubber bands for overseas children; for church we ransacked our mothers' pantries for canned goods, usually beets or beans or stewed apricots, and laid the cans under a special Christmas tree in the church basement. On Christmas Eve, we were told, they would be delivered in packages to needy families. I didn't know any needy families, but I was glad to help them, whoever they were, and I glowed a little as I placed my beans and beets on the growing pile.

At home I looked forward to the rewards of being a recipient, for all good women in Ames exchanged baked goods at Christmas. My mother baked her plain but flavorful wheat-germ bread, and sometimes kringla, a tender Norwegian pastry redolent of nutmeg. Other mothers arrived with trays of frosted sugar cookies, rum balls, fruit cakes, gingerbread men, sugar-coated nuts, jellies, and marmalade. Mrs. Kramer, that outstanding cook, always appeared at the last minute, just when we'd given up hope, with her annual offering, a Danish coffee cake so rich, butter-laden and strewn with nuts that we saved it to eat on Christmas morning. Every Christmas Mother said, "Let's just each have one piece, it's so rich, and keep the rest for tomorrow." Sneaking back to the kitchen for slice after slice, my sister and I ignored her. "How could anybody want butter on this coffeecake?" Mother added, as she resignedly put the butter in front of us on the table. We slathered it on the hot coffee cake, which immediately dissolved in warm sugary bits of icing. Then we carried our plates into the living room, where we nibbled on the last bits of pastry as we opened our presents. My sister and I, who fought most of the time, declared an unspoken truce on Christmas morning and hugged awkwardly as we exchanged gifts. For those brief moments we really wanted to please each other. We sealed our temporary bond with Mrs. Kramer's coffee cake and washed it down with lots of hot chocolate.

After Christmas, the Iowa winter settled in, long white months of cold and snow, a blur of peaceful monotony. Although spring was supposed to arrive at Easter, the season seldom fulfilled its promise, choosing instead to melt, slush and slop its way through the snows and frosts of March and April. But by Easter we children could begin to see the end, both of winter and of our school year, which began to pick up speed as the sun grew stronger, moving more rapidly toward the blaze of June. By May we could feel the penultimate beat of the surge toward summer when we celebrated VEISHEA. VEISHEA was what Ames celebrated instead of Fourth of July, presidents' birthdays or founders' days. Although it was a college holiday, its acronym formed by the major divisions of Iowa State (Veterinary Medicine, Engineering, Industrial Science, Home Economics, Agriculture), the whole town turned out for the three days of VEISHEA.

Swarming over the campus, free from school on a special VEISHEA exemption, we children wandered in and out of buildings that we only knew from their outsides the rest of the year. Although I went past the School of Home Economics four or five times a week, only at VEISHEA did I have an excuse to go inside. Every department of the college had an open house, and most of them offered souvenirs free or at a very low price. Scanning a printed guide, we roamed from one handout to another, collecting tiny evergreens planted in paper cups at Forestry, recipe sheets at Foods and Nutrition, playdough at Child Development, ice-cream cones from Dairy Industry. Among the milling crowds we located our friends, stopped to share miniature cherry pies from Home Economics, exchanged news of the best stops, looked at each other's loot, and moved on.

Although no one in Ames ever scorned the chance to get something free or cheap, not all our visits were purely mercenary. We were curious too, watching a broadcast at the college television station or studying the intricacies of the latest stainless-steel milking equipment, each polished piece part of a puzzle to us town children, who lived next door to farms but seldom knew precisely what went on there. My favorite exhibit each year was in Zoology, where in a dank basement room, gloomy even under the fluorescent lights, were ranged row after row of preserving bottles. Some of them had long swirly tapeworms, floating eerily in the yellowish light, or colorless guinea pigs or splay-legged frogs, moving lifelessly in response to the heavy beat of feet on the tiled floor. But one row of bottles, high above the floor, held a sequence of fetuses, each one slightly more developed than the last. Fascinated, I stood and examined them furtively. Whose babies were they? Did a baby really look like that? How long had they been bottled up here? Was that what it was like to be dead, a warped doll-like thing forever suspended in liquid space? My examination was never long enough, however, because I was always interrupted by the arrival of someone I knew, and, embarrassed to be caught staring, I left quickly.

After a day of scavenging all over campus, we rose early on Saturday morning, tired but fiercely determined to get good seats for the VEISHEA parade. All the dormitories, fraternities and sororities competed for prizes with their floats, which, given the engineering expertise available, were wonderfully elaborate contraptions of chicken wire and colored crepe paper, mounted on motor-driven platforms with portable phonographs blaring out accompanying music. Winding along a jammed route through campus, the parade lasted all morning, with marching bands from all the neighboring small towns, sporting gaudy uniforms and inscribed drums; prancing horses; convertibles filled with town dignitaries, college administrators, and beauty queens; and the floats, alive with square-dancers, clowns tossing candy, or pretty girls in formals smiling and waving. We all clapped, cheered, and moved restlessly on the fringes of the crowd for a better view. Perhaps it rained once or twice during the years I watched the VEISHEA parade, but I only remember how the sun shone, the bands played and the crowds cheered. Spring had come, and summer sparkled in the gleam of the passing trombones and the bare shoulders of the pretty girls. That night we sat in the bleachers of the stadium, pulled our coats around us, and rejoiced in being outdoors while we watched *Stars over Veishea*, a musical show whose words and lyrics were often lost in the night but whose appeal lay in the very fact that we were listening to music under an open sky. Before long we would be sitting in our steamy backyards, slapping mosquitoes, and watching thunderstorms crackle above us. VEISHEA was our festival of passage into summer.

Summer at the Lake

"Guess what, darling?" I said in my most enthusiastic tones. "I've managed to sign you up for a whole summer at the most wonderful day camp, where you can go swimming and ride horses and have arts and crafts. You get to ride a bus into the country and have your lunch and come home in the afternoon. You'll meet lots of children. Isn't that great?" Jennie looked at me. At seven she was too old for a day-care center, and I knew from irritable experience that in a city neighborhood without playmates her age, my only child got itchy and querulous after a day or two of vacation. Unlike me when I was young, she can't run and play in the woods, wander safely through nearby streets, bicycle all over town, or walk to a playground. "You know, Jennie, you'd be bored if you stayed home all summer," I added, watching her expressive face. She stared down at the dining room table, running her finger through the dust. Finally she looked up at me and sighed. I could see she was going to give in. "All right, Mommy," she said plaintively. She waited for a moment. "But do you suppose next year I could have the summer off?"

Her question returned to haunt me on many hot afternoons that summer. We ought to be picnicking by a pool, I thought. Or I should be teaching Jennie how to play tennis. What was I doing to my child, I wondered, by depriving her of lazy, unplanned summers? And yet what alternative did I have? I had to get some work done. Damn. I began to feel guilty. By August, when day camp ended, I had determined

to make one of those gestures that well up from the collective unconscious of working mothers. If I couldn't give Jennie the kind of summer
I'd known as a child, at least I could give her a few days of real vacation. I could take her to a Minnesota lake. We'd fish, swim, listen to
the loons cry at night, sleep to the sound of waves washing against the
shore. When I mentioned my plan to Jennie, she got excited too, and
the following weekend we set out for Gull Lake. It would be like my
summers on Lake Carlos, I thought, only of course shorter. I could
spare only three days.

I wish we hadn't stopped at the Paul Bunyan amusement park, but I
couldn't help it. Even though she didn't read well yet, Jennie could
easily spot tempting billboards. Once I had admitted I knew there was
a giant statue, and yes, probably some rides, I was caught. Paul Bunyan speaks! Say hello to Paul Bunyan! For over an hour we waited to
hear Jennie's name, which I'd slipped to the attendant, emerge from the
awkwardly manipulated head of the statue. It never did. Scuffling in
the dirt, we then stood in line to watch a trained chicken cross a rope to
the other side of its cage. "Doesn't it ever get out, Mommy? Does it
have to stay in there all day? I think that's mean," Jennie said. After
the burning smell of the Dodge 'Em cars, the tinny merry-go-round
music, and the droning voice of mechanical Paul, I was anxious to
leave. This was no lake vacation.

But outside town our luck wasn't much better. I hadn't thought to
make reservations, and on an August Friday in Minnesota the lake
was as filled as a parking lot in downtown St. Paul. Circling the water
on a busy highway, peering for something set back into the woods, we
finally stopped at a promising "VACANCY" sign. A handful of trim
cabins, not too close to each other, and I could see a line of rowboats
pulled up on the shore. Beyond, the lake looked blue and inviting. But
no cabin was available for such a short stay. The only vacancy was in
the motel unit, a row of six rooms facing the highway, thirty dollars a
night. "And a boat?" I asked. "Sorry," the man said. "Boats just come
with the cabins."

It was late, Jennie was tired and understandably complaining, and
my eyes hurt from squinting into the highway sun. So that night we

cooked hamburgers on a hot plate and ate them in front of our motel, sitting cross-legged on a strip of grass that separated us from the stream of cars pouring by us. Gas fumes mixed with the breeze from the lake. After supper, Jennie and I took a walk on the edge of the highway, counting dead monarch butterflies. We found twenty-two. Jennie shook her small fist at one of the passing cars.

Saturday wasn't much better. We went swimming, but there was no beach, and the water was scummy with algae and with oil slicks from motorboats. Jennie screamed and left the water when a bloated dead fish drifted near her. In the afternoon Jennie wanted to use the resort's miniature golf course, but the owner said that was an additional five dollars, so we went back to Paul Bunyan, circled the lake again, made a trip to the grocery store for hot dogs, stopped at a roadside rummage sale, and returned, hot and dissatisfied, to our stuffy room. "Mommy, why can't we go out on the lake? Why not?" Jennie asked as we munched our hot dogs and watched the cars. "I haven't got a boat, that's why. Now stop begging," I said crossly. A man passing the motel on his way to the cabins stopped. "Pardon me," he said politely. "Did I hear your little girl ask about a boat? I'm not using mine tonight. Would you like to borrow it for an hour or so?" Jennie began to crow with delight.

As I settled into a rowing rhythm, bending my stiffening back, I watched the resort dwindle behind us. It was almost sunset. Few boats were on the lake tonight, perhaps because it was so still. No fish would be biting, except perhaps close to shore, and there the cabins were too thick, children splashed too loudly, and motorboats dripped gas. This far out the lake was glassy, broken only by the stroke of my oars. Sometimes I let them hang in the air and watched the drops of water fall quietly into the lake. Jennie dabbled her finger over the side of the boat and looked for dragonflies. From here the lake seemed big, the cottages and resorts small. When we were almost in the middle of the bay, I put the oars in the boat and let it drift. Leaning back against the prow, I looked up at the darkening sky, now shot with gold and orange as the sun began to dip behind the far horizon. One distant loon called to another, who answered mournfully. The only other sound was the *soft slap of water against the boat. Even Jennie was quiet. If I half-closed my eyes, and looked at a wooded section of shoreline, I could almost pretend we were alone on the lake, adrift in the dusk, free to float wherever the currents took us.*

"Mommy," Jennie said. "Sssssh," I answered. "Mommy," she insisted gently, "I just wanted to know. Was it like this at your lake when you were little?" "Yes, Jennie," I said, closing my eyes entirely. "It was just like this."

When school let out in June, we raced into the sunshine with whoops of glee, scattering test papers like confetti and wadding up gym clothes like used Kleenex. Anything that reminded us of school would be shoved into the closet as soon as we got home. Now we could see the long summer yawning ahead, with its lazy afternoons, balmy evenings and late bedtimes. In the bright sunshine my head beat with possibilities: I would try to get a regular baby-sitting job, read ten books a week, take swimming lessons, coordinate my wardrobe, keep my cuticles oiled, sew school outfits for fall. Afternoons I would go to Summer Playground, and nights, of course, I'd play kick-the-can.

After supper children of all ages on our street met at the largest backyard for kick-the-can, a game that continued until mothers whistled us indoors for bed. We cowered under bushes and behind houses, hollering loud enough to wake old Mrs. Miller as someone raced out of the blackness to kick the can off a low stump and free the prisoners. I can still hear the excitement of someone calling, "Ollie ollie oxen, all in free," a cry that sounded as thrilling to me then as "Damn the torpedoes!" or "Remember the Alamo!" It rang through the summer nights of my childhood.

Although my summers always offered dizzying freedom on those first few days in June, before long I found my time well organized. As soon as Summer Playground began, I spent all my afternoons there, first as an eager participant, and then, when I was older, as an assistant in the dramatics program. When I was fifteen, I left the playgrounds forever, but by then I had learned as much about painting ceramic miniatures and braiding plastic lanyards on wooden spools as I'll ever want to know. Girls took Arts and Crafts at Summer Playground, sitting on high stools beneath the basement windows in the cool dark "shop" at Welch School. Only boys were allowed to use the tools on the tables behind us, running electric saws, and under close supervision, turning out jigsaw puzzles and birdhouses. The buzz of an electric saw still seems to me, regrettably, a masculine sound.

Sometime during July, when I had braided enough lanyards to give three to Mother and two to each of my friends, I began to look forward to our trip to the lake. In August we would take two or three blissful weeks and drive to Alexandria, Minnesota, Mother's childhood home, where we stayed in an old frame farmhouse, perched high on a hill overlooking Lake Carlos. There my mother and her two brothers and three sisters had spent their summers as children, decamping from their winter house in Alexandria to the "summer place." Later my grandfather had given each of his children a lot adjoining the farmhouse acreage, and two cottages, a quarter-mile from each other on the wooded shore, meant that my sister and I had cousins to play with there.

Going to Lake Carlos was an all-day trip, starting as early as we could manage to get up and ending in late afternoon or early evening, when, tired and dusty, we finally unlatched the chain at the driveway almost completely hidden by birch woods, and eased down the grassy hill to the farmhouse. It was a major expedition not only because it took so long to drive to Alexandria, but because we had to plan carefully what we would take. The old farmhouse, almost derelict now except for occasional summer visitors, was for many years without running water or electricity. Since the ten-mile trip into town meant having to leave the lake for a whole morning or afternoon, we brought as many supplies as possible: sheets, towels, dishrags, a favorite saucepan, canned goods, utensils. Then we each had our individual requirements: my sister's sketch pad and paints, my dolls or games or crossword puzzles, mother's typewriter, and all of our books. Our prevacation trip to the Ames Public Library depleted at least two of its shelves. On the ledge beneath the rear window of the car, my mother piled all her *New Yorkers* from the past year. Though we were strictly limited to one suitcase each for clothes, none of us could argue the other out of any books. If Mother complained, we pointed sternly to her *New Yorkers*. We also carried a "medicine kit," an old overnight case used for rubbing alcohol, calamine lotion, Band-Aids, flashlight, toothpaste, shampoo, hairbrushes, aspirin, and anything else that might come in handy in case an epidemic swept the shores of Lake Carlos.

And then there was the dog. For several summers we took Gypsy, a part-collie mongrel my sister fiercely loved. We could leave our cat behind, but not Gypsy. So very early on the morning of departure, proud of my family reputation as an efficient organizer, I took charge of packing the car. Surrounded by suitcases, duffel bags, paper bags and cardboard cartons, as well as stacks of books, I began methodically tugging, squeezing, rearranging. The back seat was the biggest challenge. There we needed a pillow for whoever's turn it was to sleep on top of the two duffel bags. The lunch basket and thermos had to go in the back seat for instant access, as did Kleenex, books, Karen's pastels, and the medicine kit in case of en-route accidents. But room was needed to sit or nap, and then there was Gypsy. Finding such space in the crowded back seat of a 1949 Oldsmobile coupe was a challenge to which I rose with determination. An intuitive grasp of solid geometry deserted me in the classroom but got the car packed by eight A.M.

Every year of my packing I stormed into the house in protest. "Can't we leave Gypsy across the street with the Smiths this time?" I argued. "She'll never fit!" But my sister, rising instantly to Gypsy's defense, yelled and cried, and my mother finally said, "Well, you know, dear, Gypsy will be a good watchdog for us." The farmhouse was surrounded by woods, invisibly set back from the road, not even in shouting distance of our relatives, if they should happen to be staying in their cottages. One summer an alarmed friend of Mother's, hearing of our isolation, made her take his old collapsible shotgun, just in case. "You three girls out there all alone, without a *man?*" he said disapprovingly. We kept the gun disassembled in a drawer near our beds, and Mother put the bullets in a coffee can in the kitchen. None of us knew how to shoot it anyway. Gypsy did bark, usually in the middle of the night at noises we couldn't hear, and she at least terrified us. So Gypsy came.

When the car was scientifically loaded, we rolled down the windows for air that would turn hot by noon, unbearable by three o'clock. Off we started, high with excitement, already looking for a place to stop to eat breakfast. On the morning of a long car trip we were allowed to choose a truck stop or cheap cafe, where we could order a stack of hotcakes and sausage, drowning everything in butter and syrup and stuffing ourselves so that we would have little appetite for lunch. Though breakfast at home would have been faster and cheaper, eating pancakes out was a vacation tradition.

After breakfast my sister and I settled down, reading or dozing or looking out the window, watching for Burma-Shave signs and X-Marks-The-Spots, white wooden crosses an insurance company piously erected on the site of traffic fatalities, one cross per death. At one bad curve near Jewell, strung with six white X's, Mother slowed to a crawl for miles afterward. Those bleak white crosses in the midst of a green fertile landscape sobered us children too. In all those years of driving to Minnesota we never saw a serious accident, but I envisioned them whenever we passed those silent markers.

Before we were old enough to bury ourselves in our private worlds of books, my sister and I passed the time by singing songs, all the verses of "Clementine" or "Down in the Valley" or "She'll Be Coming 'round the Mountain," or by playing "Ghost" or "Alphabet." Many miles would whizz by as we watched fruitlessly for Q's and Z's in Quaker State or Pennzoil signs. Whenever we drove through a small town, we had a new distraction, eagerly searching for a five-and-dime store where we could begin to spend our vacation money. Mostly we collected miniatures, tiny china dogs or salt-and-pepper shakers that looked like tiny china dogs, but we also haunted the souvenir counters for birchbark canoes stamped "Spirit Lake," or inch-long beaded moccasins, or, if all else failed, colored postcards. Mother, always reasonable, allowed us two or three stops before she announced firmly, "Now, that's it. Either we spend all day in Woolworth's and Ben Franklin's, or we get to the lake. How about it?"

For many miles, and five or more hours, the landscape didn't change: rolling green cornfields, with the corn so high in midsummer that it cut off any side view; small towns, truck stops, more cornfields, silos and farmhouses and barns, then more cornfields. But after we passed the Minnesota border, where we always raised a cheer, we began to sense differences. We were surrounded by foreign license plates. Small lakes appeared, at first muckylooking large ponds encircled by pasture or corn. But soon the lakes grew bigger, and the steady cornfields gave way to more varied fields, wheat, alfalfa, and pastured hills that had nothing planted on them at all except scrub evergreens. By Glenwood, with its soaring sweep of highway that looked down on miraculously blue Lake Minnewaska, we knew we were almost there. Despite the heat baking us inside the small stuffed car, the air seemed clean and fresh. Birch trees dotted the shores of the lakes we passed now. We watched the signs carefully, counting the miles to Alexandria.

Once in Alexandria, we had to pay a courtesy call on my grandfather, Oscar Erickson, whose guests we technically were when we stayed at his farmhouse. For some years he had lived alone with his Irish setter, Ada, in the old family home in town. My sister and I dreaded these visits, for my grandfather was a crusty, partially deaf old man, never very affectionate, with a gruff bark that may have hidden a loneliness we were too young to recognize or understand. He was retired now from his years as deputy and recorder of deeds. His house smelled damp and moldy, with a faint lingering odor of urine, and we girls perched awkwardly on a sagging sofa in the dark little living room, patting Ada and staring at a yellowed photograph of F.D.R. on the wall, while Mother valiantly carried on a conversation. "We won't stay long," she had promised us as we drove into his yard, "but he *is* my father and your grandfather. I want you girls to give him hugs and be nice to him." We did our dutiful best, but Oscar did not know what questions to ask us, and we were too intimidated to ask any in return. So we hugged him on entering and leaving, and let Mother do all the talking.

Finally, after counting the minutes restlessly, we piled with relief into the packed car. Leaving the stuffy house behind us with its closed windows and pulled shades, we began to anticipate the cool breeze that would be blowing off the lake in the early evening. Now, in half an hour, we would be there.

Passing quickly through town, we soon found ourselves on a blacktop road that circled the Carlos group of lakes. We began to watch for them, wanting to be the first to cry out joyfully: "There's Lake L'Homme Dieu! There's Little Darling!" and the ultimate, "There it is! There's Lake Carlos!" We knew all the summer cottages, the bait shops, even the grouped signposts pointing to resorts on parts of the lake we had never seen nor indeed would ever visit. We were heading to a private stretch of Lake Carlos, a long Erickson-owned sweep of land bounded by a Bible camp at one end and a state park at the other, reached by a narrow dirt trail you could easily miss if you didn't watch for the turnoff.

Before we reached the turnoff, we passed a row of five or six large houses, summer residences so grand we couldn't even imagine the wealth of families who could afford to use them for just a few weeks a year. Some of them had boathouses and guest cottages that were bigger than many houses in Ames. Though we never met anyone who owned one of these houses, we gave each a name, making Mother slow down as we drove by so we could greet them and peer for signs of the enchanted people who lived within. My favorite was "The Chinese Pagoda," an architect's extravaganza trimmed and painted with Oriental curves and arches. Even its birdhouse was a miniature black-and-gold pagoda. My sister's choice was "The Swiss Chalet," a rambling mansion with heavy stone foundations and an encircling porch, dotted with wicker chairs and settees overlooking the lake. Abruptly this row of houses ended, a dusty gravel road began, and for a few miles we lost any sense that a lake lay behind the impenetrable trees.

Now we watched for the white salt-lick. At the corner where the dirt trail began stood a stone-strewn, miserable-looking pasture, where in a shady corner a few bedraggled cows stood, switching off flies. Near the road were a water trough and a huge block of salt, its white square corners looking incongruously neat and clean among the scrubby brush and sparse grass. Some summers we didn't see any cows, but the salt lick was always there, a mute reminder of man's intrusion. After this pasture, the field turned rapidly into a tangled woods, so thick we couldn't see more than a few feet into its dark depths. For half a mile or more we bumped and jogged along the narrow trail, bouncing over a wooden culvert whose rattle always made my sister cry, "Trolls! Watch out for trolls!" and passing a large swamp whose cattails waved temptingly among moss and slime. Then we were there, stopping abruptly at the small entrance hacked in the woods, unlocking the chain, winding down the curving drive that hid the farmhouse from the outside world.

The first few hours at the lake were always an anticlimax. Closed up for a year, the farmhouse was filled with dust, dead flies, and mouse droppings. Before we could unpack, we had to give it a fast cleaning, at least enough so we could fix dinner and make up our beds. First Mother had to build a fire in the rusty black cookstove so we could heat water. Hot water was a luxury. Even after the farmhouse was electrified, it had no plumbing and no hot-water heater. Drinking water was ferried from town in a tall milk can, but all other water was scooped from an old oak rainbarrel outside the house or hauled a quarter-mile from the lake below.

We scattered to our tasks, Karen heading down to the lake with pails, Mother swabbing out the icebox on the back porch so perishables could be stored quickly. I took charge in the kitchen, washing enough silver and dishes for supper, mopping down counters, wiping off the oilcloth-covered table. We always ate outside on the screened back porch, an arm's length from the icebox, unless a cold rain drove us into the gloomy small dining room. Later my sister and I took turns shaking out mattresses and blankets, spreading sheets, and fighting over who got which pillow. When it got dark, Mother lit the two kerosene lamps. We were too tired to read that first night, but most evenings we squinted in their yellow circles of light as we devoured the books we each had brought with us. After supper it was too dark to unpack anymore, so we brushed our teeth, peed on the weeds outside the house rather than climb the overgrown path to the outhouse, and crawled into bed. As I fell asleep, I could hear the wind rustling the grass in the field next to the farmhouse, a far-off lapping of water against the shore, and mice scurrying up the walls to the attic. Though I was frightened of meeting a live mouse, the skitter of tiny feet in the walls was oddly soothing.

When I was grown and married, and had not seen Lake Carlos for some years, I returned one summer with my husband to camp on my mother's lot. Grampa was long dead, and an aunt now owned the farmhouse. My husband and I went in to visit her and my uncle, as well as to see "the old place," as my mother always called it. They had done some remodeling, installing running water and even a flush toilet. But, despite their efforts, I could see how shabby the old place was. Had I really slept happily on such gray, stained mattresses? Could I have put my head on pillows that must have been rank with mildew? Knowing how I scream involuntarily when a mouse runs across my own tidy kitchen floor, could I really have been so accepting of the dozens, maybe hundreds, of mice who shared that farmhouse with us? I was struck, and not happily, by a sense of the interfering fastidiousness I had acquired.

After the farmhouse was cleaned and settled, my sister and I were free to spend the rest of our time at the lake as we wanted, with the exception of occasional trips to town to see Grampa, get the mail, and buy groceries. Sometimes we had cousins who played card games with us, took us on motorboat rides, helped us hunt for raspberries or Indian arrowheads, or who took sides in the various games all children invent of if-you-get-us-we'll-get-you-back. But my sister and I were happy by ourselves as well, reading, swimming, or just lazing in the old canvas hammock, swatting mosquitoes and shooing deerflies.

Some days I managed to go fishing on the lake. This was not an easy matter to arrange, since we had no boat. One summer my mother, tormented by my pleas, drove to the nearby Bible camp and managed to beg the use of a rowboat for an afternoon. In return, we went to town and bought the director a canned ham. "You'd better enjoy your fishing," Mother said with a touch of understandable grimness. "Get out there right now and just be back by dark." Some summers I borrowed a boat from my generous Uncle Lloyd, and then I fished most sunny days.

Though I hoped I might somehow snag a big walleye accidentally drifting into my hook, Mother and I knew that wasn't really why I went fishing. I did like to bring home a few nice-sized sunfish or crappies, a modest acknowledgment that my time hadn't been wasted, though I couldn't share Mother's appreciative murmurs as we dabbed for the little bits of speckled white meat among the myriad tiny bones. I really fished mainly because I wanted to be alone on the middle of the lake. With a can of worms and some bacon, a few spare hooks, a pail, sunglasses, a book and some peanut-butter sandwiches or cookies, I could stay out all afternoon. I rowed straight out from shore, then turned until I was hovering in front of an aunt's cottage. There, in the midst of dark green water, was a rock bar, which I found by lowering the anchor until I could hear it clink on the stones. From shore I could see my uncle waving, a tiny stick figure, perhaps motioning me farther out or more to one side if he thought I hadn't found the rock bar yet. Then I anchored, letting the line out so far I wondered if I could hold my breath and swim all the way to the bottom. Carlos was deep, I knew, and a mile wide here. After threading a worm or some bacon on my hook, I paid out line from my wind-up reel and sat and waited. Tiny fish nibbled often enough to keep me awake, and sometimes I felt a frightening jerk on the line. Almost always when I pulled it up, the bait was gone. Mildly excited, knowing a fish was down there, I didn't really think I'd catch it. Nonetheless I rebaited the line, dropped it down, and jerked it around to make it look as though the bacon were alive. Once in a while I did bring up a fish, which I prayed hadn't swallowed the hook, since that meant such unpleasantness I hauled anchor and rowed inshore for my uncle to deal with it.

For most of my fishing time, however, I didn't handle fish at all. I stretched out on the wooden plank seats, making myself a prop from a life-preserver cushion, and I dreamed. Few boats were out on the lake in those early years, and aside from the quiet thrumming of a trolling motor as a more serious fisherman edged by me, looking for his own drop-off or rock bar, I could listen to the sounds of the lake. Waves lapped gently against my boat, lulling me into a drowsy trance as the sun shone on my shoulders and bare legs. Though I was never allowed out on the lake in rough weather, sometimes a storm began to brew suddenly, and then the waves slapped and broke noisily as I hurriedly headed in, waving reassurance to my beckoning mother on the dock. If it was a quiet day, dragonflies buzzed around the boat and lit on my bobbing line. Sometimes a fish jumped nearby, as though it knew it was safe. Loons circled over the lake, their eerie cry a companionable call in daytime but strange and mournful at night. As I sat in my gently rolling boat, twitching my line, staring at the green water that turned to brilliant blue in the sunny distance, I knew that I was out of sound of any human voice. If someone from shore wanted me, he or she could only wave. It was an exhilarating feeling that made me want to shout aloud. From here the woods looked as they must have years ago, except for the few cottages that were such familiar features they seemed as natural as the trees. I could imagine Indians peering behind the birches, or my own mother as a child wading waist-deep into the lake with the laundry.

Summers at Lake Carlos seemed timeless. Although I grew and changed, eventually packing Tampax in the medicine kit and caring more intensely about mail from boyfriends at home, I lapsed into the lake's quiet life with an unconscious comfort that was like a sigh of relief. Much of my pleasure sprang from my awareness that we were living much as my mother had. The past and present connected at Lake Carlos in a way I didn't know anywhere else. When I trudged up the hill to the outhouse which still had an old Sears, Roebuck catalog lying on the plank floor, I was wearing down the same path my aunts and uncles had tramped years before. I even wondered about the layers of excrement piling up like archeological evidence of past generations. On cold rainy mornings, when my mother struggled with damp wood to fire up the potbellied black stove in the living room, we huddled around its warmth as her family had done, listening to the same rain beat against the same glass. She cooked us bacon in an old iron pan on top of the same cookstove, brewed coffee in a speckled blue porcelain pot with a rusty handle, wrestled with ice tongs from the disused icehouse next to the empty barn.

In one of the farmhouse cabinets my sister and I found a box of love letters and pictures belonging to one of our aunts. Even in the faded brown snapshots we could see her black glossy hair and dramatic deep eyes; when she came to the farmhouse now to visit, still a handsome woman, a romantic past hovered like a dark halo over her neat gray braids. She laughed as we read aloud from the letters, acting passages out, falling to the floor with exaggerated devotion and sorrow. "I wonder whatever happened to Isaiah Stokes?" my mother asked her. "I don't know," my aunt said carelessly. "I think he took over his father's farm in Wadena." She had traveled with another aunt to Japan in the 1920s, and some of Isaiah's faded plaintive letters were addressed to their ship. My aunt had married later, but we conscientiously never teased her about Isaiah's love letters in front of Uncle Anton.

One uncle, a silver prospector in Colorado, never came to the lake. He lived too far away and could not leave his mine. But my aunts told stories about him, and he haunted the house too, a friendly ghost. One night he saved us from a spanking. Cousin Mary, staying overnight, had to sleep on a creaky fourposter bed on the front porch. A window just above the bed led into the side bedroom, where my sister and I slept. Though Mother closed the connecting window at bedtime and warned us to be quiet, we were too excited. We opened the window and crept into Mary's bed. With the door to the house closed behind us, we three felt we were alone in the great outdoors, separated by a mesh screen, with only mosquitoes, loons, and grasshoppers to keep us company. It was so dark that night we couldn't see beyond the pine trees at the front doorstep. Far below us the lake lapped softly against the shore. It was a night for stories, secrets, private games, scorn of grown-ups. Late into the night we crawled back and forth from bedroom to porch, bouncing on the creaky bed, giggling and talking, standing on the windowsill to dive onto the sagging springs. Finally Mother marched onto the porch, an unusual sternness in her voice. "I *warned* you children," she began, but then she stopped. In the pause someone piped up a meek apology. Then she suddenly laughed. "You know, my brother Bill used to sleep out here," she said. "And he could bounce so high he almost hit the ceiling." She looked at the opened window. "We crawled back and forth too, and passed secret messages. My father got furious if he caught us." She leaned over and tucked the covers around my cousin. "Now scoot back into the bedroom, you two," she said to my sister and me. We scooted.

Though we loved our days at the lake, nights were even better. After dark the woods seemed to close in around us, with rustlings and murmurings that didn't frighten us as long as we were together. Sometimes we stayed late at a relative's cottage and walked home in the dark with a single flashlight among us. The

stars shone above us as we passed through a clearing or an open
field, but most of the woods were pitch-black. We could hear
frogs croaking by the lake, and the sound of the water against the
dock, lessening as we moved away from the cottage up the hill.
When we got home and curled beneath the sheets, pulling them
over our heads to escape the mosquitoes, we knew that no one
was awake for miles around. It was a peace so deep and so safe
that we floated into sleep as though we were magically stretched
out on the waves of the lake below.

One night before we were to leave Lake Carlos the next day,
my sister and I sorrowed together. "Let's run away," Karen whispered. "Let's hide outside where no one can find us, and they'll
have to stay and look for us." Leaving Mother asleep in her bed,
we crept past her through the living room and out the front door.
In the darkness the wild wheat in the front yard seemed almost as
tall as we were. Flattening ourselves onto our stomachs, we crept
through the wheat. No one could see us if we stayed on our stomachs, we reasoned, not bothering to remember that no one was
around to see us anyway. After a while we grew tired, and stopped.
We only had on our cotton nightgowns, and the air was chilly, a
late August breeze blowing off the lake. We whispered together
for a few minutes, nestling close for warmth. But there didn't
seem much point to staying longer. The wheat was rough under
my cheek. The grasshoppers hummed and whirred, and the loons
called as always, but somehow they sounded different. The cold-
ness of the night seemed to remind me of fall coming soon,
school starting, my life at home in Ames beginning again. Pro-
tests and plans were useless; tomorrow would come, and we'd
have to leave. So we crawled back, still whispering, still on our
stomachs. Mother was sleeping soundly, and we went quietly to
our separate beds. As I fell asleep, I could hear a motorboat, a
night fisherman, far out on the lake, its throbbing a reassuring
and familiar sound.

As we retraced the road to town next day, my sister and I hung
out the windows as we had on arrival, now each wanting to catch

the last glimpse of the water. "Good-bye, Chinese Pagoda!" we called and waved at the people standing in its front yard, who, surprised but friendly, waved back. "Good-bye, Swiss Chalet! Good-bye, Lake Darling! Good-bye, Lake L'Homme Dieu! Good-bye, Alexandria!" After Mother turned onto the cement highway, we settled down for the long trip home. I sorted through the shells I'd collected, my sister fiddled with her pieces of white birch-bark she had turned into tiny canoes, and my mother watched for a truck stop that would serve good hotcakes.

Soon my sister and I cheered up. The lake would be waiting for us next year, and the year after that. As the car carried us farther away, I let myself listen to the hum of tires on pavement, an intermediate rhythm that would rock me home. The summer was almost over, September almost here. What would I wear the first day of school? What had all my friends been doing while I'd been gone? Would we be able to get down to Blaine's Pool once more before it closed? I looked ahead, not at the straight highway heading between fields of corn, but to the months before me. The car lulled and rocked, and I lay back on the duffel bag and closed my eyes. Somewhere ahead lay the promise of Christmas.

The World Outside

I didn't think anyone had to tell me, "You can't go home again." After twenty years, my Ames, small, friendly, fully knowable, is now almost lost in an exfoliation of subdivisions, college dormitories, shopping centers, retirement villas, factories, car lots, freeways. Driving into Ames I have learned to wait patiently for some familiar sign, Lundgren's Furniture Barn, an old Phillips 66 station, a rusting underpass where trains used to thunder overhead, the vet's kennels that once stood as a quiet outpost but are now restlessly nudged by Burger King and Kentucky Fried Chicken.

I thought I had adjusted. I could still take long walks and orient myself by old landmarks. No matter if the West Street Grocery was now Dugan's Deli, or Rexall Drug a beauty parlor called Hairy Krishna. They were still neighborhood shops. Inside the Collegiate Presbyterian Church where I was married, the nave had been reconstructed, so that the front was now the back, but from the outside it remained ivy-covered and solid. Lincoln Way had been enlarged, but traffic still hummed along it, carrying travelers who preferred to cut through town rather than whiz by on the encircling freeways. I could walk down West Street, past the church, back along Lincoln Way and feel my past still faintly alive around me.

But last year my mother forgot to tell me about Welch School. Home for a holiday, I was driving with her across town, following a route I had traveled by foot, bicycle and car so many times that once I knew its very cracks and potholes. Out of the corner of an eye I glanced toward Welch, the ancient prison-brick square school that had always loomed on a hilltop overlooking the Arboretum. There I had entered fifth grade when we moved from the other elementary school district on the college side of Ames, and there I had stayed through junior high school. I had known that some years ago Ames had built a new junior high, and I remembered that Welch was now simply a grade school. But I didn't think that mattered. I still planned to go back some time, maybe next visit home, and wander through those dark halls, past my sixth-grade classroom, into the art room, across the gloomy gym where I had cheered and danced, through the concrete playground where I had spent summers as a recreation worker.

When I glanced absentmindedly out the window that afternoon, I jerked the wheel so violently that my mother gasped and grabbed the door handle. "Mother!" I said accusingly. "What has happened to Welch?" Where there had been an imposing building was now a gaping hole. Welch had been torn down, the rubble removed, every last brick carted off. I looked again, and again. I had always seen the old school so strongly in my mind's eye that as I looked at that glaring vacancy, it seemed to me the faded brick still rose above it.

It doesn't matter, I told myself. Just another example of time moving on. If I'd wanted to, I could have gone back any number of times in the past. I wouldn't have known anyone there anyway. All my old teachers were long since gone, dead, retired, moved away. Probably the art room, with its huge gray ceramic pots filled with damp clay and its crowded stacks of easels, had long since been turned into something else. Maybe a teachers' coffee room. They had always wanted one, I remembered. But all during my visit to Ames, I avoided driving by that barren patch of ground. Soon, my mother said, the city would turn it into a parking lot.

A year later I took my daughter Jennifer to Ames to visit her grandmother. This trip, I told her, I had a special project. I wanted to bring my camera and photograph some familiar places before they were torn down and lost forever. She could come with me that day if she liked. She was mildly curious and agreed.

Several of our stops were predictably disappointing. The little yellow house where I had lived until fifth grade was still there, but even tinier and more rundown than when I'd last seen it. I tried to tell Jennifer about its orchard and back lot, how I'd climbed among bees and cherry blossoms, how my father tilled and cultivated our Victory Garden during the war, where we'd grown sunflowers and sweet peas. Now all she could see was the gnarled skeleton of one old tree, stripped by winter, and an asphalt parking space where I assured her sunflowers had once towered bravely. When we knocked at the sagging back door, and peered through the window at the bare wooden staircase, I was glad no one was home. Jennifer was disappointed. She was ready to return to Grandma's house.

But when we pulled up next to a small two-story school, brick and cement like the old lost Welch, Jennifer became excited. "There are swings, see!" she called. "Can I get out and swing?" Of course, I said, and followed her to the playground. Almost nothing had changed. As far back as I could remember, I had never wanted to revisit Louise Crawford Elementary School, where I had begun kindergarten and stayed until Welch. My memories of those early years were dim, and I had felt no need to burnish them. But now I was struck by a haunting sameness that had eluded me in my other treks to childhood shrines. The swings were in the same place, anchored as far as I could tell in their original cement moorings. The jungle gym where I'd carefully guarded my swinging skirts had been replaced with a surrealistic structure, but it too stood in the same spot. As Jennifer swung happily, I walked across old basement gratings, where I'd once lost pennies, to the kindergarten windows. Inside the room looked shockingly familiar: tiny furniture, though plastic rather than maple, large wooden blocks, blackboards, stick-ups all around of bright felt letters and numbers. For thirty-five years perhaps nothing had changed. I stared blindly now in the windows, remembering friendships, losses, shrieking games, even a trip to the principal when I had been late to school three times. Swinging the big brass tardy bell on the school steps, E.Z., the white-haired janitor, used to hold its clapper silent when he saw me running down the tracks. But he couldn't wait forever.

The tracks. That was what seemed wrong, I thought, turning back to look at the playground again. Now Jennifer was scrambling high on the climber, heedless of her skirts. A railroad track had run along the rear of the schoolground. By the time I was at Louise Crawford, few trains ran along them, mostly freights. Sometimes at night I could hear them faintly from our house some blocks away. But frequently we would see one or two workmen on a small bumper car, as we called them, quietly putt-putting by the school on their way to some unknown rendezvous. Maybe they were going to repair tracks. Maybe they were going all the way to Marshalltown or Keokuk or Chicago, as one boy claimed. They always wore railroad-striped overalls and genuine rail-road caps, tall with visors, just as in Lois Lenski's books. All of us lucky enough to be at recess when the bumper car passed ran to the tracks, as close as we dared, while the teachers shrilly called us back. We shouted and waved frantically to the men. They always waved back and grinned.

Jennifer had seldom seen trains. I knew she had never seen a bumper car. Now I wanted her to come and walk along the tracks with me, balancing precariously, one foot ahead of another on the bright gleaming rails. But of course that was what had changed. No rails ran there. At the edge of the schoolyard was a fence, dividing its property from some messy back gardens on the other side. No scars, no trace. The tracks had probably been torn up so long ago that few of these homeowners knew that the Chicago & Northwestern had once run at the foot of the garden, whistling in the night, beckoning small children.

Now I have a picture of Jennifer on the Louise Crawford play-ground, poised high on a metal climber, smiling as I did when I had reached the very top of the dangerous jungle gym. Behind her I can see the swings we both have now swung on, the same trees I used to make leaf boats, the darkened windows of my old kindergarten room. I don't know what she will make of this picture when she is grown, but I am glad I have it.

When I was growing up in Ames, nothing changed very fast except the weather. The Little Store, a one-room shack next to

Welch School, underwent transformations every few years: Bob's General Store, Sally's Superette, Dayton's Dairy. We just continued calling it "The Little Store." Its sign disappeared and reappeared with new lettering and new names, but inside Bob, Sally, or Mr. Dayton still stocked Twinkies, Juicy Fruit, Wonder Bread, Coke, Tide, Ivory Snow, milk and eggs. We didn't care who took our nickels and dimes, just as long as someone was there when we needed something. And someone always was.

Because the town seemed to stand still in those years of the late forties and fifties, growing slowly but not in any disturbingly visible way, we thought the small center of our universe was stable and secure. If we knew little else, we certainly did know Ames. Though no village, in fact then a town of some ten thousand, Ames was plainly laid out and easy to move around. Its two business districts, a handful of elementary schools, two junior highs, one senior high, one hospital all sat in logical places. When our boyfriends got cars, they could drive us around for hours without thinking in an endless circle of familiar houses, schools, stores, the A&W Root Beer stand, the Maid-Rite, the Ranch Drive-In, and home again.

When I finally left Ames to go east to college, my new friends teased me about how I always introduced myself. I never just said my name, they told me. Instead I always announced, "I'm Sue Allen from Ames, Iowa." That was how I saw myself, an emigrant and ambassadress, trailing a town behind me. Being from Ames meant you were *from* somewhere, from a place that, if your listener only knew about it, would explain a great deal about you. It is a sense of place my daughter, who has lived for varying times in California, London, and different parts of the Twin Cities, will probably not share. I have not yet decided whether she has suffered a loss or an enlargement.

If there *was* a world outside Ames, it was easy to forget about it. As a child, I thought no one in Ames went anywhere. Most families I knew had always lived there. Every September we anticipated the one or two new kids in our class. We regarded them in a romantic light, at least temporarily until we could sort them into one of our various "sets." In eighth grade I carefully watched Peggy O'Reilly as she settled shyly into her seat: she was Irish, Catholic, red-headed. An exotic background, but she seemed eager to please. My social antennae having received favorable signals, I decided to walk home with her after school, and we became close friends. We still are. But twenty-eight years later, both living in different cities, I still half-consciously think of Peggy as a new girl in town. Having grown up in Mason City, a hundred miles away and somewhere I'd never been, she was a constant reminder to me that, in fact, people did come from somewhere besides Ames.

Sometimes my friends took trips to visit grandparents, as Peggy often did to Mason City, but no one traveled much for pleasure in those years. Families with a sense of obligation to their children's cultural vistas drove to a national park: Yellowstone, Grand Teton, or the more accessible Mount Rushmore and Badlands. Many of us spent an August week or two in Minnesota. But otherwise we stayed home.

The only foreign place most of us saw with any regularity was Des Moines. Although it was only thirty miles away, Des Moines was an hour's trip along narrow curbed highways, through two small towns, past turnoffs to other, unvisited small towns. Central Iowa, which we thought of as rather densely populated, was a series of suns and satellites. Ames glowed benignly upon the hamlets of Randall, Huxley, Jewell. We in turn looked to the bright lights of Des Moines.

My own personal pilgrimages to Des Moines usually led to Younkers Department Store. An avid shopper like my mother, I would beg her several times a year to ask her friend Vanessa Harbinger if we could all go to Des Moines. Mrs. Harbinger's daughter Kristy and I were good friends, as were Vanessa and my mother, and if we all went together, my mother wouldn't have to drive alone. My mother hated driving; she clutched the steering wheel so tightly her knuckles were white. I don't know how she managed our yearly trips to Minnesota. She always spoke of going to Des Moines as if it were a dangerous safari from which we might not be likely to return. Mrs. Harbinger was more sanguine.

A day shopping in Des Moines was a great occasion. Early after breakfast we'd set out, dressed in our best as though we were off to church, a snack packed in a paper bag, car carefully stoked with gas and oil. Past the outskirts of Ames, into the open countryside, we picked up speed exhilaratingly until we eventually found ourselves stuck behind a slow-moving semi-trailer truck. Then, if Mrs. Harbinger drove, we braced ourselves, peered out the window, watched for coming traffic, and shouted encouragement. "It's okay!" "There's a yellow line ahead!" "I can't see over the next hill!" Finally Mrs. Harbinger pulled out, stepped on the gas and we held our breath for the endless wait alongside the truck until we were safely back into our own lane. If my mother drove, we had a different tactic. We followed the truck until one or more of us became visibly restless. "Hazel," Mrs. Harbinger would turn and say gently to my mother. Then my mother was forced to act. But she didn't pass. Instead she looked for some place to pull off the road, preferably a truck stop or gas station. "Let's just take a break," she said, turning off the ignition. Then we climbed out, used the bathroom, bought a Coke or a candy bar. It gave the semi enough time to pull far ahead of us so we wouldn't run the chance of getting stuck behind it again.

Once inside the city limits of Des Moines, we followed a maze of streets none of us except Mrs. Harbinger really knew, block after block of bedraggled-looking houses, small warehouses, strange churches. Central Des Moines was not especially attractive. When we reached a main street near downtown, we looked anxiously for the one parking lot we always used, hoping it wouldn't be filled. Then Kristy Harbinger and I walked as fast as we could, urging our mothers along, until we got to Younkers.

Younkers Department Store was a confusing marvel to a young girl from Ames. Occupying a small city block, it had not just one but several entrances. We always used the one with a visitors' book, where you could leave messages for friends: "Hazel—come to the French Room at 4 P.M."; "Vanessa and Kristy: wait for us in the Tearoom at 11." Shopping in Younkers was a social affair, punctuated by coffee in the morning, lunch in the Tearoom later. Inside the store I wandered in a happy daze among infinite departments. Unlike any store in Ames, Younkers had more than one counter that sold sweaters, more than one dark corner for shoes. I never completely mastered its layout. Just when I thought I had compared every price and variation of short-sleeved, round-collared white cotton blouses, an item which in Ames would have one coarse broadcloth style cheap at Penny's and a fancier pocketed style less cheaply at Marty's, I would find a new strain blooming in an overlooked corner of Younkers.

Bargains seemed to leap out at me from unexpected places: heaps of reduced Irish-linen handkerchiefs on top of the shiny glass notions counter, "End-of-the-Month Clearance" signs over dirndl skirts in Misses' Separates, and of course always the possibility of a hidden wonder in the French Room. There my mother and I would meet before lunch, knowing whoever had been there first would have already culled its possibilities for the other to consider. The French Room was Younkers' version of elegance. It was a large room, thickly carpeted, lined with mirrors, entered through heavy gold-framed glass doors that swung shut to close off the ordinary bustling world of everyday Younkers. Usually you had to ask to have clothes brought out, a tactic that effectively discouraged casual bargain-hunters like Mother and myself. But sometimes the French Room had a Special Clearance, advertised by a discreetly lettered sign on the heavy glass door. Then we would go in, heading straight for the rack with telltale price tags against the wall. We looked at the tags first, then at the clothes. Sometimes my mother would try on a dress, while I looked, almost always in vain, for something that wouldn't look too old or funny but would still say, quietly, "The French Room" on its gold-and-white label. Once, in high school, I bought a long-sleeved rayon shirt with gay multicolored flowers on a white background.

It came from a different world from the one of white round collars. But the first time I wore it, and perspired—in a French Room blouse, a lady didn't sweat—all the colors ran together, so I had to keep my arms pinned close to my sides whenever I wore it. Still, I knew it was elegant, and once, before it had been reduced, it had cost $14.95. Just for a blouse. That was what one expected from the French Room.

After our foray to the French Room, Mother and I would lunch in Younkers' Tearoom, among a roomful of ladies, all talking loudly. We ordered things we couldn't get at the Rainbow Cafe at home: onion soup, chicken à la king, English muffins. For dessert, gingerbread with lemon sauce. Joined by the Harbingers, we would compare purchases, pulling each one triumphantly from its dark green Younkers sack for inspection. Then we would map out our afternoon, dividing it among the handful of smaller but intriguing shops that lined the block across the street. Regretfully, since I'd always see some unvisited counter, some last unexamined "Bargain" sign, we'd ride the escalators down two floors to the main exit. Escalators were unique to Younkers in all Iowa then; there was a single escalator in Younkers' Cedar Rapids store, I'd heard, but I'd never been there. As a child I was thrilled by the folding stairs that disappeared into flatness. But even when older, I loved to ride majestically up and down, surveying Younkers below as if its spread-out departments were my private fiefdoms. In the car on the way home, we'd open all the packages again, exclaiming over each other's surprises, marveling at reductions, and comparing successes. To have found a size 12 navy-blue pleated skirt when the only one seen in Ames had been size 8 was a vindication of our whole trip. If only, we thought, we could shop in the Des Moines Younkers every day.

But since it was a difficult hour's drive away, especially in uncertain Iowa weather, Des Moines was never a daily experience. Aside from shopping expeditions with our parents, it had to be saved for special occasions: basketball tournaments, family reunions, church assemblies, or, during later high-school years, perhaps dinner and the theatre on a Big Night. If a boyfriend could borrow his father's car—no parent would let a son drive a jalopy all the way to Des Moines—he might take his girl to Jimmy and Lou's, then to the KRNT Theatre. Jimmy and Lou's was a steak house where they would serve set-ups if you brought your own liquor. By the time we were seniors, many of us had been able to savor the sophistication of sitting in a booth at Jimmy and Lou's, watching a date carefully remove a flask from its brown-paper sack and pour a little rum into a glass of Coca-Cola. At Jimmy and Lou's, no one ever asked for your i.d.

After dinner at Jimmy and Lou's, we sometimes saw a real Broadway show, in its second or third year around the country, with live New York actors and fancy stage sets. The cavernous KRNT Theatre, a reverberating dome, was more suitable for massive revival meetings or the Ice Follies than it was for the human voice, however much amplified by a battery of hung microphones. But we didn't care. Seated at a dizzying distance from the stage, we listened raptly to the songs or carefully laid plots of the shows we knew had been Big on Broadway. We laughed as much as possible at any joke and applauded wildly at the end. I had read about *The Bad Seed* in *Time*, I had heard the songs from *The Pajama Game* on the radio, I had seen pictures in *Life* of Deborah Kerr in *Tea and Sympathy*. When the lights in the auditorium dimmed, I could get a sense of what it might be like to be on 42nd Street, which seemed to twinkle all the way from New York to the giant marquee outside the KRNT Theatre.

Such vibrations from a world outside Ames were rare, but we knew the world was there. It was tangibly connected to us by Highway 30, "Lincoln Highway," running through town east to west. One of my earliest conceptions of distance came when someone told me that if you drove along Lincoln Way in either direction and never stopped, you arrived at an ocean. The East and Atlantic one way, California and the Pacific the other. I was impressed. Sometimes I stood thoughtfully for a few minutes on the edge of Lincoln Way, then a plain two-lane city street tamely

passing through Campus Town, past our junior-high football
field, off into the country. On this very pavement cars ended up
in California. Or New York. I could drive and drive and then I
would be at one of the oceans. One nation, indivisible, linked by
this road that unrolled from shore to shining shore. But I didn't
drive, and it was hard enough to get Mother to Des Moines. After
paying Lincoln Way a few minutes' homage, I looked both ways
and crossed it.

We had other indicators of distance and connections. Trains
ran through Ames then, and on our trips to Des Moines, or to
other Iowa towns, we had glimpses of highways heading off to unknown places. Outside of town, even a few miles' drive past cornfields differentiated only by the color of a barn or by the number
of windbreak evergreens convinced anyone who used her eyes
that such fields probably rolled on forever. At least for days and
days, until the Rockies, or New York City, loomed suddenly on
some startling horizon. Iowa farmland gave an impression of un-
hurried time and space. The world, I knew, was out there all
right. It would just take a long time, a long way, to find it. I was in
no hurry.

If my sense of larger geographical boundaries was hazy, it was
sharply focused on the smaller and more easily encompassed pe-
ripheries of Ames. With a trip to Des Moines a major expedition,
lesser journeys became adventures. Everything was magnified in
my eyes when measured on the scale of Ames. Because Ames had
no high hills, for example, even a gentle rise had its own name. I
lived on top of Oakland Hill, steep enough so the city fathers
held an occasional soapbox derby there. The real measure of a
hill's height for children was whether you dared to ride down on
your bike without braking and then could ride back up. Coasting
down Oakland Hill, I braked all the way, and, except standing on
the pedals and teetering in a slow zigzag from curb to curb, I had
to walk my bike to the top. Living on Oakland Hill, I felt, was a
real distinction.

My definition of "wilderness" was formed early, based on two patches of woods in Ames. When I was young, they seemed like forests. The Pine Woods was hidden in a valley belonging to the college Agronomy Station, a tract of experimental fields and orchards at one edge of town. Every neighborhood on the college side of Ames was close to the country, but ours was literally only a block from the Agronomy Station, and on sunny days, or in the crisp cool weather of early fall, my sister and I set out for the Pine Woods. At the end of our paved block was a locked gate leading to a cinder road. Beyond the gate was the countryside of the Agronomy Station. Climbing over the gate, we crunched on cinders until, a few bends in the road later, we completely left the town behind. All its houses were now hidden by tall evergreens that marched beside us until the cinders turned into a dusty dirt path. Behind one row of evergreens ran some ordinary-looking cornfields, which we ignored, but on the other side of the road were gnarled rows of grapevines, twisting and turning over a slight hillside, beckoning us to a foreign land. We walked on the grapevine side of the road. Soon we came to a clump of ancient lilac bushes, so tall they towered like trees, tangled together in a green disorder that invited us to dive into it. At six or eight we were small enough to take alarm at the sight of a man pruning in the grape arbor opposite, burrow out of sight under the lilacs, and watch cautiously until he had disappeared down the field. Then, a luxurious time later, we continued along the road, scuffing up sand, watching for ants, picking dandelions, smelling the lilacs or the profuse wild pink roses.

It seemed like hours before we arrived at the Pine Woods. First we had to pass through an orchard, buzzing loudly with bees if the cherry and apple blossoms were out. Then, one curve in the road later, we suddenly came out on the top of a small hill, looking down on a creek that ran at the foot of the Pine Woods. Though the Woods were simply a large rectangle of trees, planted by the Agronomy Station for some unknown purpose, they were the largest grove of pines we'd ever seen. Once inside the grove, it was dark and smelled of pitch. There wasn't much to do in the grove but explore its strangeness. We rolled in the pine needles that carpeted underfoot. Sometimes we took off our shoes to dip our toes into the moss. Mostly we tried to build secret hideouts, dragging fallen branches, piling up mounds of pine needles, drawing room boundaries with lines made by twigs, doing our best to fortify whatever corner of the Pine Woods seemed to us most hidden.

When the Pine Woods palled, we ran down to the creek. Unlike the larger streams that ran through town, Squaw Creek and Skunk River, this one was too insignificant to have a name. Perhaps four or five feet across, it was still deep enough for wading, and in a few spots the water came up to our knees. Even in midsummer the water seemed icy cold, just as the Pine Woods always seemed cool, and we splashed, threw stones, floated leaves and sat down on the pebbly bottom. For a time we were just the right size for the little creek.

A few years after these summer expeditions to the Pine Woods, we moved to a different part of town, far enough so we couldn't easily walk back to the Agronomy Station. Sometimes Mother took us on group picnics there. With grown-ups along, we couldn't hide under the lilacs or try to lie flat on our stomachs behind barriers of pine needles. "Come along out of there, let's go," they'd call. "Come and eat your lunch. Don't spill the lemonade. Don't go in that creek, I'm sure there's broken glass on the bottom. See, what did I tell you? Does anyone have a Band-Aid? Stop crying. Now just sit quietly on the blanket and stay out of trouble."

Near our new house, however, we found compensation for the loss of the Pine Woods. This edge of town bordered on several respectable hills, uncleared and wild, drained by a wandering rivulet called Clear Creek. Mother once said all this forest was owned by Mr. Gibbs of Gibbs Lumber, who lived in an imposing white house downtown. It didn't seem possible to us that anyone could own the forest. It was too big. We called it the North Woods, a name that suggested fairytale lands, something with unknown extent, rather forbidding. You could actually get lost in the North Woods, something that would never happen within the neatly defined boundaries of the Agronomy Station, and we children who played there never roamed too far. Sometimes we could hear gunshots; someone was hunting squirrels or rabbits, and the sound always sent us scurrying home, unless we were dabbling in Clear Creek, which had not only a name but also sinkholes deep enough to float in for a few feet. Then we ducked under water, holding our breath, hiding as we had years ago under the twisted lilac branches, until we felt sure the grown-ups had passed us by.

In fall we wandered through the North Woods to gather brightly colored weeds, watching conscientiously for poison ivy, wondering what would happen if we ate the shiny orange or red berries that hung on wild bushes, collecting gold and red maple leaves that seemed too beautiful to be left to rot on the ground. In winter the neighborhood children gathered to sled at the biggest hill, where we steered a dangerous course that veered past a giant oak, scarred and dented with crash marks, and narrowly avoided the frozen banks of Clear Creek.

Early spring was probably the most exciting time in the North Woods, for then Mother took us to hunt for May-basket flowers. On a chilly Saturday morning when the sun finally broke from gray skies into the thin clear sunshine of early spring, Mother hung an old willow basket over her arm and led my sister and me to a hidden entrance into the woods a half-mile away from our house. Down a winding path, barely visible under the last patches of melting snow and moldly leaves, we followed Mother's sure steps, looking carefully as we walked for nearby flowers. Mother taught us how to find the delicate white Dutchman's-breeches and snowdrops and we gathered them into small bouquets with wild purple violets. At the end of the path, deeper into the woods than we ever dared go alone, was a small clearing with a large flat-topped stone in the center. Scattered around the stone were old cigarette butts, beer cans, and bits of paper. Mother said college students knew about this place and sometimes came here to

have parties, so we must never go this far by ourselves. It was disappointing to know that someone had been here before us. But,
protected by Mother, we weren't frightened about meeting any
strangers, and we soon turned to scamper home, running ahead of
her now, yelling and racing, while she followed slowly with the
picnic basket full of flowers. When we got home, we had hot rolls
and cocoa while we constructed little baskets out of colored paper to fill with flowers and leave at our neighbors' doors.

The Pine Woods, the North Woods, and a lake in Minnesota
were what I knew of wilderness as a child. When I was in third
grade during my mother's year at Claremont Graduate School,
my sister and I both got some kind of flu. We had to stay in bed
while Mother prepared for her master's orals. She was working on
Faulkner, and in desperation, she decided one long afternoon to
read aloud to us from "The Bear." Of course we understood little
of his complexities, but we were able to follow the compelling
story of the hunt, and whenever Faulkner soared into his long
breathless descriptions of the infinite forests harboring an immor-
tal bear, what I saw in my own mind was a larger, but recogniz-
able, version of the North Woods.

Today most of the North Woods has been razed and developed,
with expensive contemporary homes artistically planted on steep
slopes we once skimmed in the wind on our sleds. Clear Creek
has long since been polluted and virtually dried up. Fragments of
the woods remain, but even now I have never fully explored
them. I do not want to know where they end.

Not only the Pine Woods and North Woods but other periph-
eries of Ames also helped shape my notions of size and grandeur.
Though I later revised my sense of scale, basic geographic pictures of Ames remained in my mind like negatives. From them I
formed composite images of what the world outside was really
like. Although I saw real mountains for the first time when I was
eight, when we crossed the Rockies, I was not entirely unpre-
pared for their craggy heights. I had been many times by then to
the nearby Ledges State Park. This sudden outcropping of bluffs,

worn into caves and niches by a quiet river, was such a significant break in the level landscape of central Iowa the bluffs had been given a name, and park, of their own. On one of the highest, the legend went, an Indian maiden had leaped to her death to escape something, no one remembered what, perhaps an unwanted lover or an enemy tribe. Most Midwestern parks, I later learned, have similar legends, but I was moved by this first glimpse of long-ago romance at the Ledges. Despite the scrawled, crude initials carved into the rock, I sat there and looked out over the park benches below, gazing above the trees, wondering what it must have been like for that doomed Indian maiden.

If the Ledges were my mountains, Iowa's two resort lakes, Spirit Lake and Okoboji, prepared me for another kind of American landscape. Our family almost never went there, but both lakes were close enough, two or three hours' drive, so some of my friends visited relatives or even rented summer cabins there. Occasionally I was lucky enough to go along. Once in a while parents drove a carful of us to Okoboji for the day, leaving at dawn and returning long after dark. Surrounded by cottages; lined with docks; covered with trolling motorboats and racing speedboats; disgorging fishermen, swimmers, and sightseers from cars parked bumper-to-bumper at every public beach; Okoboji had a gaudy, tawdry, noisy atmosphere that reminded me of our yearly trips to the State Fair. We didn't pay much attention to the actual lake. It was green, rather murky, usually cold, and wherever we wanted to swim we had to worry about hidden weeds that clutched at our ankles like water spirits. Instead we visited the Dairy Queens and popcorn stands, loitered in corner drugstores looking for postcards, nagged the parents to let us try the roller rink, which they never did. I was in my twenties when I first saw Las Vegas, but I was not surprised. It was, after all, something like Lake Okoboji.

Travel inside Ames, or even to a lake near the boundaries of northern Iowa, was not the only way my images of the outside world were formed. The Ames educational system did something to broaden our horizons too. That was the phrase our social-studies

teachers often used, "broaden your horizons," words that implied
a painful stretching process. To do this they had the help of the
Weekly Reader and then, by junior high, *Current Affairs*. These
were succinct, summary publications of news-of-the-week-in-
review from which schoolchildren read, underlined, made notes,
and finally were tested. We read one or two paragraphs about democracy in India, self-government in the Philippines, Senatorial
debate about whether Alaska or Hawaii deserved to become
states, bulletins closer to home about record corn crops or dis-
rupting blizzards. None of it compelled our interest. The *World
Map*, which we achieved in high school, was more challenging. It
was a large poster hung in the school library each week, from
which we had to read not only short news dispatches, as innocuous
as those in the sixth-grade *Weekly Reader*, but on which we had to
find the geographical location of each story. Searching out obscure
places like Indochina, Formosa, Manchuria did give me momentary
tremors at the size of the flattened globe. But the accompanying
stories, written in simple, unambiguous prose, always reduced those
tremors to the safe level of the *National Geographic*. One of my
friends' fathers took the *Geographic*, whose pictures often drew us to
carry an issue off to her bedroom. Most foreign places, we decided,
had women with bare breasts, bright-colored costumes, quaint customs, and, as the prose told us, high hopes of improving things in
the near future. Seeds of democracy were planted everywhere these
days, the *Weekly Reader* or *Current Affairs* or *World Map* or *National
Geographic* assured us, and soon they would undoubtedly sprout into
flourishing worldwide representative government.

Of course, we all knew there was Communism. As early as
sixth grade our teacher warned us about its dangers. I listened
carefully to Mr. Casper describe what Communists wanted, which
sounded terrible. World domination. Enslavement. Destruction
of our way of life. But when he described the meaning of the political system, which he said was "communism with a small *c*," it
sounded oddly sensible: owning everything in common, sharing
resources, doling things out in equal parts. I hung around school

one afternoon hoping to catch Mr. Casper, whom I secretly adored, to ask him why communism was so bad. He stayed in another teacher's room so late I finally scrawled my question on our blackboard: "Dear Mr. Casper, why is communism so bad? . . . Sue Allen," and went home. Next morning the message was still there. Like a warning from heaven, it had galvanized Mr. Casper. He began class with a stern lecture, repeating everything he had said about dangerous Russians and painting a vivid picture of how we all would suffer if the Russians took over the city government in Ames. We certainly wouldn't be able to attend a school like this, he said, where free expression of opinion was allowed. At recess that day one of the boys asked me if I was a "dirty Commie"; two of my best friends shied away from me on the playground; I saw Mr. Casper talking low to another teacher and pointing at me. I cried all the way home from school and resolved never to commit myself publicly with a question like that again.

By the time we were in high school, our knowledge of world affairs was slightly more informed, but our sense of the dangers of Communism had been heightened by the Korean War. Now we knew about Red China. When my friend Jerry Slater volunteered in Debate Club for the positive side of the question, "Should the United Nations admit Red China?" I asked him in private how he could get up and say all those things that sounded as though he believed Red China could be treated like an ordinary country. It seemed unpatriotic, even immoral. Jerry said not to worry, it was just an intellectual game. "Think of it like points," he said. "I just try to get more points than the other side." I understood.

Far more important than current-affairs bulletins or *National Geographics* in forming my picture of the world were, of course, movies. Ames had four movie theatres, the New Ames downtown, the Campus and Varsity near the college, and the Ranch Drive-In west of town, built when I was young and hence regarded as something of an innovation. I never did get used to going to movies at the Ranch, for which you needed a car. Going to the other movies was a simple matter of walking or taking a city bus to a weekend matinee. Each theatre had its own clientele. At the Varsity we saw intellectual movies, mainly British, like *The Red Shoes* or *Tight Little Island* or *The Man in the White Suit.* Mother took my sister and me to these, giving me a feeling I still hold dear that anything starring Alec Guinness was somehow Art. The New Ames had the first-run Hollywood epics like *The Robe*, which our Sunday-school teacher recommended, or *Quo Vadis*, after which I told her that I now thought I knew what it meant to be a Christian. The Campus featured second-rate movies with Barbara Stanwyck or Dana Andrews in compromising poses on the full-colored posters outside. Mother always had to approve my movies until I reached high school, and even then she often questioned me sharply about plots. "Did you really enjoy that, dear?" she would ask, patient but puzzled. "It sounds rather silly to me."

Soon after I began going steadily to movies, I discovered movie magazines. I quickly learned that Mother didn't approve of these, either, so I restrained myself to buying only two a month, *Photoplay* and *Modern Screen*. The others I read standing up at the magazine counter at the near-by Rexall Drug. Through the chit-chat of Hedda Hopper and Louella Parsons, as well as through the chummy, confidential articles, I began to feel I was a Hollywood insider. Avidly I collected data, memorizing facts that still float back to me at odd times, like Tony Curtis's real name, Rock Hudson's home town, or Kathyrn Grayson's bust measurement.

In ninth grade I focused my star-struck attention on one particular movie star, Robert Wagner, who combined, I thought, youthful friendliness with sophistication, and whose sexiness wasn't as frightening as, say, Cornel Wilde's or Clark Gable's. The magazines described him as the boy next door. I pasted his pictures all over my bedroom wall so his smiling face beamed down on me in the morning and gently wished me goodnight. I spent even more of my allowance on movie magazines, and I remember looking anxiously in *Screen Stories* for the plot of the movie *Titanic*. I couldn't bear to see it if Bob Wagner died in the end.

Soon I discovered in *Life* to my alarm that Bob was having a tempestuous romance with the starlet Terry Moore. No, no, I thought in horror, she's all wrong for him. Too blatant, too ripe, not at all the sweet trusting girl he really needed, like Debbie Reynolds or Ann Blyth. She had enchanted him, I surmised, as Gloria Grahame or Rita Hayworth might have done. Someone needed to alert him to his mistake. So I sat down on Saturday morning and wrote my first and last fan letter. "Dear Mr. Wagner," I began politely, and went on to tell him that I knew all about his affair with Terry. I didn't think she was right for him, I said, avoiding specifics, but I surprised myself by adding loyally that if he really loved her, he ought to marry her anyway. I loved his movies and wished him all the best, Sincerely yours. When I mailed the letter, I was pleased with myself. Although I didn't approve, I had let Bob know I supported him, whatever he did. It was what my mother might have done. I waited for his reply. Some weeks later it came. It was a printed card, thanking me for my letter, and enclosing a snapshot of Bob. Enlargements could be ordered, it said, for the prices printed on the reverse side. I do not think the card was signed. I stared at the small black-and-white photo, the card, the printed prices; he hadn't even read my letter, or he couldn't have answered like that. He didn't know who I was. He didn't care. Soon afterward I tore down his pictures. Hollywood had become irrevocably part of the world outside.

Besides introducing me to beautiful people, Hollywood gave me my first, and often indelible, pictures of faraway cities and foreign countries. I have never been able to escape entirely the notion that Chicago is a city of gangsters, San Francisco of fog and loneliness, Paris of sidewalk cafes, London of wartime romance and espionage, and New York—well, New York is still emblazoned in my mind in the lights of Broadway, the Empire State where true lovers meet their fates, the Grand Central Station of heartbroken leavetakings, Central Park with dances in the grass and hansom cabs all holding Fred Astaire.

When I was fourteen and my sister fifteen, Mother decided we should take a trip to New York City. Since we had already seen the Grand Canyon and Yellowstone, New York would complete our geographic education. Mother found a modest hotel with special rates for teachers, bought us coach train tickets, and then spent many evenings arbitrating between my sister and me about how we would spend our time. Karen wanted to go to all the art museums, I wanted to see all the stores: the Metropolitan versus Lord and Taylor's, the Cloisters versus Saks Fifth Avenue. Mother preferred theatres, but we all agreed on basics: the Empire State, the Staten Island ferry, the Statue of Liberty, and Times Square. Once in New York, somehow we managed to please everyone, dashing from store to monument to museum to theatre with the energy of first-time tourists. But most of New York, while exciting, was unsurprising. I had already seen it all in the movies, and sometimes, I had to admit to myself, it didn't look quite as shiny and colorful up close. An old woman, dribbling at the mouth, tried to take my arm in Grand Central Station until Mother snatched me away. Our hotel room was dark and dingy, and we never did find a restaurant in which we felt comfortable.

What I most remember of our New York trip was my sense of being close to the center of all bargains. My targetshooter's eye for reductions, end-of-season clearances, and special purchases, trained by my many excursions to Younkers, zeroed into every window along Broadway that featured cheap napkins, tableclothes, drip-dry hangers, and jewelry boxes. Never had I seen so much wonderful junk. I felt it was almost criminal to leave it there in the shop windows when it would all cost so much more back in Iowa. Hoarding my small fund of money carefully, I comparison-shopped in store after store, trying to decide among coaster sets, ceramic pins, fuzzy slippers. My most exciting day in New York was not, alas, in a museum or theatre, but in an open dressing room at S. Klein's. There, surrounded by seminaked women and heaps of rejected clothes, I found a white tulle formal, almost strapless, with just the thinnest halter of net to hold the dress over my slight bosom, for the unbelievable price of $8.95. I didn't have anywhere to wear it, just yet, but I knew in high school there would be dances and proms. To have a New York dress in my closet, for only $8.95, was an investment in the future. I carried it with me in a special box all the way home on the train. I never wore it. By the time of my first formal dance, I wanted something more sophisticated than a white dress.

Other than the tourist sights whose imprint had already been made by the movies and the heaped bargains in store windows, New York quickly became a blur. It was not the only major trip I took as a child; in third grade, after my father died, my mother took my sister and me to Claremont, California, while she earned her master's degree. Claremont was so exotic, so unlike anything I'd seen in the movies, that it too became a blur. I registered the open, Mexican architecture and learned to say "arcade" instead of "halls" at school; I got used to finding my nostrils black with soot from the smudge pots; I saw fields of orange groves and once, on a day's trip to Corona Del Mar, the ocean. But none of it really fit together in my mind. I was waiting to get back to what I knew in Ames.

My real introduction to the world outside did not come until I was seventeen and ready to go away to college. For years I had known I was not going to stay home at Iowa State; somehow I was convinced that I should go east, or west, far away, to a college that would fit me for something absolutely different. As a sophomore in high school, I wrote to almost every small liberal-arts college I could locate, requesting catalogues, studying curricula, and, most important, finding out if they offered large scholarships. Eventually I chose Smith College. I had met one young Smith student I liked, who was dating the boy across the street, now at Amherst. She was lively, unpretentious, and easy to be with. Then I had dinner one night with an older alumna, who had actually worked for *Time* in Paris, and that touch of world adventure decided me. Clearly Smith was a place that could harbor me, whatever I decided to become.

Naturally, since Smith was in Massachusetts, I had never been there. But I knew about "back East," a kind of hallowed, ivied museum. "Back East" was Paul Revere and the Boston Tea Party, Harvard men and white New England churches, culture and literature. It was a place where women wore black silk cocktail dresses and men smoked pipes. In the East people commuted, a word as foreign to me then as Manhattans. "Out West," less exciting, implied a wide-open country of space and opportunity, bright sunshine and cheerfulness. At a college there, I thought, I'd join a high-toned sorority, edit the college newspaper and learn to drink beer at football games. It would be like Ames, I supposed, but bigger, louder, booming. And richer. Family friends didn't approve of my college plans and warned me that, East or West, I would be humbled by the snobs around me. "Won't you feel out of place?" someone kindly asked me. "I mean, all those girls with all that money?" I didn't know. Smith, the two alumnae had promised me, was very democratic. I preferred to believe them. One reason I had chosen Smith was that I was frightened about leaving Ames. With its catalogue pictures of Gothic spires, towers, and massive gates, Smith offered reassurance. The glossy-haired, casually rumpled girls on page after page smiled widely, wore tweed skirts, rode bicycles; I could do that too, I thought. It was a look I wanted to acquire, that easy, confident air of belonging.

Before setting off on the train in September that freshman year in 1957, I spent a long time organizing my wardrobe. I wanted to look just right when I arrived. For the first time Mother and I drove to Cedar Rapids, where I wanted to meet another girl from Iowa who'd been accepted at Smith and where I hoped I could find just the right shade of fawn gloves to go with the reddish-brown tweed suit I had been laboriously sewing on our old Singer treadle machine all summer. Our social visit completed, Mother and I headed downtown. There, in the other Younkers with an escalator, I bought gloves, an almost-fawn-colored felt hat, and expensive wooden buttons to sew on the front of my suit. Years later, I can still see myself getting on the Chicago & Northwest-

ern train in Ames for the first leg of the long, two-day trip,
dressed in my tidy homemade suit, little hat and fawn gloves, sitting up all the way, careful not to run my nylons when I curled
my legs under me and slept.

At night I woke fitfully, watching the lights of Cleveland, Buf-
falo and other strange cities flash by my grimy window, blurring
into each other, sprawling and sooty, with identical factories,
smokestacks, and apartment buildings. This was neither my Midwest nor my East, but a shadowy corridor whose character I could
not label. Before I went back to sleep, I pulled my raincoat carefully over my lower legs, tucking it in so no one could see anything, as though I were a child again on top of a jungle gym. Just
before I left Ames, Mother's friend Mr. Sanders had told me
about an Iowa girl who, waiting between trains on a bench in
Chicago's Union Station, had unwittingly crossed her legs and
forgotten to rearrange her skirt. Quick as a wink a woman had
slipped onto the seat next to her, whipped out a hypodermic nee-
dle, and shot her in the thigh. She had fallen unconscious to the
floor. If a friend who was traveling with the girl hadn't come out
of the ladies' room just then, Mr. Sanders said, the girl would
have been immediately carried off to a house of prostitution.
Once there, she would of course have been too ashamed ever to
leave. She would have been lost forever. Keep your eyes peeled
and your legs together, he warned me. I did my best.

Sometimes two or three girls my age, in pairs or groups, hurried
through my car on their way to the smoker or diner. One of
them was the girl from Cedar Rapids, who was traveling Pullman.
She politely invited me to come to see her compartment, but the
porter firmly turned me aside. Only first-class tickets here, he
said. The girls I saw were chatting, laughing, looking much like
those catalogue pictures of breezy "Smithies" on bicycles. They
occasionally glanced at me curiously where I was curled up
against the window, reading a book, chewing on one of the now-
musty apples my mother had carefully packed in my large food
box. Have some meals on the train, my mother had urged me, at

least once eat in the dining car. But I was shy and worried about money. I felt more comfortable munching apples and eating peanut-butter sandwiches, especially when I saw those laughing girls pass by. I heard one of them say with a giggle, "I'm sure up for a brandy Alexander." I didn't know what that was.

On the morning of the third day, I went into the restroom early so I could freshen up. I straightened my seams, brushed crumbs from my skirt, washed my face carefully, and applied lipstick. Outside the window Massachusetts was rushing by; soon it would be time to get off in Springfield and find the train to Northampton. More and more girls had flooded into the train and they spilled, a shrill, shouting, pushing crowd, onto the Springfield platform. I was tired and frightened. Everyone else, I thought, seemed to know where she was going, so I dug my nails into my palm and determinedly followed the crowd into a tiny Boston and Maine car waiting on a side track. For half an hour we rumbled along a brown rushing river that flowed between steep hills, a landscape so dramatic I knew I was at last in the East. The trees had begun to turn color and flung masses of orange, brown and gold against the green hillsides. Unfamiliar signs whirled by me speaking in a foreign tongue: Hadley Falls, Holyoke, Howard Johnson's, Mount Tom, Wiggins Tavern. At least I had heard of Howard Johnson's. According to an Ames girl who'd eaten at one, it was like a fancy version of Jimmy and Lou's, only with a million different flavors of ice cream. My throat felt dry. It was an unusually hot day for late September, and the sun beat harshly through the glass windows. My stomach heaved, and I breathed hard to keep my equilibrium.

When we pulled into the small station at Northampton, I stepped uncertainly down the steps of the train and wondered what to do next. My wool suit stuck to my legs and clung to my underarms. Inside my gloves my hands were sweaty from heat and nervousness. As I looked around me, I could hear a jumble of slightly strange accents, clipped and assured, mixed with glad cries of recognition and greeting as girls who knew each other tumbled off the train or jostled each other on the platform. I didn't know anyone. Most of the girls were wearing plaid skirts or kilts, knee socks, loafers. No one else was wearing a hat. As I stood uncertainly by my blue shiny Samsonite suitcase, a tall girl in a striped man's shirt and olive Bermuda shorts edged her way toward me. "Are you a freshman?" she inquired. "I'm here from Freshman Advisers to help you get back to campus." I looked at her gratefully and took off my gloves so I could shake her hand. "Hello," I said. I wanted to flee back inside the train and go home as fast as possible. I wanted my mother, my friends, my landscape. I didn't know what I was doing here. I clearly didn't belong. But this was the world outside, and I would try. "Yes, I'm a freshman," I managed to continue. Then I took a deep breath and went on. "I'm Sue Allen from Ames, Iowa." That was all there was to say.

© Dana Wheelock

ABOUT THE AUTHOR

SUSAN ALLEN TOTH has written for *The New York Times*, *The Washington Post*, *Harper's*, *Victoria*, *Vogue*, *McCall's*, *Travel and Leisure*, and many other publications. Her books include *Blooming*, *Ivy Days*, *How to Prepare for Your High-School Reunion*, *My Love Affair with England*, *England as You Like It*, and *England for All Seasons*. She lives with her husband, James Stageberg, in Minneapolis.